# Innovation, Entrepreneurship and Culture

# Innovation, Entrepreneurship and Culture

## The Interaction between Technology, Progress and Economic Growth

*Edited by*

Terrence E. Brown

*Associate Professor of Entrepreneurship and Innovation, Royal Institute of Technology and the Stockholm School of Entrepreneurship, Sweden*

Jan Ulijn

*Jean Monnet Chair, Eindhoven University of Technology, The Netherlands*

**Edward Elgar**
Cheltenham, UK • Northampton, MA, USA

Published by
Edward Elgar Publishing Limited
Glensanda House
Montpellier Parade
Cheltenham
Glos GL50 1UA
UK

Edward Elgar Publishing, Inc.
136 West Street
Suite 202
Northampton
Massachusetts 01060
USA


A catalogue record for this book
is available from the British Library

This book has been printed on demand to keep the title in print

**Library of Congress Cataloguing in Publication Data**

Innovation, entrepreneurship and culture: the interaction between technology,
  progress and economic growth/edited by Terrence E. Brown, Jan Ulijn.
    p.  cm.
  Includes bibliographical references and index.
  1. Technological innovations. 2. Organizational changes. 3. Entrepreneurship.
  4. Economic development. I. Brown, Terrence,. 1962–  . II. Ulijn, J.M.
  HD45.I5374  2004
  338'.064—dc22                                                     2003061589



ISBN 1 84376 346 X

Printed and bound in Great Britain by Marston Book Services Limited, Oxford

# Contents

# Figures

# Tables

# Contributors

Erik Baark, University of Science and Technology, Hong Kong
Jean François Boujut, Laboratoire GILCO and Laboratoire 35, Grenoble, France
Terrence E. Brown, Royal Institute of Technology and the Stockholm School of Entrepreneurship, Sweden
Ivy Chan, National University of Singapore
Alain Fayolle, INP Grenoble – ESISAR, EPI, France
Koen Frenken, Utrecht University, the Netherlands
Takahiro Fujimoto, Tokyo University, Japan, and Harvard University, USA
Geert Hofstede, Tilburg University, the Netherlands
Jérémy Legardeur, Laboratoire LIPSI, Bidart and Laboratoire 35, Grenoble, France
Loet Leydesdorff, University of Amsterdam, the Netherlands
Niels G. Noorderhaven, Tilburg University, the Netherlands
Naubahar Sharif, Cornell University, USA
A. Roy Thurik, Erasmus University, the Netherlands
Henri Tiger, Laboratoire CRISTO, Grenoble, France
Lorraine M. Uhlaner, Eastern Michigan University, USA
Jan Ulijn, Eindhoven University of Technology, the Netherlands
Robbin Te Velde, Delft University of Technology, the Netherlands
Alexander R.M. Wennekers, Erasmus University, the Netherlands
Ralph E. Wildeman, Erasmus University, the Netherlands

# Acknowledgements

We would like to acknowledge here the first international ECIS Conference (Eindhoven Universities of Technology, NL) held in September 2001 from which we invited some of the authors of the best papers to adapt them as chapters in our book.

We would also like to thank two of Jan's graduate students at Eindhoven University of Technology – Arijan Konings and Wouter Kunst, whose editorial assistance in getting this book to it final stages was invaluable.

It goes without saying that we are very grateful to Elgar, and especially Dympha and Caroline, for sticking with us.

Finally, we would like to thank Pieta, Signe, Greta and Annica who have generously allowed us to be a bit antisocial for the purpose of completing this book.

# 1. Innovation, entrepreneurship and culture, a matter of interaction between technology, progress and economic growth? An introduction

**Jan Ulijn and Terrence E. Brown**

Not all technological innovations lead to start-ups, whereas an estimated 75 per cent of the new employment is created there. This is a global phenomenon. Why are there no more entrepreneurial successes? Are innovators just too technology driven, so that they forget about the market for their ideas? *Failing to prepare for the market, is preparing to fail your business.* Or are innovators predominantly hidden in research and development (R&D) laboratories of large multinational corporations (MNCs), so that the market perspective is too far away? With all of the activities surrounding technological spin-offs geared to foster entrepreneurial spirit, why is it that so many technology companies fail to sustain this spirit? Could it be that a *special* or certain mindset is needed at the individual level for entrepreneurs and/or a certain organizational culture for entrepreneurial firms? If so, what elements make up that culture? Are you assisted by your national culture (NC) background, your previous corporate culture (CC) experience or your professional culture (PC) (c.f., *once an engineer, always an engineer*) or a combination of all these? Furthermore, are these issues related to high levels of innovation, the development of technology, (social) progress and economic growth, and, if so, how are they related?

This book discusses these questions and more, and attempts to answer some of them: *Une mer à boire* indeed, but basically rests with the question, *what culture is necessary to create new enterprises out of promising technological ideas and to what extent is that a matter of an interaction between technology, economic growth, and social progress?*

So you get an innovative idea, you decide to become an entrepreneur, but not all innovation leads to successful venture creation; in fact, many of them fail. How does the entrepreneur learn more quickly from his/her mistakes? To initiate the creation of new venture, you may need a special culture, climate or mindset. Underneath this progress there are interactions going on which can be symbolized in the iceberg metaphor which is also used for the hard facts of structure and the *soft* ones of culture (see Mintzberg, 1979; Ulijn and Kumar, 2000; Ulijn and St. Amant, 2001). Technology and (economic/financial) growth related to structure are in the visible top of the iceberg: progress related to society and culture are in the bottom below sea level and may have a larger impact than expected.

How can this interaction between technology innovation, entrepreneurship and culture be researched? Even defining the terms is problematic. Innovation, entrepreneurship and culture are studied in many disciplines and hence lead to many conceptualizations, including economic, sociological and psychological approaches. In addition, culture draws less from economics, but more from anthropology and linguistics (discourse studies), which are seldom applied to innovation or entrepreneurship. Organization and management studies seem to be the ideal interdisciplinary meeting place for all this. Furthermore, one may say that culture is a relative old research topic and entrepreneurship a relative new field of scientific investigation with all its problems of delineation, scope, paradigmata for theorizing, model design and testing, etc. Although the ambitions of this book are high, in that it attempts to bring together these three areas, instead of ending the discussion by answering all the questions, we extend the discourse by posing even more questions to be explored in future research.

## 1.  INNOVATION

The problem with exposing new concepts to scientific analysis is that they cannot easily be made directly applicable in model building and theory development. Cumming's (1998) historical overview of definitions of innovation demonstrates well that there is a long way from Zuckerman's definition of a series of technical, industrial and commercial steps (see Robertson, 1974) via Kuhn stressing creativity that shapes something into products and services, and the belief that invention only becomes innovation if it succeeds in the marketplace. Creativity is an important element anyway of innovation management (see Euram Conference, 2002). Ulijn and Weggeman (2001) also reviewed some definitions within the framework of innovation management, but the bare minimum would be:

> Innovation is creating something new and implementing it successfully at a market.

Innovation deals with processes, products and services and technology. As Wheelwright and Clark still view it (discussed by Ulijn and Weggeman, 2001), and as confirmed by Cummings (1998), the innovation management process is still often regarded as a linear and continuous process: the R&D department has an idea, throws it over the wall to the design group and manufacturing department and marketing/sales only get interested if and when they believe there is a market for it. However, reality may be a bit different, as demonstrated in recent design studies reviewed by Van Luxemburg, Ulijn and Amare (2002). Furthermore Delinchant et al. (2002) revealed that there is a growing cooperation between the design function and the R&D department of the supplier and/or of the customer. Innovation, therefore, may be seen as resulting from collective efforts including both the business internal and external actors working more in cyclical loops of improvement rather than in a mere linear process. This would suggest that innovation can be a slow incremental or almost natural/evolutionary process (see Fujimoto, Chapter 10 in this book), or a revolutionary process. Vanhaverbeke and Kirschbaum (2002) illustrated this with the DSM (De Staatsmijnen) case, a Netherlands (NL) based mining and petrochemical company developing into the nutri- and pharmaceutical sector using nano-molecular technology. This transformation required radical innovation and organizational change rather than incremental innovation.

Scholars ranging from economics to sociology are currently interested in the role of government in assessing and fostering innovation. In addition, organizational and management scientists, marketers, engineers and others are interested in how to manage innovation and technology in an effort to determine the best way to manage innovation. Given the interest in this topic, we will briefly discuss both innovation policy and management. What can governments do?

In his survey of innovation studies in the twenty-first century, Smits (2001) lists a couple of problem spots for innovation. For example, small and medium sized enterprises (SMEs) find it difficult to transform knowledge into successful products and services, and a high number of high-tech firms in life sciences and information, communication and technology companies (ICT) have difficulty in getting full value from their innovations. An analysis of the decision-making process in this area could be helpful to businesses in developing a strategic innovation management process. Mairesse and Mohnen (2002) indicate for seven European countries that there is not a one-to-one correspondence between the innovativeness of a country and the observed innovation intensity, in other words, between what is possible and what happens in reality. Some countries do much better than predicted (NL and Ireland), others do not do as well (Belgium). The statistics in surveys often do not tell the entire story, because the countries concerned are not selected randomly. Also, the interpretation of the survey results is less than straightforward. For example, what does it mean if Germany is the champion of observed innovation intensity (43.8 v. a

European intensity of 34.7). In this case the innovativeness rank predicts exactly the innovation intensity rank, but other numbers show (see Table 9.1 in Ulijn and Fayolle, Chapter 9, and Hofstede et al., Chapter 8 in this book) that the percentage of self-employed people and new start-ups in Germany is comparatively low compared with Japan, the USA, France and NL. However, sometimes a country study can at least guide the innovation policy of a local government and explore critical success factors in organizing firms, as Sharif and Chan show in Chapter 2 of this book. Accordingly, it also seems that the European Union (EU), is able through its extensive Eurostat service to create a comprehensive and meaningful statistic called the innovation scoreboard (*Innovation and Technology Transfer*, 2001a).

One major concern of this unique supranational economic community has been how to turn R&D investments into new jobs. One can say that scientometrics is one indirect means, as Chapter 4 by Frenken and Leydesdorff in this book illuminates. But how can this lead to a higher innovation performance, expressed in the number of start-ups etc?

The Eurostat statisticians have concluded that Western Europe (UK, NL and Germany) is losing momentum, Southern European countries such as Greece and Spain are catching up and that the Nordic countries and Ireland are moving ahead, whereas Portugal is falling further behind, with the remaining member states taking intermediate positions in this innovation scoreboard. Their conclusion is that the trend for the entire EU is favourable, showing an improvement over the last five years in seven indicators, a minimal increase in one and a decrease in three (public R&D, business R&D and the share of manufacturing value-added from high-tech sectors). What does it mean for future entrepreneurship development?

Europe is becoming more and more a union of regional economies instead of national ones. Within the 15 top regions/provinces Oberbayern (Germany), Uusimaa (Finland) and Noord Brabant (NL) at the higher end and Ile de France and Oberpfalz (Germany) at the lower end. Of course, this can be the effect of the MNC R&D laboratories as from Siemens/ BMW (Munich, Oberbayern), Philips (Eindhoven, Noord Brabant) or Nokia (Helsinki, Uusimaa). The Netherlands and Germany seem to score better regionally than nationally here. The Southern European countries are not represented in the July 2002 issue of the above source. European Union policy-makers hope to reduce these differences by developing internal and external networks of cooperation. Perhaps some regions act more as engines of innovation and entrepreneurship than other regions?

Once governments have created the right policy in which innovation might lead to new business, how do you increase the innovation performance of SMEs in the ICT and biotech sectors, for instance? Darsoe (2001) presents, on the basis of some Danish biotechnology firm cases, a few guidelines to foster creativity and innovation through communication and cooperation. The building sector where ICT is still underused might be a case in point for innovating SMEs. Chapter 3, by Baark, exemplifies to what extent the knowledge conversion process between the different actors shape innovation as a social and cultural process through engineering consultancy. How does innovativeness relate to entrepreneurship?

One may conclude, for instance, from Davidsson (see Fayolle, 2002) that innovation and entrepreneurship have creativity (and communication to develop it) in common, and that in most technology-based entrepreneurship a high degree of innovativeness is required. A study by Utsch and Rauch (2000) among 201 entrepreneurs from West and East Germany pointed to innovativeness as a mediator between achievement orientation and venture performance, while initiative was not. So, is the level of initiating behaviour related to German entrepreneurial culture? Does taking the initiative disrupt routine and standard processes too much? Chapter 7 by Legardeur, Boujut and Tiger signals a paradox of innovation in a routine design process in a French case, which might need entrepreneurship.

## 2. ENTREPRENEURSHIP

As with innovation, defining entrepreneurship is also problematic, which is well reflected by a recent European research conference on the matter (Fayolle, 2002). From a large overview of definitions presented at that conference (by Davidsson) we distil a common core:

> Entrepreneurship is a process of exploiting opportunities that exist in the environment or that are created through innovation in an attempt to create value. It often includes the creation and management of new business ventures by an individual or a team.

There are elements in the concept of entrepreneurship that derive from the economic and social context and from behaviour (is it innate or learned?). There is a link with creativity and innovation (see previous section), with new markets, products, processes and technology. Entrepreneurship involves competitive actions to win the market, involves acting to exploit opportunities and involves actors to bear risks. Economics is needed to study the market process, psychology to study the motivation and sociology, management science, and organizational behaviour to study the innovation aspect of entrepreneurship. The concept of an entrepreneur, however, is much older than that of innovation or innovator. In his comprehensive review of more than 30 definitions, Gartner (1989, p. 57) goes back to the one by Britain's J.A. Say (1816):

> The agent who unites all means of production and who finds in the value of the products ... the reestablishment of the entire capital he employs, and the value of the wages, the interest and the rent which he pays, as well as the profits belonging to himself.

This is a normative definition: what an entrepreneur should do, but it is surprising that after the Second World War the more empirical definitions take over (22 out of the total), starting with the distinction with the manager (still a normative one with Hartman, 1959, and an empirical one with Litzinger, 1965). It seems as if by then a distinction between the more daily operations management and the rather innovation-based entrepreneurship was born. In the same piece Gartner concludes that 'Who is an entrepreneur?' is the wrong question; one should no longer verify (personality) traits (innate or learned) to predict what this person should do to make an enterprise a success, but study what the entrepreneur is actually doing.

Why is innovative entrepreneurship so important around the world? One answer is that it commercializes public knowledge and it contributes to productivity and employment growth. The concept of entrepreneurship is not only limited to small business development (Cummings, 1998; Pinchot, 1985; Thornberry, 2001). Vanhaverbeke and Kirschbaum (2002) concluded, based upon the study by Roberts and Berry (1985), that business as usual would only lead to incremental innovations, but that radical technological innovations in a strongly R&D driven business require strategic corporate entrepreneurship in order to succeed. This would also include spin ins/acquisitions and, in our opinion also spin-outs/sales of companies/ start-ups. Entrepreneurship and/or intrapreneurship are also needed in large firms to sustain innovation management. The Legardeur, Boujut and Tiger study in Chapter 7 demonstrates that the production of a unique composite fibre-reinforced material, sheet molding compound (SMC), could lead to a paradox of innovation in a routine design process in the French automotive sector. Entrepreneurship is needed to break away from routine. The concept of the skunk works outlined and exemplified in Chapter 6 by Brown might be seen as another way to stimulate intrapreneurship/entrepreneurship and out-of-the-box thinking in an existing firm.

Based upon Gartner (1985; 1989), Bruyat and Julien (2001) and Fayolle and Bruyat (Fayolle, 2002), Fayolle tried to develop a conceptual framework and a field of research to study the foundation and the development of innovative business processes. After an outline of the paradigm context (including Bachelard, Feyerabend, Kuhn and Popper) and a philosophical perspective, Kyrö and Kansikas (Fayolle, 2002) review 337 refereed journal articles from 1999 and 2000 in the field of entrepreneurship. They concluded that this field is strongly US based once more, with 12 top journals publishing about it. Apart from a variety of qualitative and quantitative research methods, the studies can be distributed over (by order of decreasing importance) the firm, the business, the relation between the individual and the business, between the firm and the economy, and between the individual and the firm. Other targets such as links between society, economy and individual got far less attention. Chapter 5 by Te Velde fills a little gap here in a historical/conceptual sketch of true entrepreneurship based upon Schumpeter's theory of economic development.

Another gap is the study of entrepreneurial behaviour as a (strict) psychological phenomenon. Although Kyrö and Kansikas (2002) concluded there was a nice balance of quantitative/statistical and qualitative studies, it is difficult to isolate the more rigorous experimental or clinical psychological approaches in this comprehensive survey and that of Shane (2002). Another recent critical perspective on business and management, however, presenting a published journal article by Kreuger (2002) and the conference by Fayolle (2002), addressed both the process and the psychology of individual entrepreneurship. Addressing such questions as 'Are women more successful than men as entrepreneurs?' and notwithstanding the social context factor which might not always be very beneficial to female entrepreneurs, Gundry, Ben-Yoseph and Posig (2002) could ascertain a dramatic increase of women-owned businesses worldwide: one-quarter to one-third of all businesses in the formal economy are headed by women. They have to cope with discrimination, prejudices and certain skill deficiencies (c.f., financial competency; for details see Hisrich et al., 1997), but at the same time demonstrate successful management styles such as open communication and participative decision-making. In a comparison of the USA and Central (Poland) and Eastern Europe (Romania), family and culture appeared to have a large impact on the rate of female start-ups. Cromie (2000) found a significant difference between reasons given by men and women to establish an enterprise, relating to career dissatisfaction and child-rearing: a mother can more easily work at home for her own enterprise where she seems to care less about making money than men. The sample of entrepreneurs studied in West and East Germany had autonomy, job dissatisfaction and achievement in common as the top three motives to be self-employed (see also Hofstede et al., Chapter 8). This helps confirm that traits research here is less important than the study of actual motives and behaviour. In this sense the clinical observations by Kets de Vries (1996) are unique: the entrepreneur on the couch. Such psychoanalyses might explain, why so many (high-tech) start-ups fail (50 per cent within 10 years according to a recent Dutch study). A need for control, a sense of distrust, a desire for applause and resorting to primitive defensive mechanisms, such as splitting, projection, denial and a flight into action (manic defence) seems to be quite common among entrepreneurs. How can they be helped?

Different actors might be available at the local, state and global (government) levels. In a US/EU comparison Fonseca, Lopez García and Pissaride (2001) found not only more high-tech start-ups in the USA, but also start-ups in the area of financial and communal service, which is normally the domain of governmental concern/action in the EU. In an index of start-up costs expressed by the number of regulations and weeks needed to set up a company (see also Ulijn and Fayolle, Chapter 9 in this book), they found only Denmark and the UK ranked lower than the USA. All other EU members ranked higher, with Spain, Germany and Italy having the highest start-up costs.

It also appears that large MNCs may gain by helping small start-ups and SMEs. There is some contradiction here. On the one hand, Jones (2001) demonstrates a growing internationalization trend of small high-tech firms: think local, act global. Is this only for general management and not innovation management? On the other hand, Acs, Marck and Yeung (2001) strongly recommended that SMEs leave the international innovation to MNCs and share the international direct exporting profits with them instead. Does this imply that there is a critical mass of R&D required for innovation? Van Luxemburg, Ulijn and Amore (2002) showed some Dutch cases that seem to point in that direction. An international entrepreneurial orientation of SMEs is definitely required in any case, for which Knight (2001) gives a strategic model. International comparative entrepreneurship studies, such as the ones by Dana for Pacific Asia (1999) and China (see also Shi, 1998), the Central Asian Republics, Myanmar and the Nations of former Indochine Française (Dona, 2002) might facilitate the global learning in this area. International entrepreneurship and innovation seem to warrant further investigation.

What can academia do to help start-ups? Apart from indirect stimulation (research) technology-based entrepreneurship can be stimulated directly through education and incubators. The work by Birley and MacMillan (1997) and Birley (1998) at Imperial College, London, might be a case in point here. In a recent survey of (university) incubators EU-wide (*Innovation and Technology Transfer*, 2002b), the UK, Germany and Italy rank among the highest density of SMEs, with a corresponding number of incubators in this decreasing order: Germany, the UK and Italy. Most of the businesses in these university-based incubators were in the field of software development, computer technology, and e-business and biotechnology. Fayolle's work (2000) showed that engineers are seldom entrepreneurs; perhaps they lack the critical mass skills and competencies needed. In this sense high-tech incubators can be a big help. Additionally, entrepreneurship education as part of technology management and industrial engineering curricula can provide some of the missing skills and competencies technologists need to increase their chance of entrepreneurial success.

In sum, the creation of economic value through the entrepreneurial and/ or venturing process is quite complex. Furthermore, the results seem to vary greatly across countries. This may not have been surprising in the past when education (skills, competencies, capital, etc.) was not readily available to some parts of the globe; however, given that this has changed substantially, especially in Europe, these differences still persist. Given this, it appears that national differences (that is, culture) has a powerful effect on the process of creating innovative and entrepreneurial people and firms.

## 3. CULTURE (NATIONAL CULTURE, CORPORATE CULTURE AND PROFESSIONAL CULTURE)

Not all innovative people are entrepreneurial, it seems a special mindset (and environment) may be required for this. Within the framework of managing high technology and innovation, Levy (1998) outlined how to create an organizationwide culture of innovation and intrapreneurship/entrepreneurship through identifying and encouraging champions and entrepreneurs and using different management methods, such as high management involvement, listening to the customer and entrepreneurial greenhouses. But what is innovation and entrepreneurial culture? A comprehensive recent handbook on entrepreneurship such as the one by Shane (2002) does not deal with psychology or culture, which is amazing given some breakthrough studies by Shane earlier in his career about innovation culture (1992; 1995; 1997; Shane, Venkataraman and MacMillan, 1995).

The link between culture and economics has generally not been very well studied. Lavoie and Chamlee-Wright (2000) for instance talked about the development, representation and morality of business, but do not use any recent cultural theories. Culture can be seen, of course, as a selling item in the domain of music, theatre, films, literature or artefacts (see Gray, 1998), but this represents only the outer layer of the onion of culture, which is the explicit expression of deeper norms, values, beliefs, attitudes, perceptions and implicit assumptions. In the Netherlands, however, it was surprising that recently the Minister of Economic Affairs organized a national values committee to stop society from further cultural degeneration. Is this the best way to close the gap between innovation, entrepreneurship and economic growth?

If innovation and entrepreneurship are related concepts, it is important to make the connection also at the cultural level. In line with the earlier study by Ulijn and Weggeman (2001) and Ulijn and Fayolle (Chapter 9 in this volume), the various authors in this book handle culture at three different levels: national culture, corporate culture and professional culture.

Moreover, the link between culture and psychology will be discussed to relate innovation and entrepreneurship to each other not only at the group level, but also at the individual level. Both need cooperation and teamwork. Innovation and entrepreneurial culture would then be, to follow up Hofstede's definition of culture, the programming of the mind of innovators and entrepreneurs. What is the overlap?

## National Culture (NC)

Innovation and entrepreneurship is an interesting subject to compare across national borders, but what, if anything, can countries learn from each other? We look here at NC from a business perspective, as is suggested by Crane (2000) who looked at business culture in Germany, France, Spain, the UK, NL, Sweden, Switzerland, Hungary and Russia, with views from the USA, India and Japan. He concluded that there seems to be a European business culture encompassing all, as there is in North America, the Middle East, Asia and Africa (although drawing strict lines between them may sometimes be difficult). Different chapters in this book deal with innovation and/or entrepreneurship with a national culture perspective, including the EU (Chapters 4, 8 and 9), Hong Kong (Chapters 2 and 3) and Japan (Chapter 10), and a comparison with the USA (Chapters 4 and 8). Hofstede et al. (Chapter 8) includes other Anglo-Saxon countries, such as Canada, New Zealand and Australia. The recent Valence conference referred to earlier (Fayolle, 2002) expanded outside the EU member states, with contributions about entrepreneurship from Norway (Oftedal, Amo), Estonia (Sepp and Hankov), Bulgaria (Kolarov), Russia (Iakovleva) and Tunisia (Zghal and others). With the previously mentioned coverage of Asian and Pacific countries by Dana, a comprehensive global set of studies is available, except perhaps for Africa and Latin America.

The most recent South American survey by Lenartowicz and Johnson (2002) used the introspective Rokeach Value Survey (Rokeach, 1973; Schwartz and Bilsky, 1990) and covered 12 Latin American countries, finding some variable pertinent for both innovation (see Ulijn and Weggeman, 2001, for an independent study on innovation drive) and entrepreneurship. In general there is some homogeneity across the NC borders of Argentina, Bolivia, Brazil, Chile, Colombia, Ecuador, Mexico, Paraguay, Peru, Puerto Rico, Uruguay and Venezuela, but one should caution against the 'Latino' or 'Hispanic' stereotype. Retail managers in those countries were shown, as measured by personality indicators, to be ambitious, capable and courageous: Bolivia and Brazil rank highly there, which is promising for an emerging market. Moreover, the two economic powerhouses, Brazil and Mexico, might differ because of the difference in language: Portuguese v. Spanish. One should not overgeneralize and stereotype based upon false assumptions with respect to innovation and entrepreneurship.

While we are most concerned with national difference with respect to culture here, we recognize that there are important within-country variations related to regions and ethnic groups, as suggested above because of differences in number of patents and by a recent study by Van den Tillaart (2001) on entrepreneurship. For example, 9.2 per cent of all Dutch SMEs are run by immigrant entrepreneurs, such as Turks, Surinamese and Moroccans (in this order), mostly in services (restaurants, retail, automation and public relations).

**Professional Culture (PC)**

An individual's extensive education and subsequent career may have a significant impact on the processes of innovation and entrepreneurship. Looking at engineers and marketers one can often see these professional culture differences. For example, there is evidence, especially anecdotal evidence, that many engineers and engineering firms have difficulty understanding market needs. This *difficulty* may be deeply rooted, stemming from the education, training and career professional socialization that engineers (and other professionals for that matter) go through. Kunda (1992) proposed to engineers a new culture to make a bridge in the high-tech corporation (see for a thorough discussion, Martin, 2002). Within the development of a start-up company a unique orientation towards one PC might decrease to benefit more differentiation eventually via an integrative stage of PCs as an intermediate step. Ulijn, Nagel and Tan (2001) and Fayolle, Ulijn and Nagel (2002) concluded that Dutch engineers are quicker to accept the other PC of marketing than their German or French peers. It is even a general trend that high-tech venture starters often focus too much on their technological innovation and not enough on the market: a conflict of PCs? The Baark and Legardeur, Boujut and Tiger chapters (3 and 7) reflect on these issues in both Hong Kong and France. More cooperation is needed between the different professions and their cultures involved in a start-up process, not only engineers, but also marketers, lawyers, bankers and other financial specialists. Furthermore, there are preliminary indications that there may even be differences in professional culture across national cultures and, to complicate matters even more, these may interact in unexpected ways.

## Corporate Culture (CC)

Are some corporations more innovative then others? Yes. Certainly Ulijn and Weggeman (2001), Shane (1992; 1995; 1997; 2002), Shane, Venkataraman and MacMillan (1995), Shane and Venkataraman (2000), Nakata and Sivakumar (1996) and Ulijn et al. (in press) outline, on the basis of different dimensions linking CC to NC in corporate alliances that this is the case. The skunk works culture presented in Brown's chapter (6) in this book makes a link to intrapreneurship. Because there has already been so much research produced in the areas of corporate culture, we believe that there is not too much that we can add. However, there has been little work that examines the interaction of CC, with both PC and NC. And how these three concepts relate to the development of innovation and entrepreneurship is a new concept that we begin to discuss in this chapter and is picked up by some of the other authors in following chapters.

## Culture and Psychology

Is there a relationship with culture and behaviour with respect to innovation and entrepreneurship, and can the field of psychology inform the issue? Montalvo (2001) tried to predict through a social psychological meta-theory applied to decision-making on the basis of attitudes and beliefs. To what extent would the model he proposed change the individual behaviour of innovators? In general it has been a problem to distinguish culture and personality in innovative and entrepreneurial behaviour. Issues such as creativity, attitudes (Eagly and Chaiken, 1993), perceptions and cognitive schemata are studied in both, as the latter relates to knowledge management in an intrapreneurial context (Oftedal, in Fayolle, 2002). Is the concept of entrepreneurial spirit that leads to cognitive biases a matter of culture or personality? Is what Cavusgil and Godiwalla (1982) defined, and what Hart, Webb and Jones (1994) discussed within the framework of internationalization and export decision-making as psychic distance, in actuality a matter of cultural distance? How can it be measured? In general, there is an underlying comparison to geographical distance (i.e., the farther away the more different and difficult). In contrast, what is very near and expected to be similar, can be very different both within a multicultural society and between border countries, such as NL and Belgium, NL and Germany (see the data by Hofstede et al. in Chapter 8). What does this mean for the NC dimension of innovation and entrepreneurship?

Although it is very difficult to disentangle culture and psychology here, entrepreneurship has some personality aspects that seem rather psychological in nature (see for an overview Frank et al., in Fayolle, 2002).

Intuition is another aspect of entrepreneurial behaviour (see Frese, Chell and Klandt, 2000). Opportunities may involve dual processing by the entrepreneur: cognitive v. associative with a risk of false attributions (Chaiken and Trope, 1998). For example, an entrepreneur might not be a systematic information processor, the gut feeling counts for more. Gender might be another combined psychological and cultural aspect of entrepreneurial success (see Section 2 in this chapter). Moreover, a cross-cultural comparison of personality indicators for innovation and entrepreneurship is another blend of culture and psychology. The collection of papers by Frese, Chell and Klandt (2000) listed personality predictors of success and entrepreneurial behaviour including the transition to the social psychology of groups. How important is it to team up in innovation and entrepreneurship?

### Group/network/cooperation/conflict

The fact that strong individualism fosters creativity and innovation in its first stage (Ulijn and Weggeman, 2001, and the research they refer to) and that start-ups very often consist of smart individuals who have an idea 'to create value', might lead to the idea that sharing and teaming up with another person with complementary skills is the surest path to success. However, some entrepreneurs want to remain autonomous as much as possible. Within the EU, Ulijn and Fayolle (Chapter 9) evidence, at least within and among French, Dutch and German engineers, that cooperation between engineers needs to be encouraged strongly in high-tech start-ups. The need of a high collectivism and teamwork in the implementation of an innovation and the success of cooperative start-ups at Imperial College in London (see Birley, 1998; Birley and MacMillan, 1997), for instance, supports this recommendation.

The finding by Bond and Hofstede (1989) that the gross domestic product (GDP) in the West would correlate with a high individualism and in Far East Asian countries with long-term orientation (LTO or the Confucian Dynamism Index) was quite striking. That high LTO was often related to high collectivism and power distance seems to create a natural environment for a radical implementation of an innovation, as the Japanese example showed a couple of years ago. In parallel, it was a plausible development that the breakthrough work by Hofstede was coupled with a serious methodological update on innovation in culture theory from social psychology by Schwartz (1994). Hofstede et al. went beyond the individualism/collectivism dilemma as discussed above within the framework of innovation and entrepreneurship in this book. While the initial steps of business creation involve often the individuals, generally a group, or at least

cooperation among a few individuals, is needed for success, especially in
high-tech based entrepreneurship.

It comes as no surprise that, in particular, Western authors such as
Kanter (2000) make a strong plea on the basis of examples for collaborative methods to build a culture of innovation, such as networks, cross-
boundary teams, supply-chain partnerships and strategic alliances (SAs).
In particular social networks help entrepreneurship (Aldrich and Zimmer,
1986), since family, friends and fools are often the initial investors in new
business ventures. Networks can also be important for opportunity identification and in the internationalization of the venture (see Dana, 2001). A
strong interpersonal trust (Dibben, 2000) and commitment is required for
cooperating in the entrepreneurial venture. Even among start-ups strategic
alliances can stimulate an innovation culture, as Park, Chen and Gallagher
(2002) have demonstrated.

Just a good technological idea is not enough. Success depends again on,
among other things, cultural fit, a key but routinely neglected source of
failure. It is important to spot such cultural sources in time and, once they
occur, to solve them by the correct conflict management styles. In the Chinese
culture, where networks (through *guanxi*) are the most natural things to do
(see Gesteland and Seyk, 2002, for the pros and cons of the different options,
such as joint ventures), team conflict could mostly be avoided to preserve
harmony and face. The book by Selmer (1998) contains several chapters on
partnership management to handle such situations on the basis of
American–Chinese joint ventures both intra- and inter-culturally. How can
an innovation and entrepreneurial culture handle all this?

**Innovation and Entrepreneurial Culture**

It appears that the commonalities between innovative and entrepreneurial
spirit can override the differences between organizational differences.
Cooperation between European start-ups seems to be a key to it (Ulijn and
Fayolle, Chapter 9 in this book) and the EU supports this (see the different
issues of *Innovation and Technology Transfer*). Increased mobility of innovative and entrepreneurial engineers and scientists within the EU is needed
to avoid a further brain drain to the USA (Ulijn and Gould, 2002). If it can
be shown that there is a correlation between mobility and innovation, how
would that put pressure on EU policy-makers? The chapters by Hofstede
et al. (8), Sharif and Chan (2), Baark (3) and Fujimoto (10) also show how
different firms, sectors and countries can learn from each other here. It
seems as if a strong innovation and entrepreneurial drive is needed as a
basic cultural dimension intersecting NC, PC and CC. Apart from creativity, empathy and persistence, this drive seems to be one of the key charac-

teristics of the successful entrepreneur starting up (Waasdorp, 2002). It often requires technology-based innovation and entrepreneurship to make substantial social progress and/or economic growth. We briefly discuss these issues over the next few sections.

## 4. TECHNOLOGY

Advances in technology lead to many innovations and new enterprises. Nobody would deny that. But compared to other sectors, technology-based entrepreneurship seems still to be ripe for investigation. Given its importance to social progress and economic growth, how can more technology-based business creation be encouraged? This is a question with which many are struggling. In a recent study, only 28 per cent of the top 110 fastest growing companies in the Netherlands, appeared to be high tech in recent years, with only 13 per cent of those top 110 in the industrial sector (Waasdorp, 2001). Is this just a Dutch phenomenon? How does it relate to low and medium technology or even biotechnology? The Dutch seems to lag behind in some sectors, such as biotechnology, which is strongly dominated by the USA, Denmark (DK) and the UK. Even in the field of environmental technology, where the Dutch invented the windmills in the seventeenth century, DK is now the leader in producing equipment for wind energy. Edquist, Hommen and McKelvey (2001) adapted Organization for Economic Cooperation and Development (OECD) data from 1996 to show the higher the technology, the more employment there is. Is that still true, and could the job rate be higher, if there is more technology-based entrepreneurship? Fayolle (2002) indicated that in France only 2 per cent of the engineers create high-tech businesses. Therefore, it seems there is a gap between (potential) technological innovation created by engineers and the attempts to exploit those technologies. Why does this gap exist and how can it be closed?

Technology goes more quickly beyond national borders than anything else. For example, ICT is an important source of innovation with a strong impact on human communication (Ulijn, Vogel and Bemelmans, 2002) and negotiation (Ulijn and Kersten/Tjosvold, 2004). Everybody wants to have the most advanced technology, but on the innovation side it is still very much a one-way transfer from West to East or North to South. A study by Shi (1998) shows for the tape recorder sector that Chinese recipients of imported technology were able in 61.3 per cent of cases to do new product development assisted by local organizations as a result of a technology transfer project with a non-Chinese firm. For 90.3 per cent the localization rate was 80 to 100 per cent. Sixty-four per cent reported that they were not imitating the imported equipment, but 96.8 per cent confessed that there was no innovation at all based upon the imported technology. Why in a country with radical innovations in the past, such as the clock, the compass and gunpowder (fireworks), is there not more high-tech entrepreneurship? Innovation is available in many Chinese sectors (Du and Farley, 2001), but technology transfer from outside China does not seem to lead to much learning in the sense of start-ups (Warner, 2000). Or is it just a matter of time?

Technological innovation is directly related to economic performance in countries such as the USA, Japan, Germany, France, the UK and Scandinavia, but seldom to emerging economies, as Steil, Victor and Nelson (2002) indicated. That study covered a wide range of sectors, where technological innovations take place: the Internet, computers and semiconductors, banking and financial intermediation, securities trading, venture capital, pharmaceutical and agricultural biotechnology, electrical power and automobiles. For the European context the book by Jones-Evans and Klofsten (1997) concluded that technology-based small firms become increasingly important for future European industrial employment, and technologically innovative SMEs contribute largely to wealth creation. Multinational companies seem to require more radical technical innovations than they can produce themselves. Apparently SMEs and high-tech start-ups seem to be better able to innovate radically than MNCs, especially if they are helped to do so by the larger firms. How can cooperation between MNCs and SMEs in the area of innovation be encouraged?

One of the roadblocks may be that SMEs traditionally are less internationally orientated than MNCs. If MNCs set up a research agenda for cross-border innovation as suggested by the study by Zander and Sölvell (2000), they could include SMEs to facilitate the international technology transfer needed. Yli-Renko, Autio and Tontti (2002) demonstrated clearly that the international sales growth of technology-based new firms was strongly correlated with internal social capital and knowledge intensity. He further found that management contacts led to significant correlations with foreign market knowledge, geographical diversity and entry mode experience. In addition, one of the strongest correlations was between customer involvement and foreign market knowledge. So one lesson for SMEs could be: become the supplier of MNCs and they will give you more opportunities to innovate internationally. How can culture play a role?

One cultural layer in this is often overlooked: that of the PC of the different fields of expertise involved within MNCs, SMEs and start-ups and across sector borders. Legardeur, Boujut and Tiger (Chapter 7) give the example of design cooperation within the automotive sector where different competencies and PCs have to match. Dr J. Mena de Matos, director of the European Design Centre in Eindhoven (NL) indicated that in a project between seven countries the biggest misunderstanding turned out to be across disciplines, not across national borders (*Innovation and Technology Transfer*, 2001b). Engineers no matter where they came from, saw things in much the same way. Technology appeared to be a unifying factor once more. So the view of economists on technology might be a bit biased. Multinational companies can help high-tech start-ups with their R&D potential and share in the profits of such cooperation. More research is needed to look at how professional cultures affect the innovation process. One hopeful outcome of this research can be the identification of innovation process bottlenecks. The elimination of these problem areas could facilitate innovation and entrepreneurship, especially in MNC/SME joint projects. What additionally can be done to foster international cooperation?

From different sources (Steil, Victor and Nelson, 2002; Ulijn and Gould, 2002) one gets the impression with respect to the innovative and entrepreneurial engineer that the USA still ranks ahead of the EU. One reason for this is the freedom the American workforce has to follow opportunities. The mobility of EU citizens (even within their own countries) is very poor. There might be one exception, Germany, which attracts the most immigrants from other EU member states (25 per cent in 2001) apart from Turks (28 per cent) and 15 per cent from the former Yugoslavia out of a total of 7.7 million foreigners. Steil, Victor and Nelson (2002) showed for Germany that the foreign students are attracted equally to science and engineering and humanities and social sciences.

In general there is a brain drain from new member states in Central and Eastern Europe to the EU and the USA. This amounts to a substantial transfer of human capital, because much of the science and engineering education investment is often done in the home country. Similar trends are to be observed in South Africa and China. The USA remains more popular than Europe. One reason might reside in the following slogan uttered by a Dutch European Parliament member.

> The EU is very good in investing euros into R&D, but when does R&D return those euros by new employment, new businesses as a part of the internal market?

Cross-border cooperation and integration goes slowly (but surely) through Euroregion developments. More recent development also include some countries in Central Europe, such as the virtual incubator of new firms in the border region of Austria, Hungary and Slovakia (see *Innovation and Technology Transfer*, 2002b) and the Phare programme for an infrastructure for economic and social cohesion.

What is true for the EU, may be even more true for the East. Russian engineers, for example, can be very inventive, as the recent Cybiko example shows: a hand-held computer which displays an awesome multifunctionality (www.cybikoxtreme.com), with Taiwanese manufacturing and American marketing. Why can Russian entrepreneurs do all three? Should they? A careful analysis of five entrepreneurial ventures in Russia by Puffer and McCarthy (2001) may have indicated why. They have to navigate through a hostile maze of a political, economic and legal nature. They have to be opportunistic and optimistic and are seen as *different* from other Russians who might envy their success and see the entrepreneur's profit as their own loss (see also Iakovleva, in Fayolle, 2002). So, how do we create a new entrepreneurial spirit for engineers in Russia and in the rest of Europe?

A final reason for the gap between technological innovation, entrepreneurship and the low rate of high-tech venture creation might be the perceived risk involved and the fear of failure. Risk is strongly related to the Hofstedian dimension of uncertainty avoidance, which normally has to be low in the initial stage of innovation and entrepreneurship but should become higher towards the implementation into the market to avoid unnecessary risks (Nakata and Sivakumar, 1996). The innovator in a big firm probably takes less risks than the high-tech venture creator. This is not the place to review the extensive literature on strategic and technological risk perception in entrepreneurial ventures (see Forlani and Mullins, 2000; Busenitz, 1999; Hauptman and Roberts, 1987). We will just summarize some of the general entrepreneurship characteristics touched upon so far and try to relate them to technology entrepreneurship.

Entrepreneurs tend to be individuals with high motivation, risk-taking and proactive behaviour, who seek to create value for themselves and their customers by exploiting innovations, by exploiting opportunities and perhaps by creating new ventures. If they are engineers dealing with innovative technology, they may rely heavily on their formal education and previous experience to help them. The business environment for high-tech venture is usually dynamic/turbulent, heterogeneous and hostile. Success for these ventures often depends on the organizational systems, the strength of the innovation and marketing. As we have stated before, technology-based ventures seem to need a high degree of internal cooperation, perhaps because of the complexity involved. In a very comprehensive book, Dibben (2000) proposed a model of cooperation for the entrepreneurial venture backed up by types of trust in the entrepreneur's interaction with the different actors: (1) dependence (outside), (2) familiarity (both in- and outside), (3) comprehensible situational cue (both inside and outside), and (4) faith (outside). The idea is that trust can facilitate coordination and cooperation in the innovation and venturing process.

With such a high number of uncontrollable factors, augmented with the ever-changing technological perspective for the engineer, there are a lot of risks involved. Entrepreneurs have a generally high-risk propensity, but they do not view themselves as risk-takers. To reduce risks they use more heuristics in their decision-making than innovation managers in big firms. In this context, biases and heuristics are decision rules, simplifying strategies, cognitive mechanisms, and subjective opinions in uncertain and complex situations (see Busenitz, 1999; Kahneman, Slavic and Tversky, 1982). If risks are not taken well and trust has been betrayed, a start-up might fail. What happens then? Waasdorp (2002) quoted from EU sources the results of an EU–US comparison among business managers on the stigma of failure. What is the relationship between the following:

1. One should not start a business, if there is a risk it might fail.
2. Someone who has failed should be given a second chance.

Two extremes show up. Dutch, Austrian and German business managers would say: 'Don't even try to start your own business, if there is a risk to fail.' Irish, American and British peers would say: 'If you fail, just try it again.' Brown's skunk works concept (Chapter 6) certainly helps to convert an obvious failure into a new sign of hope: one should learn from his/her mistakes. In this light it is significant that Dutch bankruptcy law, which dates from the late nineteenth century, recently changed to make trying again easier for the entrepreneur (www.ez.nl/faillissementswet).

All in all, technology and entrepreneurship is still a challenging relationship, which this book can only partly cover (see also Butler, 2001, and Phan, 2000, for more specific studies, including the field of e-commerce). Highly mobile, innovative and entrepreneurial engineers should be encouraged in MNCs, SMEs and start-ups to cooperate across industrial and country borders, to trust new ventures and to take risks. When you fail in start-ups in any part of the world, you should be able to just try it again. How strong is the link between innovation and entrepreneurship as an indicator of economic growth and to what extent is this link seen as social progress? An answer to those questions in the next sections might fuel the need for a true global innovative and entrepreneurial culture.

## 5. ECONOMIC GROWTH

**Is Progress Synonymous with Economic Growth and is it Fostered by any Technological Development?**

The economic growth engine that has innovation and entrepreneurship at its root, can be responsible for wealth creation, wealth redistribution and employment. It can also create substantial value for the customers as well.

In addition, economic growth can be a source of foreign direct investment, development of a country's infrastructure, a strong tax base, etc. It can even lead to the development of a county's art and culture. However, *can* is the operative word. Although economic growth and (social) progress can go hand in hand, it would be naïve of us to think that progress and economic growth are synonymous; but others continue to make that mistake. Growth can certainly help society progress, but it does not guarantee it, especially social progress that is evenly distributed across the population. Innovation, entrepreneurship and growth just provide the potential for social progress. The system of government and the strength and will of the people are largely responsible for whether or not economic growth is translated to social progress.

## 6.   (SOCIAL) PROGRESS

### What is Progress with Respect to Innovation and Entrepreneurship?

One of the first things that comes to mind is that much of the world's innovation comes from the developed countries, while social injustice, unequal wealth distribution, etc. is generally relegated to the less innovative parts of the world. Is this a coincidence? There are entrepreneurs all over the world, even in the poorest regions, but some of them seem to be better connected for technological innovation than others. Could this be one of the reasons?

Do national culture, innovation and entrepreneurship interact in a way that affects social progress? Kolarov's case study of an innovative Bulgarian firm (in Fayolle, 2002) confirms the low to middle individualism of former communist countries (Romania, Serbia, Slovenia, Croatia, Russia, Bulgaria, Hungary, the Czech Republic and Poland in increasing order), the rest of Europe being more individualistic (IND). Is this because of the former communist/capitalist distinction or does it date back to (Slavic) tribal cultures? Kolarov concluded that the innovative culture in these countries implied loyalty, tradition, internal support, family environment teamwork, respect for seniority and formal structure. The collectivism of Central/Eastern European and Asian countries may even assist innovative entrepreneurship, given a stable social cohesion.

The EU has programmes to support such social cohesion. It is clear that an equal balance of innovation and entrepreneurship across country and regional borders could contribute to social progress and justice. The ideas of sustainable entrepreneurship and environmental and social responsibility are a part of social progress. The position of the Scandinavian countries is very peculiar in this respect. They are small, but rich, economies and are also very democratic and generally philanthropic. What is their position in the East–West and North–South social progress scale? The national culture research by Hofstede evidences a lot of similarities between Scandinavian countries such as Sweden, Norway, Denmark and Finland and NL (non-Scandinavian). All those countries share a low power distance (PWD), uncertainty avoidance index (UAI) and masculinity (MAS), and a high individualism.

Looking at the sources Waasdorp (2001) quoted, Finland is the only country with a strong correlation between innovation and start-ups; all the others have a weaker correlation, with Norway having the lowest. When it comes to risk and failure the Nordic countries seem to favour risk and failure avoidance with the exception again of Finland, Denmark and NL. Why is this?

Bjerke (1999) compared American, Arab, Chinese, Japanese and Scandinavian (only Denmark, Sweden and Norway) cultures. The USA with the highest innovation and start-up relationship, displayed a culture where (social) progress and (economic) growth are almost synonyms and the role of the company is to promote personal goals, while in Europe companies would pursue rather societal goals. Bjerke used some of the above Hofstedian dimensions, such as PWD and UAI (important for innovation and entrepreneurship) and related them in one model to attitudes towards time and environment, people relations, expressed through communication, measure of success, attitude to trust, aims, skills wanted and societal orientation and, finally, to problem-solving and attitude to change. In particular, the interaction between social and time orientations between the above five culture groups and the PWD–skills interaction (both very relevant for converting innovation into entrepreneurship) may give insight into why Scandinavian countries may lag behind the USA in innovation and start-ups. Scandinavian countries have a long-term/individual orientation; they are *learners* (see Lundval, 2002). The Americans have an orientation towards the future, but are short-term/individual (opportunists), the Chinese believe in reputation, with a short-term/group orientation, whereas Japanese and Arabs believe in dominance: a long-term group orientation. Both the Japanese and Scandinavians share a desire for equality among people, while Americans prefer equal systems skills. Finally, Arabs are loyalists, because they have unequal systems skills, while the Chinese are adapters, because of their unequal people skills.

As a conclusion Bjerke stated that the US system be considered a *shareholders' capitalism*. The Scandinavian countries' system cherishes *stakeholders' capitalism*, which bears a responsibility to contribute to a social cohesion. However, this *socialist* attitude does not seem to be very beneficial for the start-up rate.

Finally, one other dimension might be relevant in this social progress dis-cussion linked to innovation and entrepreneurship: a low MAS or high femininity in the Scandinavian countries in the broad sense. This implies a high degree of empathy, affiliation, open communication and participative decision-making (see Gundry, Ben-Yoseph and Posig, 2002) which men in 'feminine' societies also display. It comes as no surprise, then, that 4200 female Swedish entrepreneurs did not underperform at all compared to their male peers (Du Rietz and Henrekson, 2000). Birley (1998) found that there are far more psychological and demographical similarities between women and men entrepreneurs than earlier research suggested. The number of minority female start-ups is increasing: by 1996, 13 per cent of women-owned businesses in the USA were owned by women of colour (Gundry, Ben-Yoseph and Posig, 2002; and see Inman, 2000 for a further overview). It should be obvious that women have to play an important role in social progress. Although female entrepreneurs may underachieve more in some areas such as international entrepreneurship, perhaps it is because of their (over)dependence on family capital (Gundry, Ben-Yoseph and Posig, 2002.).

In sum, innovation and entrepreneurship play a significant role in the economic growth of a country. In fact, innovation and entrepreneurship may be the most important factors that drive the process of economic development. However, while ultimately economic development is vital for the advancement of a country, we cannot confuse economic growth with social progress. Although both economic growth and social progress vary across countries and are related to particular details such as national culture, history, tradition and so on, social progress is also affected by things such as wealth distribution, individual/human rights, equalization of gender rights, which are not directly affected by economic growth.

## 7.    SUMMARIES OF CHAPTERS

We would like to acknowledge here the first international ECIS Conference (Eindhoven Universities of Technology, NL ) held in September 2001 from which we invited some of the authors of the best papers to adapt them as chapters in our book.

### Innovation

Chapter 2. Sharif, Naubahar (Cornell University, USA) and Ivy Chan (National University of Singapore), 'Conceptualizing innovation manage-ment and culture in the Hong Kong Special Administrative Region

(HKSAR): an exploratory study of organization-specific critical success factors'.

Sharif and Chan attempt to identify the building blocks at the organizational level that may contribute to national innovativeness using Hong Kong as setting and the concept of a National System of Innovation as a framework.

In summary, the chapter theorizes that organizations' learning initiatives, rooted in management culture and their staff's individual learning styles, are positively related with internal cooperation. Innovators and creative thinkers should be encouraged. They also posit that there are a few other activities which if an organization were to engage in, would foster the requisite culture necessary for innovation. In addition, they argue that organizations that have active relationships with other organizations contribute towards development in a macro-culture of national innovativeness. Next, they discuss how and why the government has a key role to play in the development of national innovativeness in the areas of SME policy as well as knowledge dissemination and distribution. Ultimately, they conclude that while firms are at the center of the innovation process, the development of national innovativeness is dependent on many factors that can vary across country, networking and collaboration among organizations seems to be the most important.

Chapter 3. Baark, Erik (University of Science and Technology, Hong Kong), 'Knowledge management, institutions and professional cultures in engineering consulting services: the case of Hong Kong'.

Baark explores the context of innovation in engineering consultancy, again using Hong Kong as the setting. He accomplishes this by examining key contingencies shaping innovation processes based on a taxonomy of four major dimensions of engineering consultancy business: professional culture, institutional framework, knowledge creation and information technology infrastructure.

His findings suggest that the professional culture of engineering consultancy in Hong Kong, has attempted to distance itself from the questionable practices of some local Hong Kong contractors and subcontracting entrepreneurs. As a result the professional engineering culture has maintained its Anglo-American roots and traditions of professional autonomy and ethics, and thereby has established a framework that seeks to maintain international standards for quality of services and innovation.

In addition, trends in the institutional framework of engineering consultancy in Hong Kong, like a greater complexity of project-based services, new procurement approaches and building codes, have tended to constrain innovative efforts of engineering consultants.

Baark links knowledge creation and accumulation in engineering consulting with innovation in the field and describes how important specially crafted knowledge management systems are key success factors for engineering consultant firms. He ends the chapter by pointing to the expanding information technology infrastructure for engineering consultancy firms in Hong Kong, and suggests that in the growing technology infrastructure there exist unexploited opportunities for firms, especially smaller firms, to innovate.

Chapter 4. Frenken, Koen (Utrecht University, NL) and Loet Leydesdorff (University of Amsterdam, NL), 'Scientometrics and the evaluation of European integration'.

Frenken and Leydesdorff, confront the issue of European integration. At the root of this issue are the fundamental questions of the existence of a European union and how well the European Union is doing against its primary objective. The lens through which they examine this issue is scientific research. More specifically, they use scientometrics to determine quantitatively the level of integration of the European science system. As a result, issues such as collaborative research efforts, national science policy, national culture and professional culture are discussed.

But, as with most of the chapters in this book, this chapter is intended to facilitate, supplement and encourage discussion rather than to definitively answer questions regarding whether or not European integration *exists in the sciences*.

**Entrepreneurship**

Chapter 5. Te Velde, Robbin (Delft University of Technology, NL), 'Schumpeter's theory of economic development revisited'.

Te Velde tackles the legendary Schumpeter but, unlike the vast majority of researchers that often cite him, Te Velde has read both his early works and his later works in great detail. As a result, he can make the bold claim that Schumpeter was consistent throughout his career with respect to his views on economic development and the entrepreneur as the central agent for technological and economic change. Te Velde states that Schumpeter's theory of economic development not only rightfully puts the activities of the individual entrepreneur at the centre of the analysis, but that the theory is not just a treatise on entrepreneurial activity, but rather a *general* theory of economic development.

Te Velde spends most of the rest of the chapter describing the Schumpeterian entrepreneur in detail, in context and in light of today's economy, which is very interesting given that Schumpeter first wrote about it over 90 years ago. He concludes by outlining the characteristics of this special entrepreneur. He then calls to whoever is listening (governments?) to provide the environments so they can multiply.

Chapter 6. Brown, Terrence E. (Royal Institute of Technology and the Stockholm School of Entrepreneurship, Sweden) 'Skunk works: a sign of failure, a sign of hope?'

Co-editor Brown focuses on a special type of administrative innovation, new product development and organizational culture. As we move to even more dynamic business environments, he states that it has become increasingly important for business to be innovative, not just to gain a competitive advantage, but to survive. As a result, organizing for innovation has become a key business objective. Of the many organizational innovations to emerge, one of the most well known is the skunk works.

The evidence, at least anecdotally, is that great innovations are often the result. However, this chapter begins by taking a slightly different view. Influenced by the perspective of Schrage (1999) this chapter takes the view that the creation of a skunk works is often a signal of management dysfunction. The formation of a skunk works is a signal that the regular organization's structure, systems, process, etc. are no longer able to handle innovation or radical change, so, as a result, must form a new, separate organization, built on exclusivity, in order to be innovative. Furthermore, not only does the creation of a skunk works signal management dysfunction, but also may even accelerate the dysfunction.

However, the chapter does not stop there. The skunk works concept and practice is actually confused, complex and misunderstood. As a result, this chapter attempts to begin to define, clarify and structure the concept. This results in the creation of the skunk works matrix, the research activity continuums and group of key success factors. Ultimately, it seems that the skunk works-like programmes that are the most effective are those that create the most value for the organization as a whole. To create this value there is a greater emphasis on development rather than research. Furthermore, this development is product development and, as a result, has a strong emphasis on the market. Despite the fact that many skunk works-like programmes are created under less than ideal circumstances, for less than ideal reasons, the use of skunk works of all types by large corporations seem to be accelerating. Therefore, it is a ripe area for further research. This chapter raises more questions than it answers and by that helps in spurring the dialogue.

Chapter 7. Legardeur, Jérémy (Laboratoire LIPSI, Bidart and Laboratoire 35, Grenoble, France), Jean François Boujut (Laboratoire GILCO and Laboratoire 35, Grenoble, France) and Henri Tiger (Laboratoire CRISTO,

Grenoble, France), 'Entrepreneurship and the design process: the paradox of innovation in a routine design process'.

Legardeur, Boujut and Tiger present an empirical study based on the development of design process. More specifically, it is about how knowledge, learning, and entrepreneurial competence come together to create innovation in the design process. The authors found that there are considerable problems and complexity for the innovative process within a highly constrained environment.

The result of their analysis calls for a rethinking of the roles, competencies and actors required to innovate the design process. Furthermore, the problem of product and process integration is highlighted through questioning the role of external suppliers in the early design phases.

### Culture

Chapter 8. Hofstede, Geert, Niels G. Noorderhaven (both Tilburg University, NL), A. Roy Thurik, Alexander R.M. Wennekers, Ralph E. Wildeman (Erasmus University, NL) and Lorraine M. Uhlaner (Eastern Michigan University, USA), 'Culture's role in entrepreneurship: self-employment out of dissatisfaction'.

Hofstede, Noorderhaven, Thurik, Uhlaner and Wennekers and Wildeman examine in depth the influence of cultural, economic and psychological attitudinal variables on differences in the level of entrepreneurship in more than 20 Western nations and Japan, for the period 1974–94.

After integrating data on entrepreneurial and economic variables with data on cultural variables, their results showed that, across nations, dissatisfaction with society and with life in general are the main determinants of the level of entrepreneurship. Specifically, countries where people are less satisfied have more self-employed individuals. Furthermore, these are the same countries that have a larger power distance, stronger uncertainty avoidance, more bureaucracy and corruption, and which are relatively poor.

Next the authors test a model that predicts the level of entrepreneurship using economic and dissatisfaction variables. Among the many results was support for the conclusion that dissatisfaction with life and with society are key determinants of the level of entrepreneurship across nations. At the end of the chapter, by using the well-known Hofstede indices of national culture, they demonstrate that culture seems to serve as an important moderator variable in relationships between economic factors and level of entrepreneurship.

Chapter 9. Ulijn, Jan (Eindhoven University of Technology, NL) and Alain Fayolle (INP Grenoble–ESISAR, EPI, France), 'Towards cooperation between European start-ups: the position of the French, Dutch and German entrepreneurial and innovative engineer'.

Co-editors Ulijn and Fayolle explore directly the issues of innovation, entrepreneurship and culture. While the chapter certainly raises more questions than it can answer, the authors try to develop a model of the entrepreneurial and innovative European engineer and his/her interaction with the environment through networks and cooperation. This is backed up with some answers to eight research questions related to data about the entrepreneur's economic environment, the rate of self-employment and some of its difficulties, and the possible effect of national culture on willingness to start a new venture in France, the Netherlands and Germany. Moreover, the research on which this chapter was based examines how national culture and professional culture and differences affect how engineers, innovators and entrepreneurship collaborate.

The authors go further by attempting to address the question of how to foster cooperation between European start-ups for a better enterprising and innovative culture. In this effort they address issues such as mobility and immigration. Because of the problems of cross-functional communications, it seems there are new virtual borders preventing cooperation that might lead to venture creation. As a result, the authors present a summarizing model of a new cultural identity of Europe based upon entrepreneurship, innovation and mobility using the onion culture metaphor by Hofstede (1991) and Schein (1991) to increase the mobility of the European engineer (Ulijn and Gould, 2002). In the end the authors believe that a new culture is needed to foster the cooperation between high, low and other technology start-ups to facilitate a truly European technology entrepreneurship.

10. Fujimoto, Takahiro (Tokyo and Harvard Universities, Japan and USA), 'Multi-path system emergence: an evolutionary framework to analyse process innovation'.

In the final chapter Fujimoto examines long-term process innovation that creates a new and competitive manufacturing system. Fujimoto posits that one of the key questions in process innovation is whether manufacturing routines are pre-planned or do they emerge dynamically? With this in mind he proposes a kind of evolutionary framework that may be applicable to an artificial system that he believes is *ex post* rational: for example, a manufacturing system of Toyota Motor. By evolutionary framework he means a 'dynamic perspective that separately explains an observed system's survival (i.e., the functional logic) and its formation (i.e., the genetic logic)'. In addition to this, Fujimoto attempts to add two new main concepts to the existing evolutionary framework to innovations – *multi-path system emergence* and *evolutionary learning capability*.

In the end Fujimoto presents an intriguing challenge to the so-called rational manager and management. While most decision-makers assume that most processes are rational, Fujimoto's lesson to managers is that they should not assume rational plans always solve those (rational) problems. Furthermore, given the actual process of system change is generally emergent, successful companies must develop an organizational culture of *preparedness*, if they intend to be successful in the future.

## 8.  DISCUSSION OF THE INTERACTION BETWEEN THE SIX KEY ELEMENTS OF THE BOOK

So far we have tackled interactions between the Innovation (I), Entrepreneurship (E) and Culture (C) on the one hand, and Technology (T), Growth (G) and Progress (P) on the other. This section attempts to give a brief overview of all (see Table 1.1).

Most of our chapters deal with both innovation and entrepreneurship, the more innovation-based studies by Frenken and Leydesdorf and Fujimoto are not very explicit on entrepreneurship. Innovation is linked to learning (Sharif and Chan), Baark (knowledge management), science-based (Frenken and Leydesdorf), related to the design process (Legardeur, Boujut and Tiger) or process innovation (Fujimoto). The chapters by Te Velde and Brown deal basically with entrepreneurship/intrapreneurship. Entrepreneurship comes back in SME (Sharif and Chan) and services contexts (Baark); it links up to intrapreneurship (Brown) or is needed to innovate routines (Legardeur, Boujut and Tiger). Both innovation and entrepreneurship are often technology related (see Sections 4 and 5).

Do our chapters discuss the link between technology and economic growth? In this book a wide variety of technologies are discussed including R&D (Sharif and Chan), engineering consulting and construction sectors (Baark), IT (Te Velde), aviation technology (Brown), sheet molding compounds and the automotive sector (Legardeur, Boujut and Tiger, and Fujimoto). The link with (economic) growth is explicit in Hofstede et al. and Ulijn and Fayolle who use features such as GDP, population density and labour productivity. This link with growth is less direct in Sharif and Chan (SME policy) and Frenken and Leydesdorff (long-term EU success). The advancement of technology brings about uncertainty and change. The best practices model by the EU (see *Innovation and Technology Transfer*, 2001b) covered well many managerial and techno-organizational aspects, including participation, structural and labour components, and a commitment to change for effective knowledge and innovation management. The study by Shenhar (2001) in 26 high-tech case projects in the USA pinpoints well that the intensity of communication tends to increase with technological uncertainty to achieve such cultural change towards more innovation and entrepreneurship. Brown, Legardeur, Boujut and Tiger, and Ulijn and Fayolle suggest clearly the need for such change.

Both innovation and entrepreneurship can create employment, but engineers could be more active start-ups than their culture seems to allow, as we have concluded so far in this chapter. Employment as part of social economics and the transition to innovation and entrepreneurship as part of social progress is obvious; everybody wants to be employed, but self-employment is another story as Hofstede et al. (with the share of female labour) imply. A comparison between the USA and Japan would be interesting here. In both countries long-term growth and progress seem to be synonymous, but the social context would be more flexible and open in the USA, whereas in Japan there is greater restraint (see Steil, Victor and Nelson, 2002), where the entire country seems to go for the type of innovation for which Fujimoto suggests a neo-Darwinian evolution which is not incremental or radical. In addition, on the basis of their further analysis Steil, Victor and Nelson (2002) recommended that Germany be more open and market flexible, and enter newly emerging fields of technology, such as biotechnology and software, with sufficient vigour to actually establish a leading position. They suggested to the French government a devolution of power and wealth to give public operators in innovation and entrepreneurship more freedom to set their own long-term strategies within a coherent subsidy scheme, instead of piling up often small and scattered financial injections.

As we have seen so far, innovation does not lead automatically to entrepreneurship; a special innovation and/or entrepreneurial culture needs to be developed as suggested in the Ulijn and Fayolle chapter (9). The growth/progress dynamics can be enforced by a cultural change, as conceptualized by Gagliardi (1986), who proposes an incremental model to go from old to new idealizations through insertion of new values to be reconciled with the old ones through stabilization, cohesion, organizational efficiency, collective experience of success and, ultimately, consolidation of new experiences. Countries, corporations and professionals can learn from each other across borders, and not only in the more traditional North–South or West–East direction, as the study on Russian entrepreneurship by Puffer and McCarthy (2001) might suggest. Weber (1958) explained the strong Western entrepreneurial behaviour by using the Protestant work ethic, but is it so different from the Muslim ethics in Arab countries such as Tunisia where an analysis of the exceptional entrepreneurship of the Sfax region (see Zghal, in Fayolle, 2002) could not be explained by geographical reasons alone? The right psychological mindset and a favourable social environment are important for start-ups. The Chinese Confucian ethic as

*Table 1.1  Which chapters cover which elements of the book title?*

| Chapters and elements | Innovation (I) | Entrepreneurship (E) | Culture: NC-CC-PC | Technology (T) | Progress (P) | Economic growth (EG) | Interaction? Comments |
|---|---|---|---|---|---|---|---|
| *Innovation* | | | | | | | |
| 2. Sharif/Chan | ++ Learning | SME | NC: Hong Kong management culture | R&D | National innovativeness | SME policy | ± |
| 3. Baark | Knowledge management | Services | PC: Engineering, NC: Hong Kong | Engineering consulting, construction sector | Colonial past IT infrastructure | NA | ± |
| 4. Frenken/ Leydesdorff | Science-based | NA | EU (several countries), USA, Japan | Scientometrics | + | Long-term EU success | + |
| *Entrepreneurship* | | | | | | | |
| 5. Te Velde | + | ++ | Claim on universatility | + IT | Is culture also gradual? | + | + |
| 6. Brown | + | + Intrapreneur? | CC: Skunk works shows a counterculture | + Aviation technology | Probably | NA | + |
| 7. Legardeur/ Boujut/Tiger | Design process | Needed to innovate routines | PC: from steel to SMC | Sheet molding compound (SMC) | NA | NA | Theory-based case study |

*Culture*

| | | | | | | | |
|---|---|---|---|---|---|---|---|
| 8. Hofstede et al. | + | ++ | ? | NC: EU, Jap, USA, Can., NZ, Austria | Female labour share employment | Link with GDP, pop. density | Strong empirical study |
| 9. Uljin/Fayolle | + | ++ | Positions of engineers | EU (Fr, NL, DK) | Employment | Link with GDP, labour productivity | Some empirical test of a model of an enterprise +innovation |
| 10. Fujimoto | Evolutionary | NA | Manufacturing | CC: Japan | NA | NA | + |

exemplified in the LTO dimension of Hofstede in Section 4 is another case in point.

Although innovation and entrepreneurial culture have much in common, there is one exception: the nature of cooperation. As Cottam, Ensor and Band (2001) indicate in their benchmark study of strategic commitment to innovation, within existing firms strong cross-functional teams are necessary. Within start-ups there is insufficient cooperation because of their minimal size, and joint ventures between start-ups are not easy because of a lack of the trust which would be required to share a smart technological idea or a niche in the market (see Ulijn and Fayolle, Chapter 9). Between existing firms cooperation is often achieved by networking and alliancing, which requires the mostly overlooked cultural fit (see Steensma, Weaver and Dickson, 2000, Ulijn, Duysters, Schaetzlein and Remer, in press). Some aspects of the Chinese guanxi concept might be very useful here (Wong and Leung, 2001), in particular the ones related to entrepreneurship, empathy, commitment and synergy. In sum, most of our 10 chapters pay attention to the interaction between some of the six elements. In most of them there is a blend of conceptualization, empirical studies and, even, case studies. What remains still to be studied?

## 9.   CONCLUSION

When you come to the conclusion section of a chapter or book as a reader, you expect the authors to succinctly summarize and highlight the major points of the preceding text and perhaps give some insightful and witty comments as they wrap up. When you come to the conclusion section as an author, you expect cogently to summarize the major points and wrap it up in a nice and tidy way. However, authors also know that this is not always possible. Some chapters do not easily lend themselves to tidy packages; this is one such chapter.

In this chapter we have made many statements about innovation, entrepreneurship, culture (at three levels), technology, social progress and economic growth. We have made a strong case that they are all important and are all related (and perhaps even interact, moderate and/or mediate each other). It is a complex and messy mix, but one that is important to investigate further. Although there have been volumes of research separately (and perhaps in dyads or triads) on many of these topics, much more work needs to be done at the conceptual level, at the methodological level, from an academic perspective and from a practical perspective.

Our primary purpose in this book is to open, push and continue the debate. We do this by posing many more questions than we attempt or even dare to answer. So, in the end, where does that leave us? (A last, final question.)

# REFERENCES

Acs, Z.J., R.K. Morck and B. Yeung (2001), 'Entrepreneurship, globalization, and public policy', *Journal of International Management*, 7, 235–51.
Aldrich, H.E. and C. Zimmer (1986), 'Entrepreneurship through social networks', in D.L. Sexton and R.W. Smilor (eds), *The Art and Science of Entrepreneurship*, Cambridge, MA: Ballinger, pp. 3–24.
Bartelsman, E.J. and J. Hinloopen (2001), 'Unleashing animal spirits: investment in ICT and economic growth', unpublished paper.
Birley, S. (ed.) (1998), *Entrepreneurship*, Dartmouth: Ashgate.
Birley, S. and I. MacMillan (1997), *Entrepreneurship in Global Context*, London: Routledge.
Bjerke, B. (1999), *Business Leadership and Culture*, Cheltenham: Edward Elgar.
Bond, M. and G. Hofstede (1989), 'The cash value of Confucian values', *Human Systems Management*, 8, 195–200.
Bruyat, C. and P.A. Julien (2001), 'Defining the field of entrepreneurship', *Journal of Business Venturing*, 16 (2), 165–80.
Busenitz, L.W. (1999), 'Entrepreneurial risk and strategic decision making: it is a matter of perspective', *Journal of Applied Behavioural Science*, 35 (3), 325–41.
Butler, J.E. (ed.) (2001), *E-Commerce and Entrepreneurship*, London: IAP.
Cavusgil, S.T. and Y.M. Godiwalla (1982), 'Decision making for international marketing: a comparative review', *Management Decision*, 20 (4), 47–54.
Chaiken, S. and J. Trope (1998), *Dual-Process Theories in Social Psychology*, Guildford Press.
Cottam, A., J. Ensor and C. Band (2001), 'A benchmark study of strategic commitment to innovation', *European Journal of Innovation Management*, 4 (2), 88–94.
Crane, R. (2000), *European Business Cultures*, Harlow: Pearson Education.
Cromie, S. (2000), 'Assessing entrepreneurial inclinations: some approaches and empirical evidence', in M. Frese, E. Chell and H. Klandt (eds), 'Psychological approaches to entrepreneurship', special issue of *European Journal of Work and Organizational Psychology*, 9 (1), 7–30.
Cumming, B. (1998), 'Innovation overview and future challenges', *European Journal of Innovation Management*, 1 (1), 21–9.
Dana, L.P. (1999), *Entrepreneurship in Pacific Asia: Past, Present, and Future*, London: World Scientific.
Dana, L.P. (ed.) (2001), 'Networks, internationalization and policy', introduction to a special issue of *Small Business Economics*, 16 (2), 157–62.
Dana, L.P. (2002), *When economies change paths: Models of transition in China, the Central Asian Republics, Myanmar and the Nations of former Indochine Française*, London: World Scientific.
Darsoe, L. (2001), *Innovation in the Making*, Frederiksberg: Samfundslitteratur.
Delinchant, B., V. Riboulet, P. Marin, F. Noël and F. Wurtz (2002), 'Cooperative design among mechanical and electrical engineers over the Internet: some implications for professional culture and human communication', in Ulijn, Vogel and Bemelmans (2002).

Dibben, M.R. (2000), *Exploring Interpersonal Trust in the Entrepreneurial Venture*, Chippendale: Macmillan Business.

Du, Y. and J. Farley (2001), 'Research on technological innovation as seen through the Chinese looking glass', *Journal of Enterprising Culture*, **9** (1), 53–90.

Du Rietz, A. and M. Henrekson (2000), 'Testing the female underperformance hypothesis', *Small Business Economics*, **14** (1), 1–10.

Eagly, A. and S. Chaiken (1993), *The Psychology of Attitudes*, New York: Harcourt Brace Jovanovich.

Edquist, Ch., L. Hommen and M. McKelvey (2001), *Innovation and Employment*, Cheltenham, UK and Northampton, MA, USA: Edward Elgar.

Euram Conference (2002), special issue of *Creativity and Innovation Management*, London: Blackwell.

Fayolle, A. (2000), 'Exploratory study to assess the effects of entrepreneurship programs on French student entrepreneurial behaviors', *Journal of Enterprising Culture*, **8** (2), 169–84.

Fayolle, A. (2002), *Entrepreneurship Research in Europe: Specificities and Perspectives*, Book of Abstracts of the first European Summer University, Valence, 19–22 September (contributions by Amo, Dana, Davidsson, Delmar, Fayolle and Bruyat, Groen, Iakovleva, Frank, Korunka and Lueger, Kyrö and Kansikas, Kolarov, Oftedal, Sepp and Hankov, Van der Veen and Wakkee, Zghal).

Fayolle, A., J. Ulijn and A. Nagel (2002), 'The entrepreneurial orientation towards technology management: the example of French, German and Dutch engineers', in D. Probert, T. Durand, O. Granstrand and H. Tschirky (eds), *Bringing Technology into the Boardroom*, Basingstoke: Palgrave.

Fonseca, R., P. Lopez García and C.A. Pissaride (2001), 'Entrepreneurship, start-up costs and employment', *European Economic Review*, **45**, 692–705.

Forlani, D. and J.W. Mullins (2000), 'Perceived risks and choices in entrepreneurs' new venture decisions', *Journal of Business Venturing*, **15** (4), 305–22.

Frese, M., E. Chell and H. Klandt (eds) (2000), 'Psychological approaches to entrepreneurship', special issue of *European Journal of Work and Organizational Psychology*, **9** (1), 128 pp.

Gagliardi, P. (1986), 'The creation and change of organizational cultures: a conceptual framework', *Organization Studies*, **7** (2), 117–34.

Gartner, W.B. (1985), 'A conceptual framework for describing the phenomenon of new venture creation', *Academy of Management Review*, **10**, 696–706.

Gartner, W.B. (1989), 'Who is an entrepreneur? Is the wrong question', *Entrepreneurship in Theory and Practice*, Summer, 47–68.

Gesteland, R.R. and G.F. Seyk (2002), *Marketing across Cultures Asia: A Practical Guide*, Copenhagen: Copenhagen Business School Press.

Gray, C. (1998), *Enterprise and Culture*, London: Routledge.

Gundry, L.K., M. Ben-Yoseph and M. Posig (2002), 'Contemporary perspectives on women's entrepreneurship: a review and strategic recommendations', *Journal of Enterprising Culture*, **10** (1), 67–86.

Hart, S.J., J.R. Webb and M.V Jones (1994), 'Export marketing research and the effect of export experience in industrial SME's', *International Marketing Review*, **11** (6), 4–22.

Hartman, H. (1959), Managers and entrepreneurs: A useful distinction?', *Administrative Science Quarterly*, **3**, 429–57.

Hauptman, O. and E.B. Roberts (1987), 'FDA regulation of product risk and its impact upon young biomedical firms', *Journal of Product Innovation Management*, **2**, 138–49.

Hisrich, R., C. Brush, D. Good, and G. Desouza (1997), 'Performance in entrepreneurial ventures. Does gender matter?', *Frontiers of Entrepreneurship Research*, Wellesley, MA: Babson College, 238–9.

Hofstede, G. (1991), *Culture and organizations: Software of the mind*, London: McGraw Hill.

*Innovation and Technology Transfer*, European Commission, Enterprise DG, Innovation Directorate, several issues, including very interesting Eurostat surveys, such as:

'Innovation scoreboard' (2001a), **5**, October, special issue (www.cordis.lu/itt/itt-enhome.html and http: trendchart.cordis.lu/Scoreboard/scoreboard.htm)

'Innovation policy: exchange of good practice' (2001b), **5**, September.

'Innovation projects' (2001c), **6**, November.

'A balance of interests' (2002a), **1**, January.

'Business incubation: growing companies' (2002b), **4**, July.

Risk and reward: changing the climate' (2002c), **5**, September.

Jones, M.V. (2001), 'First steps in internationalisation: concepts and evidence from a sample of small high-technology firms', *Journal of International Management*, **7**, 191–210.

Jones-Evans, D. and M. Klofsten (1997), *Technology, Innovation and Enterprise: The European Experience*, Houndmills: Macmillan.

Kahneman, D., P. Slavic and A. Tversky (1982), *Judgment under Uncertainty: Heuristics and Biases*, Cambridge: Cambridge University Press.

Kanter, R.M. (2000), 'A culture of innovation', *Executive Excellence*, **10**, 10–11.

Kets de Vries, M. (1996), 'The anatomy of the entrepreneur: clinical observations', *Human Relations*, **49** (7), 853–82.

Knight, G.A. (2001), 'Entrepreneurship and strategy in the international SME', *Journal of International Management*, **7**, 155–71.

Kreuger, N. (ed.) (2002), *Entrepreneurship*, (4 vols), London: Routledge, with research advice in vols 3 and 4.

Kunda, G. (1992), *Engineering Culture: Control and Commitment in a High-tech Corporation*, Philadelphia, PA: Temple University Press.

Kyrö, P. and J. Kansikas (2002), 'Current state of methodology in entrepreneurship research and some expectations for the future', unpublished contribution to Fayolle (2002), see above.

Lavoie, D. and E. Chamlee-Wright (2000), *Culture and Enterprise*, London: Routledge.

Lenartowicz, T. and J.P. Johnson (2002), 'Comparing managerial values in twelve Latin American countries: an exploratory study', *Management International Review*, **42**, 279–307.

Levy, N.S. (1998), *Managing High Technology and Innovation*, Englewood Cliffs, NJ: Prentice-Hall.

Litzinger, W.D. (1965), 'The motel entrepreneur and the motel manager', *Academy of Management Journal*, **8**, 268–81.

Lundvall, B.-A. (2002), *Innovation, Growth and Social Cohesion: The Danish Model of a Learning Economy*, Cheltenham, UK and Northampton, MA, USA: Edward Elgar.

Mairesse, J. and P. Mohnen (2002), 'Accounting for innovation and measuring innovativeness: an illustrative framework and an application', unpublished paper, ENSEA (Fr) and University of Maastricht (NL).

Martin, J. (2002), *Organizational Culture: Mapping the Terrain*, Thousand Oaks, CA: Sage.

Mintzberg, J. (1979), *The Structuring of Organizations*, Englewood Cliffs, NJ: Prentice-Hall.

Montalvo, C.C. (2001), 'Explaining and predicting the innovative behaviour of the firm: a behavioural approach', contribution to ECIS conference, The Future of Innovation Studies, 20–23 September, Eindhoven.

Nakata, C. and K. Sivakumar (1996), 'National culture and new product development: an integrative review', *Journal of Marketing*, **60** (1), 61–72.

Park, S.H., R. Chen and S. Gallagher (2002), 'Firm resources as moderators of the relationships between market growth and strategic alliances in semiconductor start ups', *Academy of Management Journal*, **45** (3), 527–45.

Pinchot, G. (1985), *Intrapreneuring*, New York: Harper.

Puffer, S.M. and D.J. McCarthy (2001), 'Navigating the hostile maze: a framework for Russian entrepreneurship', *Academy of Management Executive*, **15** (4), 24–38.

Roberts, E.B. and C.A. Berry (1985), 'Entering new businesses: selecting strategies for success', *Sloan Management Review*, Spring, 3–17.

Robertson, R. (1974), 'Innovation management', *Management Decision Monograph*, **12** (6), 332.

Rokeach, M. (1973), *The Nature of Human Values*, New York: Free Press.

Schein, E.R. (1991), 'What is culture?', in P.J. Frost, L.F. Moore, and M.R. Louis (eds), *Reframing Organizational Culture*, London: Sage, pp. 243–53.

Schrage, M. (1999), 'What is the bad odor at the innovation skunkworks?', *Fortune*, Dec. 20, p. 338.

Schwartz, S.H. (1994), 'Beyond individualism/collectivism: new cultural dimensions of values', in U. Kim, H.C. Triandis and G. Yoon (eds), *Individualism and Collectivism: Theoretical and Methodological Issues*, Newbury Park, CA: Sage.

Schwartz, S.H. and W. Bilsky (1990), 'Toward a theory of the universal content and structure of values: Extensions and cross-cultural replications', *Journal of Personality and Social Psychology*, **58**, 878–91.

Selmer, J. (ed.) (1998), *International Management in China: Cross-Cultural Issues*, London: Routledge.

Shane, S. (ed.) (2002), *Foundations of Entrepreneurship*, 2 vols, Cheltenham, UK and Northampton, MA, USA: Edward Elgar.

Shane, S.A. (1992), 'Why do some societies invent more than others?', *Journal of Business Venturing*, **7** (1), 29–46.

Shane, S.A. (1995), 'Uncertainty avoidance and the preference for innovation championing roles', *Journal of International Business Studies*, **26** (1): 47–68.

Shane, S.A. (1997), 'Cultural differences in the championing of global innovation', in R. Katz (ed.), *The Human Side of Innovation*, New York: Oxford University Press, pp. 296–303.

Shane, S. and S. Venkataraman (2000), 'The promise of entrepreneurship as a field of research', *Academy of Management Review*, **25** (1), 217–27.

Shane, S.A., S. Venkataraman and I. MacMillan (1995), 'Cultural differences in innovation championing strategies', *Journal of Management*, **21** (5), 931–52.

Shenhar, A.J. (2001), 'Contingent management in temporary, dynamic organizations: the comparative analysis of projects', *Journal of High Technology Management Research*, **2**, 239–71.

Shi, Y. (1998), *Chinese Firms and Technology in the Reform Era*, London: Routledge.

Smits, R. (2001), 'Innovation studies in the 21st century: impacts from trends in economy and society', unpublished paper.

Steensma, H.K., L.M.K.M. Weaver and P.H. Dickson (2000), 'The influence of national culture on the formation of technology alliances by entrepreneurial firms', *Academy of Management Journal*, **43** (5), 951–73.

Steil, B., D.G. Victor and R.R. Nelson (2002), *Technological Innovation and Economic Performance*, Princeton, NJ: Princeton University Press.

Thornberry, N. (2001), 'Corporate entrepreneurship', *European Management Journal*, **19** (5), 526–33.

Ulijn, J. and R. Gould (2002), 'Towards a new European cultural identity of entrepreneurship, innovation and mobility through technology (by increasing the mobility of entrepreneurial and innovative engineers): an issue and discourse analysis of the views of 41 students and 5 MEPs', contribution to the Jean Monnet conference on Intercultural Dialogue, Brussels, 20 and 21 March.

Ulijn, J. and G. Kersten/D. Tjosvold (2004), special issues of *International Negotiation* on Innovation, Culture and Negotiation.

Ulijn, J. and Kumar, R. (2000), 'Technical communication in a multicultural world: how to make it an asset in managing international businesses, lessons from Europe and Asia for the 21st century', in P.J. Hager and H.J. Scheiber (eds), *Managing Global Discourse: Essays on International Scientific and Technical Communication*, New York: Wiley, pp. 319–48.

Ulijn, J. and A. Lincke (2004), 'The effect of CMC and FTF on negotiation success between R&D and manufacturing partners in the supply chain', contribution to a special issue of *International Negotiation* on 'Innovation and negotiation: the medium' (edited by J. Ulijn and G. Kersten)

Ulijn, J. and K. St. Amant (2000), 'Mutual intercultural perception: how does it affect technical communication, some data from China, the Netherlands, Germany, France and Italy', *Technical Communication*, **47** (2), 220–37.

Ulijn, J. and M. Weggeman (2001), 'Towards an innovation culture: what are its national, corporate, marketing and engineering aspects, some experimental evidence', in C. Cooper, S. Cartwright and C. Early (eds), *Handbook of Organisational Culture and Climate*, London: Wiley, pp. 487–517.

Ulijn, J., G. Duijsters, R. Schaetzlein, and S. Remer (in press), 'Culture and its perception in strategic alliances, does it affect the performance? An exploratory study into Dutch-German ventures', *AOM Review*, special issue edited by S.O. Park.

Ulijn, J.M., A.P. Nagel and W.-L. Tan (2001), 'The impact of national, corporate and professional cultures on innovation: German and Dutch firms compared', contribution to a special issue of the *Journal of Enterprising Culture*, **9** (1), 21–52 on 'Innovation in an international context' (edited by A. Nagel, J. Ulijn and W.-L. Tan).

Ulijn, J., D. Vogel and T. Bemelmans (2002), 'ICT Study implications for human interaction and culture', introduction to a special issue of the *IEEE Journal of Professional Communication*, **45** (4) on 'ICT study implications for human interaction and culture'.

Utsch, A. and A. Rauch (2000), 'Innovativeness and initiative as mediators between achievement orientation and venture performance', in M. Frese, E. Chell and H. Klandt (eds), 'Psychological approaches to entrepreneurship', special issue of *European Journal of Work and Organizational Psychology*, **9** (1), pp. 45–62.

Van den Tillaart, H. (2001), *Monitor Ethnisch Ondernemerschap*, Nijmegen: ITS.

Van Luxemburg, A.P.D, J. Ulijn and N. Amare (2002), 'Interactive design process including the customer in six Dutch SME cases: traditional and ICT-media compared', in Ulijn,Vogel and Bemelmans (2002).

Vanhaverbeke, W. and R. Kirschbaum (2002), 'Building new competencies for new business creation based on breakthrough technological innovations', Limburg University Center and Eindhoven University of Technology.

Waasdorp, P. (ed.) (2001), *Entrepreneurship in The Netherlands*, Zoetermeer: Ministry of Economic Affairs.

Warner, A.M. (2000), *Economic Creativity: A Global Competitiveness report*, www.weforum.org.

Weber, M. (1958), *The Protestant Ethic and the Spirit of Capitalism*, New York: Charles Scribners.

Wong, Y.H. and T.K.P. Leung (2001), *Guanxi: Relationship Marketing in a Chinese Context*, New York: International Business Press.

Yli-Renko, H., E. Autio and V. Tontti (2002), 'Social capital, knowledge, and the international growth of technology-based new firms', in A. Hadjikhani and J. Johanson (eds), 'The internationalization process of the firm', special issue of the *International Business Review*, **11** (3), 279–304.

Zander, I. and O. Sölvell (2000), 'Cross-border innovation in the multinational corporation: a research agenda', *International Studies of Management and Organisation*, **30** (2), 44–67.

# 2. Conceptualizing innovation management and culture in the Hong Kong Special Administrative Region (HKSAR): an exploratory study of organization-specific critical success factors

**Naubahar Sharif and Ivy Chan**

## 1. INTRODUCTION

There has been a renewed effort in the Hong Kong Special Administrative Region (HKSAR)[1] over the past few years to transform itself into a knowledge-based economy (ITBB, 2001). At the heart of such a change is a renewal of technology policy, particularly towards Hong Kong's small and medium-sized enterprises (SMEs), and innovation management.

The concept of a national system of innovation (NSI)[2] provides a tool for analysing country specificities in the innovation process as well as a guide for policy formulation. Alternatively, management information systems (MIS) models provide a means for analysing intra-organizational cooperation and success factors.

This chapter combines two disparate bodies of literature – NSI literature and MIS literature – to conceptualize innovation management and culture in Hong Kong. In particular, this is an exploratory study of organization-specific critical success factors applicable to Hong Kong. Using the NSI as its backdrop, the focus in this chapter is firmly on the organizational level. We attempt to identify the building blocks at the organizational level that may contribute to national innovativeness. By utilizing a metamorphosis of the NSI and MIS as our analytic lens, we attempt to answer the question of what is it that characterizes an innovative organization in Hong Kong.

As its starting point, this chapter utilizes the standard schematic for a country's innovation system (Figure 2.1). While the schematic in Figure 2.1 outlines all the main actors and linkages in the innovation system, the core of the system lies at the centre, where knowledge is generated, diffused and

used. One significant component of this core is organizations. 'Firms capabilities and networks', as a major determinant on Hong Kong's innovative
capacity and thereby its performance in terms of growth, job creation and
competitiveness, are thereafter examined in detail and comprise the main
focus of the chapter.

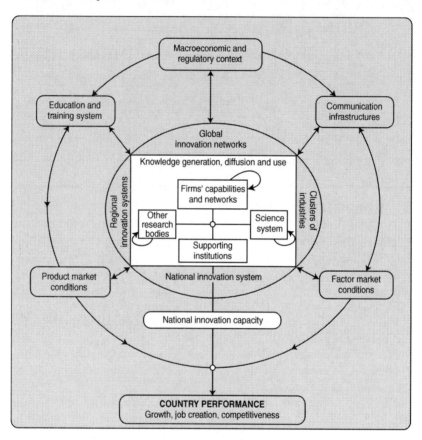

*Source:* Organization for Economic Cooperation and Development (OECD) (1999).

*Figure 2.1    Main actors and linkages in the innovation system*

In making the transition from one body of literature to the second, we
develop four constructs that we use as the innovation building blocks at the
organizational level (Figure 2.2). The first construct, organizational learning initiative can be conceptualized as functionality of employees' learning
styles and management culture. They influence the capacity of organization to generate, diffuse and use knowledge. The second construct, interor-

ganizational adherence perceives the cooperative learning and knowledge alliances between organizations to have a positive impact to national inno-vativeness. Furthermore, this chapter tangentially links the role of govern-ment (third construct) with its deliberation on innovation policies upon organizations. Finally, the fourth construct outlines common measures that can be utilized to determine a country's level of innovativeness.

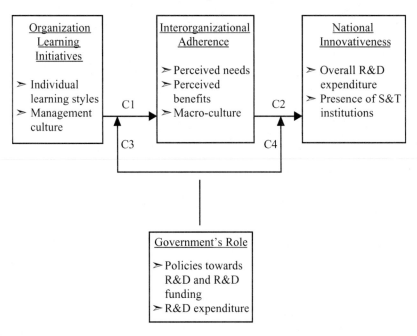

*Figure 2.2   The core of the innovation system: organizations/firms preliminary conceptual framework and conjectures for Hong Kong's NSI*

In Section 2, the NSI concept is introduced and the ways in which it relates to the remainder of the chapter is outlined. At the end of this section, the four conjectures that are used to conceptualize innovation management and culture are also stated. Sections 3, 4, 5 and 6 deals with each of the four con-jectures – the organizational learning initiatives conjecture and the interor-ganizational adherence conjectures are investigated in greater depth (in keeping with the overall concentration of the chapter), while the conjectures of government's role and national innovativeness are examined parentheti-cally. Information systems and management literature is drawn upon to form the substance of the chapter, with respect to the investigation of organiza-tions. The chapter concludes with Section 7, which summarizes the chapter.

## 2. INTRODUCTION TO THE NATIONAL SYSTEM OF INNOVATION CONCEPT

The concept of national systems of innovation first emerged from the work of a network of scholars based at the Science Policy Research Unit (SPRU) at the University of Sussex, notably Chris Freeman's studies of Japan's system of innovation (Freeman, 1987) and in related work by Bengt-Åke Lundvall and his colleagues at the University of Åalborg in Denmark. Now, more than a decade and a half later, the concept has become well established as a leading paradigm for analysing innovation processes. At the same time, though, it has also come under attack for being too broad and insufficiently theorized (Reppy, 2000).

Essentially, the market and non-market institutions in a country that influence the direction and speed of innovation and technology diffusion constitute a national system of innovation. The national system is taken to be the totality of institutions and practices that interact to produce and diffuse new technology.[3]

Innovation systems can also be conceptualized at other levels – for example, at the regional level or at the level of industries (sectoral level). These systems may or may not be confined within a country's borders, but national characteristics and frameworks always play a role in shaping them. The concept of an NSI provides a tool for analysing country specificities in the innovation process in a globalized economy, as well as a guide for policy formulation. It highlights interactions and interfaces between various actors and the workings of the system as a whole rather than the performance of its individual components (Lundvall, 1992).

In quoting Metcalfe (Metcalfe, 1995), the OECD's definition of NSI is the set of institutions that (jointly and individually) contribute to the development and diffusion of new technologies. These institutions provide the framework within which governments form and implement policies to influence the innovation process. As such, it is a system of interconnected institutions to create, store and transfer the knowledge, skills and artefacts, which define new technologies.

From the above perspective, the innovative performance of an economy depends not only on how the individual institutions (for example, organizations, research institutions, universities) perform in isolation, but on, 'how they interact with each other as elements of a *collective system of knowledge creation* and use, and on their *interplay* with social institutions (e.g. values, norms, legal frameworks)' (OECD, 1999).

The characteristics of the innovation processes differ among countries, depending on industrial specialization, specific institutional setting, policy priorities and so on. Historical experience shows that such differences persist even when countries deal with the same technological and economic developments. Countries thus have a tendency to develop along certain technological trajectories, shaped by past and present patterns of knowledge accumulation and use (Rosenberg, 1982).

A systematic analysis of technological development and innovation helps define the tasks of governments in promoting innovation-led growth by emphasizing that competitive markets are a necessary but insufficient condition for stimulating innovation and deriving the benefits from knowledge accumulation at the level of organizations and individuals. Organizations are learning organizations as well as profit maximizers, and their efficiency depends on numerous and often country-specific institutional, infrastructural and cultural conditions regarding relationships among the science, education and business sectors, conflict resolution, accounting practices, corporate governance structures, labour relations and so on.

Governments have a responsibility for improving the institutional framework for knowledge exchange among organizations and between market and non-market organizations in addition to correcting market failures (for example, providing public goods, intellectual property rights, subsidization of R&D and so on).

## 2.1 Origins of the NSI Framework[4]

The concept 'national systems of innovation' goes as far back as Friedrich List (1841). His concept 'national systems of production' took into account a wide set of national institutions including those engaged in education and training as well as infrastructures such as networks for the transport of people and commodities (Freeman, 1995). It focused on the development of productive forces rather than on allocation of given scarce resources. The concept pointed to the need to build *national* infrastructure and institutions.

The modern version of the innovation system concept was not based upon any direct inspiration from List. Rather, it emerged from within the discipline of evolutionary economics (particularly from Nelson and Winter's work, 1982). It was only after the concept had become generally accepted that Christopher Freeman and others went back and brought List forward as the intellectual ancestor. The idea of a national system of innovation was inherent in the work of the IKE-group in Aalborg in the first half of the 1980s. A standard phrase found in publications from this period was the 'innovation capability of the national system of production'. The 'innovation system' concept was introduced in Lundvall (1985) but then still without the adjective 'national' added to it. But the concept was also present in the international comparisons between national styles of management of innovation pursued at SPRU and it was Chris Freeman who brought the concept into the literature in 1987 in his book on innovation in Japan (Freeman, 1987). And it was certainly inherent in the work of Richard Nelson (1993) and other US-based scholars engaged in comparing the US system of science and technology with other national systems. Others who worked in parallel along similar lines of thought but with less emphasis on innovation were Michael Porter (1990) and Richard Whitley (1994). Whitley's concept of national business system is complementary to the innovation system approach in its emphasis on culturally embedded business practices.

The NSI concept has diffused rapidly among scholars and policymakers. Today, OECD (1997; 1999) and the European Commission have absorbed the concept as an integral part of their analytical perspective. The USA Academy of Science has recently brought the NSI into its vocabulary and now uses it as a framework for analysing science and technology policy in the USA.

## 2.2    Advantages and Disadvantages of the NSI Framework

There are four primary advantages of using the NSI framework. First, the system of innovation concept goes beyond R&D in an effort to explain innovation dynamics. The concept assumes that the rate of technical change depends on both the scale of R&D in various countries and on interorganizational learning processes.

Second, these learning processes are very much influenced by institutional set-ups that foster competition and cooperation. The concept encompasses not only stock of knowledge (R&D stock or technology capital) but also institutional elements, which strongly influence growth dynamics (Radosevic, 1998).

The third advantage is that the framework allows emphasis to shift away from the organization as the sole vector of technological innovation in a society to the role of government policy, legal institutions, education and training institutions, and even norms and regimes. That the interactive processes and feedback loops between these institutions are emphasized is a strong point of the framework.

Finally, the NSI approach is particularly well suited to analyses of technology policy. By drawing attention to the systematic features of the innovation process and their variation across countries, the NSI approach cautions against simple policy prescriptions that do not take into account cross-national differences among competing systems (Reppy, 2000).

Partly because the NSI approach is currently more of a conceptual framework rather than a formal theory, there is much debate as to whether it is even appropriate to speak of 'national' innovation systems (see, for example,

Edquist and McKelvey, 2000), when different categorizations such as regional or sectoral or transnational may be more suitable (this point is discussed in detail with specific respect to Hong Kong in Section 2.4).

Over the last decade there have been several new concepts emphasizing the systemic characteristics of innovation but with focus on other levels of the economy than the nation state. Indeed, the literature on 'regional systems of innovation' has grown rapidly since the beginning of the 1990s (Cooke, 1998). Bo Carlsson with colleagues from Sweden developed the concept 'technological systems' (Carlsson and Jacobsson, 1997) while Franco Malerba developed the concept of 'sectoral systems of innovation' (Breschi and Malerba, 1997), alluded to above. Sometimes these concepts have been presented or interpreted as alternatives to the national system approach and it has been argued that many, if not most, interesting interactions in the context of modern innovation tend to cross national borders and that there is no a priori reason why the national level should be taken as a given for the analysis.[5]

There is also argument over whether the concept is simply too 'diffuse' and 'ambiguous' (Edquist, 1997), causing it to lose its analytical powers. There is a problem related to comparison. Because the concept so closely studies individual countries, on a 'case-by-case' basis, it becomes rather difficult for cross-country comparisons to be carried out with any degree of effectiveness (as the constituent elements of the NSI may have little in common across geographic boundaries). Finally, there is the major question of how a country *arrives* at an innovation system that is effective and produces the desired results. While useful, comparisons between countries cannot provide policy prescriptions for nations, one of the main reasons being that each and every country possesses its own unique characteristics that affects its innovation system.

## 2.3 Sources of Diversity between Countries

Just as the characteristics of innovation processes differ among countries depending on various factors, countries also vary widely with regard to innovation. There are two chief sources of diversity. A first source of diversity is country size and level of development. Large and highly developed countries, for example the USA, offer markets with advanced customers and opportunities to reap economies of scale while maintaining diversity in R&D activities. Innovators in smaller high-income countries such as Hong Kong, generally have to internationalize more rapidly and concentrate on a narrower range of fields and niches that are not attractive to larger countries/multinational enterprises (MNEs) to reap these benefits. They will profit most from free flows of technology across borders and their innovation systems are often focused on capturing the benefits of inflows of technology. Hong Kong also faces proportionally higher costs for maintaining institutions that cover a broader range of subjects than can be taken up by their industries. On the other hand, technological change in information and communication technologies (ICTs), combined with deregulation and globalization, may reduce the scale advantages of large countries.

The second source of diversity relates to the respective roles of the main actors in innovation processes (organizations, public and private research organizations, and government and other public institutions), and the forms quality and intensity of their interactions. The roles of these main actors are depicted in Figure 2.1.

The actors are influenced by a variety of factors that exhibit some degree of country specificity manifested in:

- the financial system and corporate governance
- legal and regulatory frameworks
- the level of education and skills
- the degree of personnel mobility
- labour relations
- prevailing management practices, and so on.

The variable role of government is partly reflected in the levels and structures of public R&D financing. In 'catch-up' countries, government R&D expenditure accounts for a higher share of total R&D than in more advanced economies. This is very true in Hong Kong also where government R&D accounts for 0.31 per cent out of a total of 0.42 per cent of gross domestic product (GDP) spent on R&D.[6] Hong Kong still needs to build a scientific and technological infrastructure, although the business sector has moderately strong technological capabilities. At the other end of the spectrum are countries in which the business sector provides the bulk of R&D funding (such as Belgium, Ireland, Japan, Sweden and the USA).

Countries also differ in the orientation of publicly funded R&D. For instance, despite a common trend away from the 'traditional' missions of the post-war period (energy, defence) and towards new societal demands, such as ageing populations, the environment and competitiveness, the defence cluster still plays an important role in some countries, notably the USA, the UK and France. In Hong Kong, this cluster is non-existent because the People's Republic of China is responsible for Hong Kong's defence.[7]

The variable role of the higher education sector (universities and so on) serves as an indication of the relationship between the science system and the rest of the innovation system. The share of expenditure on R&D in the higher education sector (HERD)[8] financed by government is declining in the majority of OECD countries. In Hong Kong, this figure remains high and stands at 0.29 per cent out of a total of 0.42 per cent. The remaining expenditure on R&D comes from business (BERD),[9] 0.11 per cent, and from the government (GOVERD),[10] 0.02 per cent (Table 2.1).

*Table 2.1   R&D expenditure in Hong Kong, as a percentage of GDP*

| Government R&D expenditure: | |
| --- | --- |
| HERD | 0.29% of GDP |
| GOVERD | 0.02% of GDP |
| Total government R&D expenditure: | 0.31% of GDP |
| Business R&D expenditure (BERD): | 0.11% of GDP |
| Overall R&D expenditure: | 0.42% of GDP |

*Notes:*
HERD: Higher Education Sector Expenditure on Research and Development.
BERD: Business Enterprise Research and Development.
GOVERD: Government Sector Expenditure on Research and Development.

## 2.4   Appropriateness of Examining Hong Kong as a 'Country'

In light of the discussion above, relating to innovation systems, there is an element of uncertainty whether or not the *national* delimiting criterion can, in fact, be used in the case of Hong Kong. Without even considering the various technical pros and cons with utilizing the 'national' component as the demarcating condition, there are specific issues related to the case of Hong Kong that raises questions of whether the 'national' is the most suitable and practical segregating principle.

There are political as well as conceptual problems associated with using a simple NSI framework. From a political point of view, Hong Kong is *not* a nation. It is but a Special Administrative Region (SAR) of the People's Republic of China. As such, using a concept such as 'national' innovation system might well upset Beijing and local loyalists.

The conceptual problem is that there are many things which nations do (defend their territory, protect own industries, and so on) which Hong Kong does not, and perhaps should not, do. Hong Kong's is a very open system, and one could argue persuasively that many of Hong Kong's industries are placed outside the territory. The movement of these industries away from Hong Kong took place when China began its opening up in the late 1970s. This was both a blessing and a curse for Hong Kong: a blessing because Hong Kong was at the doorstep of a developing giant; a curse because Hong Kong was able to move sunset industries across the border, thereby extending their economic lives.

The key point is, however, that the NSI approach encourages the focus to be placed systematically upon the resources and networks that enable agents to innovate in a particular area. Whether one wishes to think of this in 'national' or 'regional' terms is actually not so important. What *is* important is to use a theoretical framework that gives a better understanding of the interactions and flows of knowledge that help people innovate (and innovate in a sustainable manner). Many of the networks, flows, systems and resource concepts that have been refined in relation to the NSI debate (particularly those networks and systems that are involved in innovative activities) are very useful. The NSI concept also problematizes the boundaries of those systems and the roles of their constituent players. Finally, there is the question of the difference that cultural and social contexts make.

Because the conceptual issues related to the applicability of the NSI to Hong Kong are relatively inconsequential in that they do not have direct bearings on the way in which Hong Kong firms operate (for the purposes of this study), Hong Kong is to be treated as a 'nation' or, to put it more appropriately, an *autonomous region*. This assumption is only a conceptual one, however, and utilized primarily for reasons of convenience, as it is a well-known fact that Hong Kong is, strictly speaking, another city of the People's Republic of China (PRC). Even though it is a city that is 'specially administered' (a SAR), whereby its political autonomy in all spheres of life (legal, political and social) has been guaranteed under the Basic Law, it is politically part of the PRC.

In short, the 'national' delimiting criterion will continue to be used, but the connotation is more in reference to an 'autonomous region' with its own set of values, beliefs and system 'of doing things',[11] as opposed to a fully fledged 'nation' in the commonly understood sense of the term. For instance, Hong Kong's institutions (legal, political and social) are markedly different from those of the PRC and on that basis alone, sufficiently distinguish it from the Mainland.

## 2.5   Hong Kong's SMEs

Given Hong Kong's unique nature as an entrepôt, the dominant types of firm in Hong Kong are known as small and medium enterprises (SMEs). Manufacturing enterprises with fewer than 100 employees and non-manufacturing enterprises with fewer than 50 employees are regarded as small and medium enterprises (SMEs) in Hong Kong. In June 2000, there were more than 290000 SMEs in Hong Kong. They accounted for over 98 per cent of the total establishments and provided job opportunities to over 1 390 000 persons, about 60 per cent of the workforce.

Among the various business sectors, the majority of SMEs are engaged in import and export sector, followed by the wholesale, retail, restaurants and hotels sector. These two sectors constituted 60 per cent of the SMEs in Hong Kong, employing more than half of the workforce engaged in SMEs.[12]

Hong Kong's SMEs are the basic building blocks of its economy with their relatively low start-up costs and flexibility in a changing business environment. Small and medium enterprises are a significant force in Hong Kong's economic development and they create a large number of employment opportunities. Many of today's highly successful private or publicly listed corporations have grown and developed from their relatively humble SME origin: their vision, dynamism and effective response in a highly competitive local, regional or global business environment provide the role model and inspiration for today's SMEs with similar aspirations.

## 2.6 Conjectures for Hong Kong's Organizations in the Context of the NSI Concept

According to Lundvall (1998), innovation study has to be examined from a wider perspective than learning style; knowledge taxonomy that contributes to innovativeness. This chapter attempts to do just that, by making a theoretical contribution in terms of its conjectures with respect to organization learning styles and interorganizational interactions.

As Figure 2.2 demonstrates, four specific constructs are employed to dissect the core of the innovation system. The three constructs of 'organization learning initiatives', 'organization adherence' and 'government's role' all play their part in Hong Kong's ultimate 'national innovativeness', as measured by the overall R&D expenditure (particularly expenditure from the private sector), and the presence of scientific and technological institutions.

In this chapter, four conjectures are postulated and a research plan outlined that may be used to test in particular the validity of the first two of the four conjectures. The conjectures are as follows:

*Conjecture 1*:   Organizations learning initiatives have positive relationship with interorganizational adherence.

*Conjecture 2*:   Organizations that display high levels of interorganizational interaction will give rise to a progressive development in national innovativeness.

*Conjecture 3*:   Government intervention will moderate the degree of organizational adherence.

*Conjecture 4*:   Government intervention will moderate the degree of national innovativeness.

Keeping in mind Hong Kong's efforts to review and renew its policies towards Hong Kong's SMEs, this chapter concentrates the bulk of its attention on the first two of the four conjectures. These deal with the crucial role of organizations in the overall innovation system.

## 3.   ORGANIZATIONAL LEARNING INITIATIVES

It is a widely stated argument that innovations stem from the accumulation and utilization of tacit knowledge, embedded skills and expertise from employees in organizations (Leonard and Sensiper, 1998; Nonaka and Takeuchi, 1995).[13] Based on the organizational learning perspective, organizations learn through *individuals* who act as *working agents* to assemble, detect, justify and change organizational memory and knowledge repositories (Huang et al., 2000). In addition, empirical studies show that individuals/knowledge workers are influenced by their inherent learning styles to perform various roles in knowledge production, search, reuse and application (Markus, 2001; Szulanski, 1996). Therefore, it is judicious to adapt cognitive behaviour/inclination of individuals to gain insights on innovativeness. The Kirton Adaptive and Innovation (KAI) survey is widely recognized in the field to be an important and influential work for creativity discourse. The survey is composed of 32 self-assessed items designed to investigate individuals' propensity to appropriate knowledge, tolerate uncertainty and assimilate innovative ideas found in the competitive environment.

Another thrust for organizational learning is management culture that enables initiatives and dedication to be supported and implemented. The management culture covers a systemic function and change dynamism to capitalize knowledge through a mixture of people, processes, routines and infrastructure (Abell and Oxbrow, 2000). The focus underpinning management culture includes three aspects: agenda foundation to get organizations ready on innovative track; selection and work flows to manage/utilize organizational resources; routinization to leverage resources with full strength and identify future prospects (Swan and Newell, 2000).

### 3.1   Individual Learning Styles

Many studies have recognized the KAT instrument and have confirmed its rigorousness and internal consistency (Bobic, Dais and Cunningham,

1999; Murdock, Isakesen and Lauer, 1993; Tullett and Kirton, 1995). First, rule or group conformity refers to the degree to which individuals work within the accepted structures or reject critical elements of such structures. Second, efficiency refers to the degree individuals comply with legal-rational bureaucracy, for example, precision and reliability. Third, sufficiency v. proliferation of originality refers to the number and scope of innovative ideas individuals generate. Based on the three perspectives, a continuum of innovator-adapters measurement is found and characterized as follows (Kirton, 1976; 1989).

Adapters are characterized by precision, reliability and efficiency. They are inclined to follow and accept the underlying context and seek solutions within perceived constraints. In other words, they tend to maintain stability and organizational norms, thus seldom questioning the reasons for existing practices (Cohen, 1998). Adapters also rely on knowledge that is widely shared, generally accepted, officially recorded and extensively routinized (Cohen, 1991).

Contrastingly, innovators are characterized by unrestrained and creative thinking within certain given boundaries. They are inclined to challenge the existing customs or taken-for-granted routines in order to search for alternative avenues of solutions and underlying assumptions. They may question the applicability and effectiveness of taken-for-granted behaviour and try to explore new or unlearned knowledge by tapping the incipient sources (Sadler-Smith and Badger, 1998).

Kirton's measurement, furthermore, construes implications to strategists on the strength of human capital. Theoretically, innovators are the main thrust to uphold knowledge discovery and explore alternatives. Organizations with more innovators are likely to engage in interorganization adherence, for example, learning alliances, and R&D collaboration that strengthen national innovativeness.

## 3.2   Management Culture

Culture is defined as the set of values, guiding beliefs, understanding and ways of thinking that is shared by members of an organization and conveyed to new members as an accepted code of practice (Allee, 1997; Standing and Benson, 2000). Management culture is a second organizational characteristic, in addition to individual learning styles. As stated in the above section, knowledge creation and ideas generation are instigated from individuals to the organizational context. The environment and deliberation promoted by management to inspire innovation works are therefore crucial enablers (Hurley and Hult, 1998). Interpersonal socialization, subunit knowledge exchange in documented means can be facilitated.

Management commitment towards continuous learning can facilitate knowledge diffusion and flows (e.g. know-how, best practices) from source to recipient, via channels such as interpersonal socialization and documented subunit exchange (Appleyard and Kalsow, 1999; Truran, 1998). Therefore, this study adapts three underlying management foci – agenda formation, selection and implementation of organizational resources and routinization (Abell and Oxbrow, 2000; Swan and Newell, 2000) – to investigate the organizational learning initiatives.

Agenda formation is an initial stage to prepare organizations for innovativeness. Primary actions and plans with knowledge-sharing culture, interpersonal trust, supportive mission, motivation and rewards are perceived as imperatives to inspire creative works. Organizations with such enterprise-wide readiness are characterized by openness and an encouraging learning environment (Hiebeler, 1996; Lee, Kim and Yu, 2001).

The second management culture focus is selection and implementation of organizational resources. The primary objective is to scale up the agenda to enterprise level with connections, collections and deployment of people, information, infrastructure and technology that foster a socially constructed platform to leverage innovation practices (Nonaka and Konno, 1998). Successful episodes, for example, Toshiba, Hallmark and BP Amoco, are evident and shown in prior studies (Barrow, 2001; Brailsford, 2001; Nonaka and Takeuchi, 1995).

The third management culture focus is routinization in which organizations institutionalize innovation endeavours through integration, evaluating and benchmarking organizational outcomes. Organizations may concentrate on mechanisms to infuse innovation as daily practice, for example, seminar and workshops; monitor and rectify the status quo, for example, new products/services generation; identify strengths and business opportunities and to leverage best practices such that capacity of market responsiveness and cross-functional innovation are enhanced (APQC, 2001; Hurley and Hult, 1998).

Coupled with individual learning styles, a supportive management culture imposes positive effect on organizational learning initiatives that devise a higher propensity to acquire, combine, produce and explore new ideas for innovativeness (Figure 2.2).[14]

Innovation and knowledge leverage are not limited to the intra-organization level but can be propagated within organizations also. Alliances such as joint ventures and partnerships are found in industries where cooperating organizations mutually benefit from the interaction (Inkpen, 1996). However, the fallacy of replication of benchmarking and best practices, such as blindly adopting best practices without considering the *contextual factors*, results in inverse effectiveness.[15] This is where a major contribution of science and technology studies can be found, where the importance of context is continually emphasized in various contexts, including historical, organizational and societal. In fact, one of the main reasons why *national* systems of innovation analysis continues to be the dominant form (as opposed to sectoral or other types of analysis) is because emphasis on contextual factors is maintained (which, conversely, is diminished in sectoral or technological analyses of innovation systems) (Rosenberg, 1982). Differences in country specificity (context) are displayed by actors because of the factors listed in Section 2.3.

## 4. INTERORGANIZATIONAL ADHERENCE

Certain organizations are endowed with more resources, for example, human capital and technology know-how, that enable them to substantiate a better position than those with fewer of the same resources. Business environments become more sophisticated and uncertain, and ground rules of competition and competitive advantages may rapidly become obsolete. Therefore, the capabilities to turn knowledge into practice and to uphold continuous innovation are regarded as rudiments for long-lasting strategy (Johannessen, Olsen and Olaisen, 1999; Prusak, 1996; Whadcock, 1997). Capabilities and competences building, however, are not conducted in isolation. Prior studies have shown that it is either difficult for organizations to maintain and remain self-sufficient in all knowledge (Inkpen, 1996) or expensive for organizations to endeavour to become self-contained enterprises with all sorts of capabilities (Weber, 1989). In a similar vein, organizations that manoeuvre knowledge and intellectual capital with a closed systems approach or pursue 'me too' strategies to imitate or replicate others' best practices without considering their organizational contexts find impediments to renew and extend their competences in the long run (Sawhney and Prandelli, 2000; Whadcock, 1997). Therefore, organizations are driven to engage in strategic alliances and partnerships to access skills and resources of other partners in order to strengthen their competitiveness (Morrison and Mezentseff, 1997).

In general, the partnering approach can be regarded as interorganization adherence that is instigated as a result of asymmetric possession of knowledge assets or organizational resources. Organizations are found to interact with other organizations to different degrees in terms of cooperation and partnerships with the aim to seek, spill over and integrate various bodies of organizational knowledge, to intensify their own market competitiveness (Argote and Ingram, 2000). Those adherence approaches can exist formally or informally, physically or virtually (Baltrusch, 2001), and can be perceived as a continuum of low adherence (isolated from other organizations) to high adherence (close collaboration with strategic alliance partners).

In other words, organizations with the intention of isolating themselves from other organizations, seek to prohibit knowledge leakage from inside their organizations out into the market. Conversely, organizations with high adherence aim to build a reflective learning environment where mutual transfer of knowledge and skills are possible. According to Koza and Lewin (1998), interorganizational adherence can be undertaken as either exploitation or exploration that governs the knowledge-sharing and diffusion processes.[16] Exploration refers to organizations prospecting new opportunities and alternatives for development. Usually, these sorts of organizations demonstrate behaviour on basic research, invention, risk-taking, building new capabilities and entering into new lines of business. Exploitation, on the other hand, means organizations focus on efficiency, productivity, replicating and reiterating best practices. By improving their current capabilities, standardization, routinization through systemic plans, these types of organizations experience limited innovation development (Spender, 1994).

In this study, both exploitation and exploration adherences are encapsulated and measured by three dimensions, namely, perceived needs, perceived benefits and macro-culture.

## 4.1  Perceived Needs

Organizational intentions to seek adherence from others can be driven by deficiency of knowledge and skills resources in organizations. The deficiency is primarily determined by organizations that perceive the necessity to do so or for whom the awareness of the needs exists. According to Cohen and Levinthal (1990), the perceived needs are influenced by prior knowledge that existed within organizations. Prior knowledge refers to the base of experience and repository of knowledge that resides in organizations and allows individuals to access, develop and apply the related knowledge in their work. Therefore, the more prior knowledge accumulated and available within organizations, the more intra-organizational learning and collaborative works among employees is enabled. To collate this with learning perspective, prior knowledge akin to shared mental thoughts enables organizations to be aware of the existence of new and external knowledge that is deficient in the existing repositories.[17] Also, prior knowledge stimulates the combination capacity to integrate the absorbed knowledge with associated memory (Kogut and Zander, 1992).

Lundvall (1998) suggests that knowledge epistemologies are related to search strategy and innovativeness. He suggests two forms of knowledge that can be linked with the perceived needs for interorganizational adherence. First, know-what is the objectively defined facts and artefacts that are codified and explicit to individuals. Organizations that possess this knowledge may worry about rapidly losing their competitiveness if they lose it to their strategic partners. On the other hand, organizations that lack such knowledge may not be keen to seek knowledge as they expect imitation or replication of similar skills can be easily enforced. Possible adherence may be built, underpinned by know-what in which organizations may seek short-term profits or immediate success. Second, know-how includes skills or experiences that resides implicitly in employees' minds or routines and norms that are embedded in daily practices. This knowledge is characterized as 'sticky' knowledge, is least transferable and so context specific that organizations (either as seekers or providers) may find it difficult to communicate and transfer it explicitly. The effective way for knowledge transfer and explication may be conducted through observation, close communication or apprenticeship where partners develop mutual understanding and shared thoughts through joint collaboration. In this way, interorganizational adherence is likely to result.

## 4.2   Perceived Benefits

Another factor that determines the intention towards organizational connections is perceived benefits that can be realized and grasped as the positive accrued results from adherence and collaboration. Conceptually, organizations are inspired to engage in adherences if benefits and advantages (for example, direct access from acquiring new knowledge, and potential growth for entering new markets) overcome cost and disadvantages (for example, market failure, opportunism of affiliated patterns, potential risk in losing own competitiveness, and so on) (Sawhney and Prandelli, 2000).

The perceived benefits cover a wide range of aspects, formal/informal, tangible/intangible, long/short term, where organizations can:

- respond swiftly to markets via mimicking adoption of partners' skills within a short period of time (O'Neill, Pouder and Buchholtz, 1988)
- minimize risk and failure potential by joint R&D efforts to explore wider alternatives and solutions (Armbrecht et al., 2001)
- leverage the synergetic value from sharing knowledge that yields additional value beyond the sum of the parties' individual knowledge (Makino and Delios, 1996)
- grasp the potential gains on competitiveness transcendence from assimilating new knowledge and leveraging new business opportunities (Loebecke, Van Fenema and Powell, 1999)

- reduce the overt costs incurred in consultations, experiments or simulations throughout connection processes to affect organizations' intentions to engage in such connections (Winter, 2000).

## 4.3 Macro-culture

Culture, as an imperative (either enabler or barrier) that influences the management of intellectual assets exists not only within an organization but also across organizations (Cohen and Fields, 1999; Hurley and Hult, 1998). In our study, the culture that exists *across* organizations is coined as the macro-culture where organizations impose various norms, expectations, assumptions and prevailing values upon other organizations that influence their behaviour intention to adhere with others.

De Long and Fahey (2000) concur that culture affects organizational performance with behaviour changes central to knowledge creation, sharing and use. Furthermore, they cite Chaddock's notion – knowledge management success is 20 per cent reliant on technology, with the remaining 80 per cent coming from people – to depict organizational adherence and collaborative arrangements that can be inspired by norms and practices that encourage trust and mutual support among organizations.

In the NSI context, the macro-culture can be examined in two specific areas: assumptions and norms. Organizations are found to continue to adopt poor business strategies despite the apparent evidence that relates such practices to ineffectiveness and inefficiency. Given the success of the early adopters with strategic alliances, other organizations are initiated to formulate assumption of their success and wide dissipation of innovation will come with prompt imitation of such strategic actions (O'Neill, Pouder and Buchholtz, 1998). Therefore, it is expected the interorganizational adherence will be positively impacted by such assumptions.

Similarly, the macro-culture can affect the norms that prevail across organizations. With the advancement of information communication technology, interorganizational interactions become extensive and flexible in that they are no longer constricted by time and location (Roberts, 2000). Community of practice and groups of interests with participants from diverse fields are formed and facilitated by such technology where they can exchange, share and create knowledge (Cook and Brown, 1999). The norms of communications and collaboration among organizations is extended to an informal stance that encourages open, frank interaction, collective responsibility, mutual trust and joint contribution which can be conducive to others (De Long and Fahey, 2000).

It is expected that the interorganizational adherence is influenced by the norms that promote and encourage open communications.

## 5. GOVERNMENT'S ROLE

For the most part, government addresses current challenges with administrative structures and policy instruments that have been shaped by responses to past problems.[18] Traditionally, they have intervened in the technology arena to address market failures. They should also address systemic failures that block the functioning of innovation systems, hinder the flow of knowledge and technology and, consequently, reduce the overall R&D efforts. Such systemic failures can emerge from mismatches between the different components of the innovation system, such as conflicting incentives for market and non-market institutions or from institutional rigidities based on narrow specialization, asymmetric information gaps and lack of networking or mobility of personnel.

Governments need to play an integrating role in managing knowledge on an economy-wide basis by making technology and innovation policy an integral part of overall economic policy. This requires contributions from a variety of policies in order to (1) secure framework conditions that are conducive to innovation, such as a stable macroeconomic environment, a supportive tax and regulatory environment, and appropriate infrastructure and education and training policies, and (2) remove more specific barriers to innovation in the business sector and increase synergies between public and private investment in innovation.

New approaches or institutional arrangements, including public/private partnerships may be needed to coordinate the formulation and implementation of policies. Better techniques and institutional mechanisms for evaluation are also needed to improve decision-making across traditional administrative competencies and can spur innovation in government.

In practice, many science and technology policies remain piecemeal, with insufficient attention given to fostering interactions and spillovers at national and international levels.

Ultimately, policy responses to national innovativeness are place-specific and dependent on historical heritage and on features of the economic and innovation systems. There are also important differences among countries in their capacities and traditions of their science and technology policy institutions. However, based on a common understanding of the mechanisms of innovation and technology diffusion in a knowledge-based economy (as Hong Kong is presently aspiring to be), there is room for improved mutual learning from successes and failures in addressing common objectives.

## 6.  NATIONAL INNOVATIVENESS

In essence, innovation is the ability to manage knowledge creatively in response to market-articulated demands and other social needs. Organizations are the main source of innovation; their performance depends on incentives provided by the economic and regulatory environment, their access to critical inputs (via factor markets or through interactions in networks and clusters of knowledge-based organizations) and their internal capacity to seize market and technological opportunities. Several trends combine to change the conditions for successful innovation:

- *Innovation increasingly relies on effective interaction between the science base and the business sector.* In all sectors, the innovative process is increasingly characterized by feedback between the science base and the different stages of technology development and commercialization. A greater part of the scientific research agenda is driven by problems identified during the course of technological development in the business sector.
- *More competitive markets and the accelerating pace of scientific and technological change force firms to innovate more rapidly.*
- *Networking and collaboration among firms are now more important than in the past and increasingly involve knowledge-intensive services.* Competition provides incentives to innovate, but networking and collaboration at local, national and international levels are often necessary to build the capabilities to do so. Clusters of innovative firms and other private and public knowledge-based organizations are emerging as drivers of growth and competitiveness. Increasingly jobs lie in services, where innovation is generally less driven by direct R&D expenditure and is more dependent on acquired technology and the quality of human resources.
- *The globalization of economies is making countries' innovation systems more interdependent.* Trade in technology is growing, as are international alliances among firms and cross-border purchases of patents and licences. Investment in foreign research facilities is also on the rise, particularly by firms based in smaller countries. In this environment, the competitiveness of firms depends more and more on their ability to link to international innovation networks. However, globalization is not leading to a homogenization of national innovation patterns. Countries still differ greatly owing to differing starting points, technological and industrial specialization, institutions, policies and attitudes to change.

In sum, innovation performance depends not only on how specific actors (for example, organizations, research institutes and universities) perform, but on how they interact with one another as elements of an innovation system, at local, national and international levels.[19]

## 7.  SUMMARY

This has been a conceptualizing chapter utilizing the NSI framework as a backdrop to investigate how organizations – which lie at the heart of the innovation system – can contribute to the innovativeness of Hong Kong. The focus has been on organizational learning initiatives and interorganizational adherence.

In summary, the chapter theorizes that organizations' learning initiatives, as manifested in their individual learning styles and management culture, are positively related with interorganizational adherence (cooperation). Innovators, rather than adapters, have to be fostered where creative thinking within boundaries is encouraged. Additionally, firms that engage in agenda formation, selection and implementation of organizational resources and routinization will be able to foster the requisite culture necessary for innovation.

Furthermore, organizations that display high levels of interorganizational interaction contribute towards a progressive development in national innovativeness. High levels of interorganizational interaction result from those organizations that perceive a need to cooperate with their fellow firms, those that perceive potential benefits from such cooperation and those organizations whose internal culture is commensurate with the prevailing macro-culture.

Finally, the government's role in national innovativeness is, crucially, twofold and has to be managed. On the one hand, the government needs to make innovation policy directed towards SMEs an integral part of overall economic policy and, on the other hand, it needs to integrate economy-wide knowledge so that national innovativeness results.

While firms are at the core of the innovation process, national innovativeness can also be affected by various other factors, as manifested in trends witnessed across countries today. Most important among these trends is the networking and collaboration among organizations. This has been one of the key motives for the focus on organizations and interorganizational adherence in this chapter.

## NOTES

1. Hereafter to be referred to simply as 'Hong Kong' or 'HKSAR'.
2. No distinction is made in this chapter between the terminology of National System of Innovation (NSI) and National Innovation System (NIS).
3. The discussion in this section is mainly drawn from Organization for Economic Cooperation and Development (1999).
4. The discussion in this section draws predominantly from Lundvall et al. (2001).
5. However, maintaining the policy dimension of the concept at the forefront makes it more sensible to employ the 'national' category as opposed to others. As long as nation states exist as political entities with their own agendas related to innovation, it is useful to work with national systems as analytical objects.
6. 1997 figures obtained from the Technology and Policy Research Group, the Hong Kong University of Science and Technology.
7. Prior to the handover on 30 June 1997, Great Britain was responsible for Hong Kong's defence.
8. HERD is an acronym for Higher Education Sector Expenditure on Research and Development.
9. BERD is an acronym for Business Enterprise Research and Development.
10. GOVERD is an acronym for Government Sector Expenditure on Research and Development.
11. Hofstede (2001) articulates specific values for Hong Kong culture that reinforce the idea that Hong Kong indeed can be treated sufficiently distinct from China, for the purposes of this chapter, to be considered an autonomous region.
12. 'Small and Medium Enterprises (SMEs) in Hong Kong', 25 November 2000 from: http://www.sme.gcn.gov.hk/english/smehk_b.htm.
13. In Pennings and Harianto (1992).
14. Hiebeler (1996) lists the knowledge-management championed enterprises with their accomplishments, for example, HP with its supportive culture where everyone is encouraged to take risks witout fear of punishment, and Buckman Lab with its effort to optimize sharing of knowledge with incentive and recognition systems.
15. This point is highlighted succinctly by Nattermann (2000) and Pfeffer and Sutton (1999).
16. Koza and Lewin (1998) and March (1991).
17. Bower and Hilgard (1981).
18. This section is drawn in its entirety from Organization for Economic Cooperation and Development (1999).
19. Organisation for Economic Cooperation and Development (1999).

## REFERENCES

Abell, A., and N. Oxbrow (2000), 'People who make knowledge management work: CKO, CKT, or KT', in Jay Liebowitz, *Building Organizational Intelligence: a Knowledge Management Primer*, Boca Raton, FL: CRC Press, pp. 1–16.

Allee, Verna (1997), *The Knowledge Evolution: Expanding Organizational Intelligence*, Boston, MA: Butterworth-Heinemann.

Appleyard, M.M. and G.A. Kalsow (1999), 'Knowledge Diffusion in the Semiconductor Industry', *Journal of Knowledge Management*, **3** (4), 288–295.

APQC (2001), 'Keys to success', *APQC*, http://www.apqc.org/best/keys.cfm.

Argote, L. and P. Ingram (2000), 'Introduction: knowledge transfer in organizations: learning from the experience of others', *Organizational Behavior and Human Decision Processes*, **82** (1), 1–8.

Armbrecht, Jr, R.F.M., R.B. Chapas, C.C. Chappelow, G.F. Garris, P.N. Friga, C.A. Hartz, M.E. Mcilvaine, S.R. Postle and G.E. Whitwell (2001), 'Knowledge management in research and development', *Research Technology Management*, July–August, 28–48.

Baltrusch, R. (2001), 'Exploring organizational learning in virtual forms of organization', in *Proceedings of the Thirty-fourth Hawaii International Conference on System Sciences*, pp. 1–10.

Barrow, D.C. (2001), 'Sharing know-how at BP AMOCO', *Research Technology Management*, May–June, 18–25.

Bobic, M., E. Dais and R. Cunningham (1999), 'The Kirton Adaptation-Innovation Inventory', *Review of Public Personnel Administration*, Spring, 18–31.

Bower, G.H. and E.R. Hilgard (1981), *Theories of Learning*, Englewood Cliffs, NJ: Prentice-Hall.

Brailsford, T.W. (2001), 'Building a knowledge community at Hallmark Cards', *Financial Research-Technology Management*, September–October, 18–25.

Breschi, S. and F. Malerba (1997), 'Sectoral innovation systems: technological regimes, Schumpeterian dynamics, and spatial boundaries', in C. Edquist (ed.), *Systems of Innovation: Technologies, Institutions and Organizations*, London and Washington, DC: Pinter.

Carlsson, B. and S. Jacobsson (1997), 'Diversity creation and technological systems: a technology policy perspective', in C. Edquist (ed.), *Systems of Innovation: Technologies, Institutions and Organizations*, London and Washington, DC: Pinter.

Cohen, H.B. (1998), 'The performance paradox', *Academy Management Executive*, **12** (3), 30–40.

Cohen, M.D (1991), 'Individual learning and organizational routines: emerging connections', *Organization Science*, **2** (1), 135–9.

Cohen, S.S. and G. Fields (1999), 'Social capital and capital gains in Silicon Valley', *California Management Review*, **41** (2), 108–30.

Cohen, W.M. and D.A. Levinthal (1990), 'Absorptive capacity: a new perspective on learning and innovation', *Administrative Science Quarterly*, **35**, March, 128–52.

Cook, S.D.N. and J.S. Brown (1999), 'Bridging epistemologies: the generative dance between organizational knowledge and organizational knowing', *Organization Science*, **10** (4), 381–400.

Cooke, P. (1998), 'Regional innovation systems: an evolutionary approach', in H.-J. Baraczyk, P. Cooke and M. Heidenreich (eds), *Regional Innovation Systems: The Role of Governances in a Globalized World*, London and Bristol, and Philadelphia, PA: UCL Press.

De Long, D.W. and L. Fahey (2000), 'Diagnosing cultural barriers to knowledge management', *Academy of Management Executive*, **14** (4), 113–27.

Edquist, C. (ed.) (1997), *Systems of Innovation: Technologies, Institutions and Organizations*, London and Washington, DC: Pinter.

Edquist, C. and M.D. Mckelvey (2000), *Systems of Innovation: Growth, Competitiveness and Employment*, Cheltenham, UK and Northampton, MA, USA: Edward Elgar.

Freeman, C. (1987), *Technology, Policy and Economic Performance: Lessons from Japan*, London and New York: Pinter.

Freeman, C. (1995), 'The National Innovation Systems in historical perspective', *Cambridge Journal of Economics*, **19** (1), 5–24.

Hiebeler, R.J. (1996), 'Benchmarking knowledge management', *Strategy and Leadership*, March–April, 22–9.

Hofstede, G.H. (2001), *Culture's Consequences: Comparing Values, Behaviors, Institutions and Organizations across Nations*, Thousand Oaks, CA: Sage.

Hurley, R.F. and T.M. Hult (1998), 'Innovation, market orientation, and organizational learning: an integration and empirical examination', *Journal of Marketing*, **62**, 42–54.

Inkpen, A.C. (1996), 'Creating knowledge through collaboration', *California Management Review*, **39** (1), 123–38.

Information Technology and Broadcasting Bureau (ITBB) (2001), '2001 Hong Kong Digital 21', *ITBB*, http://www.info.gov.hk/digital21/eng/.

Johannessen, J.-A., B. Olsen and J. Olaisen (1999), 'Aspects of innovation theory based on knowledge management', *International Journal of Information Management*, **19**, 121–39.

Kirton, M. (1976), 'Adaptors and innovators: a description and measure', *Journal of Applied Psychology*, **61** (5), 622–9.

Kirton, M.J. (ed.) (1989), *Adaptors and Innovators: Styles of Creativity and Problem Solving*, London and New York: Routledge.

Kogut, B. and U. Zander (1992), 'Knowledge of the firm, combinative capabilities and the replication of technology', *Organization Science*, **3** (3), 383–97.

Koza, M.P. and A.Y. Lewin (1998), 'The co-evolution of strategic alliances', *Organization Science*, **9** (3), 255–64.

Lee, J.H., Y.G. Kim and S.H. Yu (2001), 'Stage model for knowledge management', in *Proceedings of the Thirty-fourth Hawaii International Conference on System Sciences*, Hawaii: Computer Society Press, pp. 1–10.

Leonard, D. and S. Sensiper (1998), 'The role of tacit knowledge in group innovation', *California Management Review*, **40** (3), 112–32.

List, F. (1841), *Das Nationale System der politischen Oekonomie*, reprinted in, *The National System of Political Economy*, Longmans, Green and Co.

Loebecke, D.P., C. Van Fenema, and P. Powell (1999), 'Competition and knowledge transfer', *Database*, **31** (2), 14–25.

Lundvall, B.-Å. (1985), *Product Innovation and User-Producer Interaction*, Aalborg: Aalborg University Press.

Lundvall, B.-Å. (1992), *National Systems of Innovation: Towards a Theory of Innovation and Interactive Learning*, New York: Pinter.

Lundvall, B.-Å. (1998), 'Why study national systems and national styles of innovation', *Technology Analysis and Strategic Management*, **10** (4), 407–21.

Lundvall, B.-Å., B. Johnson, E.S. Andersen and B. Dalum (2001), 'National systems of production, innovation and competence-building', paper presented at the Nelson and Winter DRUID Summer Conference, Aalborg Congress Center, Aalborg, 12–15 June.

Makino, S. and A. Delios (1996), 'Local knowledge transfer and performance: implications for alliance formation in Asia', *Journal of International Business Studies*, special issue, 905–27.

March, J.G. (1991), 'Exploration and exploitation in organizational learning', *Organization Science*, **2** (1), 71–87.

Markus, M.L. (2001), 'Toward a theory of knowledge reuse: types of knowledge reuse situations and factors in reuse success', *Journal of Management Information Systems*, **18** (1), 53–97.

Metcalfe, S. (1995), 'The Economic foundations of technology policy equilibrium and evolutionary perspectives', in P. Stoneman (ed.), *Handbook of the Economics of Innovations and Technological Change*, Oxford and Cambridge, MA: Blackwell.

Morrison M. and L. Mezentseff (1997), 'Learning alliance – a new dimension of strategic alliance', *Management Decision*, **35** (5), 351–7.

Murdock, M.C., S.G. Isakesen and K.J. Lauer (1993), 'Creativity training and the stability and internal consistency of the Kirton Adaption-Innovation Inventory', *Psychological Reports*, **72**, 1123–30.

Nattermann, P.M (2000), 'Best practice = best strategies', *McKinsey Quarterly*, **2**, 23–31.

Nelson, R.R. (1993), *National Innovation Systems: A Comparative Analysis*, New York: Oxford University Press.

Nelson, R.R. and S. Winter (1982), *An Evolutionary Theory of Economic Change*, Cambridge, MA: Harvard University Press.

Nonaka, I. and N. Konno (1998), 'The concept of "Ba": building a foundation for knowledge creation', *California Management Review*, **40** (3), 40–54.

Nonaka, I. and H. Takeuchi (1995), *The Knowledge-Creating Company: How Japanese Companies Create the Dynamics of Innovation*, New York: Oxford University Press.

O'Neill, H.M., R.W. Pouder and A.K. Buchholtz (1998), 'Patterns in the diffusion of strategies across organizations: insights from the innovation diffusion literature', *Academy of Management Review*, **23** (1), 98–114.

Organization for Economic Cooperation and Development (OECD) (1997), *National Innovation Systems*, Paris: Organization for Economic Cooperation and Development.

Organization for Economic Cooperation and Development (OECD) (1999), *Managing National Innovation Systems*, Paris: Organization for Economic Cooperation and Development.

Pennings, J.M. and F. Harianto (1992), 'Technological networking and innovation implementation', *Organization Science*, **2** (3), 356–82.

Pfeffer, J. and R.I. Sutton (1999), 'Knowing what to do is not enough: turning knowledge into action', *California Management Review*, **42** (1), 83–108.

Porter, M. (1990), *The Competitive Advantage of Nations*, London: Macmillan.

Prusak, L. (1996), 'The knowledge advantage', *Strategy and Leadership*, March–April, 6–8.

Radosevic, S. (1998), 'Defining systems of innovation: a methodological discussion', *Technology in Society*, **20**, 75–86.

Reppy, J. (2000), 'Conceptualizing the role of defense industries in national systems of innovation', paper presented at the The Place of the Defense Industry in National Systems of Innovation, Cornell University, Ithaca, New York.

Roberts, J. (2000), 'From know-how to show-how? Questioning the role of information and communication technologies in knowledge transfer', *Technology Analysis and Strategic Management*, **12** (4), 429–43.

Rosenberg, N. (1982), *Inside the Black Box: Technology and Economics*, Cambridge and New York: Cambridge University Press.

Sadler-Smith, E. and B. Badger (1998), 'Cognitive style, learning and innovation', *Technology Analysis and Strategic Management*, **10** (2), 247–68.

Sawhney, M. and E. Prandelli (2000), 'Communities of creation: managing distributed innovation in turbulent markets', *California Management Review*, **42** (4), 24–54.

Spender, J.C. (1994), 'Organizational knowledge, collective practice and penrose rents', *International Business Review*, **3** (4), 353–67.

Standing, C. and S. Benson (2000), 'Organizational culture and knowledge management', in Thong, J.Y.L., P.Y.K. Chau and K.Y. Tam, *Proceedings to the Fourth Pacific Asia Conference on Information Systems*, Hong Kong: Publishing Technology Sector, The Hong Kong University of Science and Technology, 1103–13.

Swan, J. and S. Newell (2000), 'Linking knowledge management and innovation', in *Proceedings of the Eighth European Conference, on Information Systems*, Vienna, Austria.

Szulanski, G. (1996), 'Exploring internal stickiness: impediments to the transfer of best practice within the firm', *Strategic Management Journal*, **17**, Winter special issue, 27–43.

Truran, W.R. (1998), 'Pathways for knowledge: how companies learn through people', *Engineering Management Journal*, **10** (4), 15–20.

Tullett, A.D. and M.J. Kirton (1995), 'Further evidence for the interdependence of adaptive-innovative (A-I) cognitive style from national culture', *Personality Individual Difference*, **19** (3), 393–6.

Weber, J. (1989), 'Going over the lab wall in search of new ideas', *Business Week*, special issue, 132.

Whadcock, I. (1997), 'Don't imitate, innovate', *Supply Management*, 30 October, 40–42.

Whitley, R. (1994), 'Societies firms and markets: the social structuring of business systems', in R. Whitley (ed.), *European Business Systems: Firms and Markets in Their National Contexts*, London: Sage.

Winter, S.G. (2000), 'The satisficing principle in capacity learning', *Strategic Management Journal*, **21**, 981–96.

# 3. Knowledge management, institutions and professional cultures in engineering consulting services: the case of Hong Kong[1]

**Erik Baark**

Although engineering consulting is a knowledge-intensive business service that has been practised for many years in advanced industrialized economies, its crucial function for innovation related to the built environment has received relatively little attention. Services have only recently become a prominent item on the agenda of innovation research, as scholars gradually seek to understand the differences and similarities between innovation in services and in manufacturing (Howells, 2000). The new interest in service innovation has led to the development of more sophisticated taxonomies of innovation patterns in various subsectors of services (Metcalfe and Miles, 2000). Technical and engineering consultancy is usually classified as highly innovative, belonging to a group of technology-based knowledge intensive business services that are concerned with the production and transfer of new knowledge (Roberts, Andersen and Hull, 2000).

However, engineering consultants are often associated with the construction industry, a sector of the economy that has traditionally been regarded as very conservative, exhibiting a low rate of innovation. This image of construction as an innovative laggard has been reinforced by the low rate of explicit, formal research and development (R&D) activities and investment reported by firms in the sector. Expenditures on R&D in construction, measured on the basis of the activities undertaken by contractors and sub-suppliers, range from 0.01 per cent to 0.4 per cent of construction value-added for OECD countries, figures that are significantly lower than the 3–4 per cent of value-added spent on R&D in manufacturing (see Manseau and Seaden, 2001, pp. 9–10). This image is deceptive, however, since innovative activities are frequently carried out in relation to construction projects and tend to be integrated in system-wide work (Groák, 1992). Most new technologies are introduced as part of solutions of design problems in specific projects, rather than as a result of the output of research undertaken in specialized laboratories. The relations between parties engaged in innovation in various phases of planning, design and construction are highly complex, yielding an intricate pattern of client–agent relationships (Nam and Tatum, 1988). The processes of learning involved in construction innovation often rely on the experience that users acquire in the implementation of a project (Slaughter, 1993). The activities of engineering design are closely related to construction, and therefore linked to the patterns of innovation found in the construction sector (Gann, 1994). Given that the heterogeneity of patterns of innovation in the service sector has been recognized in recent literature (for example, Metcalfe and Miles, 2000), there is a need to further develop concepts and theories that help isolate specificities in the processes of innovation and their contingencies.

The professional culture underlying a knowledge-intensive business service such as engineering consulting has emphasized requirements of educational background, continuous training and social or ethical responsibility. The work of professional societies is therefore primarily concerned with enhancing the knowledge base of engineers and providing important legal and ethical guidelines. The practice of engineering consultancy is also shaped by cultural and institutional norms that are less explicit and that have been accumulated over a century. Cultural norms include values concerning the purpose and scope of work, the interaction with clients and colleagues, and often also the role of engineers in society. Institutional norms typically pertain to responsibilities and commitments under contract, procurement procedures and other aspects of business practices such as quality control. The global community of engineers shares many of these cultural norms, even if there may be exceptions where engineers fail to respect the norms. A range of explicit regulations and frequently a set of implicit conventions govern the institutional context.

The professional culture and institutions of consulting engineering in Hong Kong has been deeply influenced by the colonial past, that is, the British system of engineering education and practice. Hong Kong has emerged as one of the dynamic economies of East Asia where the provision of innovative engineering consulting services to the local construction sector can be seen as a crucial factor for raising quality and efficiency in construction. At the same time, however, engineering firms in Hong Kong are now largely staffed with locally born and educated engineers, and they operate on East Asian markets – including the Chinese Mainland – where many social and cultural values are deeply embedded in traditional patterns of behaviour. This raises important issues about the potential tensions between a 'global' professional culture and the cultural values of the organizations and societies in which consulting engineers carry out projects.

During the last couple of decades institutional changes have also affected design and construction processes, due to both the emergence of new patterns of cooperation and procurement of engineering services, and the challenges of ubiquitous reliance on information technology (IT) systems. These changes are shaping the innovative processes in ways that are only gradually becoming recognized in the sector. The processes of knowledge accumulation and deployment that provide the core competitive asset for consulting engineers are therefore undergoing a double transformation, one of which points to towards extended networks of knowledge exchange and integration of design and construction, while the other implies a higher reliance on systems of codified and formal information processing. The development along these trends is clearly also mediated by the cultural and institutional norms mentioned above.

The fundamental purpose of this chapter is to explore the emerging context of innovation in engineering consultancy, using the case of Hong Kong as a representative example combining global and local contexts. For this purpose, I shall examine the influence on innovation processes in terms of the characteristics of professional culture, the institutional environment for engineering consultancy, the patterns of knowledge creation and accumulation, and the availability of information technology infrastructure in the sector.

## ENGINEERING PROFESSIONAL CULTURE

The professional culture governing engineering consultancy has grown out of the historical development of engineering as a profession and the complex commercial and regulatory relationships that characterize construction projects. An important institution is that of the independent consulting engineer; independence implies that the engineer will provide impartial services to the client and help ensure the highest quality of design and implementation of projects. Engineers share with other professions a culture that involves a claim to autonomy and expert knowledge that provides them with a special status in society. These ideals are particularly manifest in private practices, which usually allows the professional to exercise independence of judgement in applying his or her technical skills. In this sense, professional culture represents key ideas that are assimilated through the professional's education, and usually adapted to the realities of practical employment in organizations (Raelin, 1986).

According to the ethical principles adopted by the International Federation of Consulting Engineers, the consulting engineer should be 'impartial in the provision of professional advice, judgment or decision', while acting 'at all times in the legitimate interest of the client and provide all services with integrity and faithfulness' (FIDIC, 2001, pp. 1–2). At the same time, the independent status of the engineer has been reinforced by a traditional division of labour in the construction process that attempted to distinguish sharply between responsibilities for design and supervision on the one hand, and practical construction on the other. This division of labour has been challenged in recent years, as industry players, clients and governments have sought to integrate design and building activities in search of lower costs and effective constructability. The traditional division of labour has also been seen as an obstacle to innovation, since it does not promote the essential communication between designers and contractors that could ensure the application of innovative design.

Engineering consultancy emerged as a distinct business service during the late nineteenth century. The primary function of the consultants was to provide clients with advanced engineering design or technical supervision services. Then, as now, the provision of these services called for superior command of analytical approaches in engineering and for a practical experience that represented years of knowledge accumulation in terms of both formal and informal learning. In the course of more than a century, consulting engineers have established themselves as a group of professionals, demarcating their role in competition with architects, quantify surveyors, and so on to take up a position within the 'system of professions' analysed by Abbott (1988).

Consulting engineers' role as independent agents directly employed by the developer has constituted an overreaching principle in Britain, which represents one of the most traditional formative grounds for the engineering profession. While normally hired to handle the design and/or management of the construction project, the engineering professional is also frequently required to assume a quasi-judicial role in interpreting the contracts between the owners and the contractors in neutral positions (Chapman and Grandjean, 1991). This way, the contractors only build; while the engineers/architects only design. The division of labour in the construction sector in Britain is unique compared to other European countries (Campagnac and Winch, 1997; Harvey and Ashworth, 1993). It can be traced back to the early development of the construction industry in Britain, at the turn of the eighteenth century when the British started to build railways. At its infancy stage, construction in Britain was not such an organized industry in which division of labour and roles that different industry participants played had stabilized. As projects progressed, the nature of the jobs of the engineers and contractors began to evolve. In those early days, the growth of the railway systems in Britain created unique opportunities for the engineers. Railways were largely developed by private companies and the persons in charge of these projects were usually the engineers. The proliferation of larger railway systems, in turn, increased the demand for new, highly specialized, construction and management expertise that engineers directly engaged in the construction process found difficult to master. The separation of duties between the contractors and engineers at that stage appeared logical. In addition, 'scamping' (that is, careless construction) and bribery were fairly common in the early railway construction projects involving developers, engineers and various contractors. As a strategy to cope with inefficiencies following such malpractices, large companies started to impose administrative measures, such as supervision protocols. The protocols introduced the engineers as an independent agent, and may be regarded as contributing to the formation of the work arrangement in the engineering profession in Britain (Linder, 1994). The British engineering profession remains characterized by its adherence to stringent division of labour in the design, supervision and construction of new projects, despite significant changes in technology and economic conditions (Harvey and Ashworth, 1993).

In the early twentieth century, professional engineering consultants primarily served a range of business sectors such as building construction and transportation, helping them to improve the design of production and construction projects. Public organizations also employed engineering consultants to handle projects of increasing complexity and stringent requirements in terms of safety. Other sectors of the rapidly growing manufacturing industries relied on corporate research and development, or production engineering divisions, to generate new product designs and to improve production methods. This became particularly noteworthy in the USA, where the development of the engineering profession took a different path following the dynamics of its own institutional and other environmental factors. During the late nineteenth century, American engineers worked primarily as independent consultants, but during the first half of the twentieth century, the number of engineers in the USA skyrocketed and many of these engineers found prosperous careers in corporate America as they often assumed high rank positions in the enterprises (Reynolds, 1991a; 1991b).

As professional occupations have gained prominence during the twentieth century, engineers have come to fill a key position in the shaping of the 'technocratic mode of administration' of modern societies (Rossides, 1998, p. 149). Some sociologists have seen this phenomenon as a consequence of an emerging meritocratic system, while others have stressed the 'occupational principle' that supports the control and power that professions may exert on the basis of a claim to special esoteric competence and to concern for the quality of its work and its benefits to society (Friedson, 1994). A common perception is that a profession requires specialized knowledge that reflects considerable preparation in skills, methods and principles. Professions also maintain high standards of achievement and conduct, encourage lifelong learning and engage in public service. These ideas have been the core of the Anglo-American tradition of professionalism, and they have been increasingly important in societies that have previously relied much more on education and status to distinguish elites (Friedson, 1994, pp. 18–19). While definitions of professional identity and its historical or sociological ramifications have generated a substantial body of literature (for example, Burrage and Torstendahl, 1990), an essential point is that professions constitute social or cultural constructs and are deeply influenced by national contexts.

Due to its status as a British colony, Hong Kong had emulated British traditions in the creation of an engineering profession until quite recently. For many years, the construction sector in Hong Kong exhibited a kind of dual configuration where civil engineering structures were primarily designed by British professionals, but were built by the local construction workers (Kao et al., 1997). The Engineering Society of Hong Kong was founded in 1947 with the aim of bringing together engineers of different disciplines. The Hong Kong Institution of Engineers (HKIE) was incorporated by Government Ordinance in 1975 and continues to develop and expand, adapting to the needs of engineers in Hong Kong.

An important development in 1982 was the Hong Kong Government's decision to recognize Corporate Members of the HKIE for civil service. Membership of the HKIE is now the primary qualification for employment as a professional engineer in Hong Kong. The procedures for registration of consulting engineers in Hong Kong remain relatively simple, and a person trained as engineer, who is able to document a basic expertise and membership of an appropriate professional organization, can register as an engineering consultant with various government authorities. The current Engineers Registration Board originates in debates about the need for a registration process that took place between the government and the Hong Kong Institution of Engineers in 1986–87. These discussions led to an agreement that registration boards should be set up for engineers, architects, surveyors and planners, primarily with the aim of ensuring consumer protection, but also for the protection of professionals. An Engineers Registration Ordinance was enacted in 1990, and since then more than 2000 engineers have been registered (Engineers Registration Board, 2000).

Another professional society, the Association of Consulting Engineers of Hong Kong (ACEHK), is a formal professional association incorporated in 1977 that was organized to promote common interests of the existing engineering consulting firms in Hong Kong. The objectives of the ACEHK are, among other things, to establish standards for the conduct of consulting engineers in Hong Kong, to promote the professional interests, rights, powers and privileges of consulting engineers, and to seek to promulgate appropriate conditions of engagement and fee scales that provide fair remuneration for the services provided. The ACEHK Memorandum of Association stipulates that a qualified consulting firm that has been established in Hong Kong for more than three years and is planning to further develop its business in Hong Kong is eligible to join the ACEHK as a full member. The memorandum also provides rules of professional conduct, including guidelines relating to independence, professional standards of practice and the manner in which the client is served (ACEHK, 1999). Thus, membership of the ACEHK may be used by a firm as an important reference for public relations or to present the firm to a client, thus providing assurance for the client that the firm observes basic professional standards. This can be an important supplementary selection criterion in addition to a membership of the HKIE.

The professional culture of consulting engineers in Hong Kong thus constitutes an extension of British and international traditions for social and ethical responsibilities, with a significant emphasis on maintaining independence and autonomy in engineering decisions. Although the construction industry in Hong Kong has been beset by problems of poor quality, such as short piling in public housing projects, these troubles have largely been related to the preponderance of excessive subcontracting arrangements among contractors, and not to design issues (see 'Construct for excellence', 2001). Professional societies encourage consciousness and training for quality work among their members and, through the allocation of an Innovation Award for Construction Industry in 2000/01, have sought to provide additional incentives for innovative design.

## INSTITUTIONAL FRAMEWORK

Several aspects of the institutional framework of engineering consultancy will influence the potential for innovation in the sector, for example, the project-based characteristics of engineering consultancy and the complex nature of the services provided. Another important aspect of the institutional framework is various approaches to procurement of design and supervision services, codes and regulations governing safety or environmental standards. Creating the design for complex systems in a heterogeneous market, where the design problems tend to call for individual solutions and idiosyncratic approaches for each project, also requires a unique practice of learning and knowledge accumulation.

Engineering consultants are engaged in the production and delivery of highly complex services. These services are produced with the aim of constructing or developing products or systems that are often complex on their own account (Gann and Salter, 2000). They participate in the construction of complex structures that require contributions from many different actors, and they are frequently engaged in the planning of systems for communication or transport that have to accommodate a broad variety of needs and/or depend on a large number of factors. Furthermore, each service tends to address very specific or idiosyncratic situations, and the solutions that the firm has to come up with need to be tailor-made in order to contribute the maximum value to the functionality of the structure or system created. The production of most engineering services also calls for the mobilization of many different types of expertise and disciplinary approaches, where the combination of these types of knowledge varies from one project to the next while the process of knowledge creation relies heavily on personal contacts and direct interaction.

The nature of work carried out in relation to these complex service products lends itself to the organizational framework of project-based activities. Project organization allows a firm to assemble appropriate expertise and exploit the synergies among the team participants; project teams are frequently provided with a wide scope of decision-making authority. Close interaction with clients and the need to carry out design or supervision in the proximity of the site of a construction project also require that project teams operate in a temporary office, further reinforcing the relative autonomy of the project organization. Organizational structures associated with mass production and large-scale manufacturing industries, including both functional divisions and various types of matrix organizations, appear ill-adapted to the requirements of advanced production methods (Winch, 1994). The project-based organization appears to be much better suited to complex systems production, which tend to focus on providing unique or bespoke products, and where the direct user involvement in the innovation process can be very significant (Hobday, 2000).

Most work undertaken by consulting engineers aim to provide services related to complex systems and structures in unique settings, and the project-led organization has long been a predominant entry level form for engineering consulting firms, as it is for construction industry in general (Stallworthy and Kharbanda, 1985). Large, international engineering consultancy firms have often created specialized divisions or even new firms to assist in concentrating efforts in specific areas of work, such as environmental engineering or IT. Nevertheless, new projects initiated by these divisions will frequently draw on resources from other divisions or subsidiary firms. The predominance of project-based organizational structure in the sector is also epitomized by the significance of the concept of a project life cycle, encompassing the stages of identification, planning and feasibility, conceptual engineering, detailed design, procurement and commissioning, in the management of engineering consulting work (Corrie, 1991). Indeed, the effective management of activities during various stages of the project life cycle is essential for competitiveness of firms in the construction business, and remains a key focus of concern for industry participants and government alike (Miozzo and Ivory, 2000; Wearne, 1993; Winch 1998).

The project-based characteristic of engineering design and consultancy has very significant implications for innovation in the sector. Projects provide the context and framework within which knowledge flows take place, and they shape the linkages between firms and other organizations (such as public or private clients). It requires collaboration or partnerships between firms (frequently firms that are competitors in other contexts), and the outcome depends on the extent to which participating firms – or, perhaps more accurately, project leaders – are able to manage networks with complex interfaces (Gann and Salter, 2000).

The complexity of production and products generated in the engineering consulting sector tends to support incremental innovations introduced in the course of project work, rather than radical innovations that would lead to a fundamental overhaul of services and business. Each new design, new material or new construction method needs to be aligned with a vast number of other variables in the final product, and there is often limited opportunities for the consultant to engage in extensive testing of the effects of an innovation. Therefore, innovative ideas are usually implemented with as much precaution as possible, and a continuous stream of incremental improvements or optimization efforts is an approach that usually lends itself better to meeting the requirements of clients than propositions demanding major, system-wide changes in the product or construction processes.

Projects involving advanced engineering design in Hong Kong have become increasingly complex during the recent decades. The construction of the Mass Transit Railway system, which was initiated in the 1970s, constituted a highly complex undertaking involving 25 major civil engineering and 10 electrical and mechanical engineering contracts, which amounted to a total sum of HK$5.8 billion, excluding interests and other finance costs during the period of construction. New technologies such as diaphragm walling and compressed air tunnelling were introduced, and complex issues of construction in congested urban areas with severe restrictions in working space, acceptable noise levels and vibration had to be solved. The complexity of planning and construction of new towns in the New Territories presented another major challenge to engineering consultants. However, the most extensive and complex project to date has been the construction of a new airport at Chek Lap Kok in the 1990s. This undertaking, known as the

Airport Core Programme (ACP), comprised a system of 10 projects, strategically designed to erect and connect the replacement airport on Lantau Island to various locations in the territory and to provide land for other developments. At a cost of US$20.6 billion, the 10 ACP projects included the construction of terminal buildings, a railway and an expressway to the Central district, and bridges, reclamation and housing projects. Although most engineering design projects in Hong Kong do not involve such extreme complexity, the difficulties associated with construction in congested areas, under difficult geotechnical conditions, and with multifarious environmental surroundings are usually challenging.

Procurement patterns in Hong Kong have undergone significant changes during the last few decades. In the immediate post-war period, procurement of engineering design services by the Hong Kong government was guided largely by informal contacts and negotiations. However, in the 1960s corruption had become endemic in both public organizations and private business in Hong Kong. After the creation of the Independent Commission Against Corruption in 1974, however, a decade-long battle to institutionalize a clean government and a censured private sector ensued. After syndicated corruption in the police force was effectively curbed, corrupt practices in the 'notorious Public Works Department', which oversaw a large part of construction work in Hong Kong, became a primary object of investigation (Lo, 1993, pp. 101–4). Housing topped the list of complaints about corruption referring to government departments during 1974–82 (Palmier, 1985, p. 167). Prosecution of senior Building Department officials served to manifest a more disciplined environment for public works and the construction business. Complaints regarding corruption involving government departments declined in the late 1980s. However, such complaints against public organizations have since increased again, while complaints involving corruption in the private sector have increased steadily in both the 1980s and 1990s. More recently, inadequate monitoring of piling for public housing construction projects created public uproar; these events led to the resignation of the Chairman of the Housing Authority in June 2000 and the disciplining of several contractors. The resurgence of such problems has prompted the Works Bureau to announce the objective of ensuring 'that the quality of consultants and contractors selected to deliver public works will meet the requirements of our projects' (Works Bureau, 2000a, p. 3).

Procurement of consulting engineering services by public or private organizations has consequently evolved into institutional frameworks that provide stringent rules for competition related to technical excellence and price (Rowlinson and McDermott, 1999). Although procurement regulations differ among countries or even local administrations, they often share a fundamental set of premises that should ensure that clients get maximum value for their money. One of the most important elements of procurement guidelines implemented in many public administrations or international organizations is the two-envelope system whereby consultants submit bidding documents separately in two envelopes containing the technical proposal and the consultant's fee respectively. This procedure is designed to ensure that the quality of the technical proposals is evaluated without consideration of price (which is only assessed after the best technical proposals have been shortlisted). However, depending on the ratio adopted by the client in weighting the technical excellence and fee cost, competition can become quite severe and tends to reduce any incentives to provide innovative (and therefore risky and costly) solutions. Most government departments in Hong Kong have utilized a ratio of 80 to 20 per cent in relative weight of technical and fee for evaluation of bids. Some departments have used a 50:50 ratio, with the result that consultants adopt a minimalist attitude to technical details while facing very severe competition on fees.

The practice of procurement in the construction industry tends to force engineering consultants to devote much time and energy to formulating a bid during the early stage of the design process. This is often a risky endeavour as only one firm/consortium is selected from a pool of contenders. Depending upon the actual project, competition could be very intense. For projects undertaken for the government of Hong Kong SAR, elaborate guidelines exist for the tendering process. For instance, with regard to equipment included in building services jobs, the government requires that at least three manufacturers should be involved; otherwise, the consultant has to request a special approval from the respective government department. Tenders are also used to increase competitive pressure on engineering consultants. In 2000, the government invited 16 consortia of international consulting firms, of which four were Hong Kong based, to bid for a state-of-the-art design of a long span bridge to link up the Stonecutter Island with the New Territories. In another recent competition, a total of 62 teams of consultants were engaged in bidding for a project. The number of competitors varies according to the project, but such numbers illustrate the intensity of competition.

Building codes represent another type of regulation influencing the scope of innovation. Quite a few engineering consultants in Hong Kong assert that considerable obstacles in pushing forward innovations related to construction projects arise from the existence and interpretation of building codes and regulations. When a new technology is proposed for a construction project, getting government approval turns out to be decisive, especially in the case of technologies that have not been used anywhere else in the world. Various consultants have expressed their sympathy with the plight of government officials, and some even think that the regulatory system related to the construction industry in Hong Kong is beneficial to maintaining and improving quality standards in the local industry. However, it is evident from our interviews that many engineering consultants regard the efforts required to provide justifications for innovative solutions as excessive. The money and time involved in such endeavours can certainly be a discouraging factor for the engineers, with subsequent major influences on their thinking process.

The problem was explicitly recognized in a recent review of the construction industry in Hong Kong. The report stated that a

> robust and comprehensive regulatory framework is necessary to ensure effective performance of the construction industry. But care should be taken that regulatory controls do not become an impediment to the industry's drive towards excellence. We urge regulators to substitute prescriptive provisions with performance-based ones, streamline procedures, minimize conflicting requirements set by different regulatory authorities and develop a service culture. The ongoing review of the Buildings Ordinance and its subsidiary legislation, which seeks to modernize the legislation and to encourage building innovation, has our full support. We encourage other regulators to similarly facilitate the construction industry's operations. ('Construct for excellence', 2001, p. 9)

The institutional framework for innovation in the engineering consulting sector in Hong Kong has been transformed by the increased complexity of projects. Furthermore, procurement approaches for projects undertaken by the public sector have attempted to increase competition, and to reduce the scope for corrupt practices. At the same time, the procurement procedures have encouraged price-based competition to an extent that may have detrimental influence on technological innovation and the level of quality attained in new projects.

## KNOWLEDGE CREATION AND ACCUMULATION

Knowledge accumulation depends critically on the resources that firms command; in particular, the knowledge that is available (internally in the organization or from external sources) or need to be created. Mobilization of knowledge includes the sourcing of knowledge through recruitment and training of engineers or other experts, by the establishment of platforms for interaction among participants in a project and with external agents, or through the professional community. Knowledge management in engineering consultancy firms impinge directly on the level and patterns of innovation. The primary characteristic is the fact that the human resources are critically important for the success of engineering consultancy firms (Boxall and Steeneveld, 1999). The competitive assets of engineering consultancy firms reside primarily in the skills of their staff, and are thus contingent on the quality and capabilities of their human resources. Many small firms in the sector are simply based on the expertise of one or a few engineers. Larger firms usually organize their production and delivery of services through project teams of certified engineers with a long-term experience in specialized areas of engineering, who embody the tacit knowledge as well as the stock of formal knowledge accumulated in the organization.

The reliance on knowledge, which is often embodied in the expertise of employees, has had a tendency to support a pattern of knowledge accumulation that is gradual and often characterized by largely tacit elements. The project team will usually be composed of senior engineers that have built up their specialist knowledge of the design through many years of practice, combined with a group of engineers who are still in the process of learning (Smith, 1995; Wearne, 1993). The profession also emphasizes this aspect of practical experience in the requirements for certification as a chartered engineer. To a large extent, knowledge management in engineering consultancy firms focus on recruitment, training and retaining of engineers who are keen to continue to expand and enhance their knowledge base. Their services rely heavily on their professional expertise, acquired through formal education, continuing professional development and hands-on experience. Through the design process, for instance, the engineers apply scientific knowledge to solve problems derived from the clients' requirements. Scientific knowledge may entail mathematical calculations, geometric analysis, and so on. Subsequently, ideas, concepts and, in some case, analyses are presented in the form of visual interfaces that call for unique computer skills. Materials are engineered in such a way that they perform to the clients' requirements. Knowledge of this kind is often explicit in nature, although it may frequently be presented in a visual form (Henderson, 1999).

Engineers acquire the sort of skills required to do calculations, prepare drawings and presentations and so on through formal channels, schools, professional institutions, on-the-job training or self-study. On the other hand, engineers also need to exercise discretion at certain points during the design process, and decision rules may not always be available. They make choices on what options to explore. Aesthetics is very much a subjective measure. Attributes like comfort cannot easily be evaluated following explicit rules.

In construction design there is a human element of instinct and subjective judgement that links processes of engineering with the creation of art. To a large extent, experienced engineers recognize that the design process can be very intuitive in nature (Hough, 1996). Imagination is part of intuitive knowledge, and the processes required to put this type of knowledge to work are frequently tacit. During the process, engineers often visualize their ideas and concepts in their mind or as draft drawings, and they base their decisions on a gut feeling about the strength of a structure, the attractiveness of a solution, and the feasibility of a new technique. On account of the inherent fragmentation of the traditional construction process, however, the production of a design is an intricate process where many considerations and demands must be considered, and the resultant configuration will embody compromises and synthesis of many strands of knowledge. Innovative consulting engineers are frequently confronted with situations and constraints that are idiosyncratic and particular for each project. At the most fundamental level, one must understand – to paraphrase Walter G. Vincenti (1990) – what it is that engineers know and how they get to know it.

Knowledge is created, integrated and applied in organizational contexts that, as Nonaka and Takeuchi (1995) remind us, reflect both the intensity and nature of interactions among individuals and a range of different types of knowledge. An engineering project will involve extensive relationships between the project group, the firm, and a host of other actors such as partners in the project, the client organization, contractors or suppliers, and government regulators. Engineering consultants depend on the interests and capabilities of other business sectors engaged in construction projects such as architects and contractors. Innovation in engineering consultancy thus occurs within the context of networks of various actors and with reference to institutions that govern relationships between actors involved in construction projects, professional and ethical codes, technical or regulatory standards, and so on. The accumulation of knowledge and the creation of new knowledge in connection with innovations in the sector can therefore be analysed with reference to the model for knowledge creation proposed by Nonaka and Konno (1998). They argue that knowledge creation is a spiralling process in which knowledge is continuously created and recreated within the work team and the organization through four modes of knowledge conversion, continuously turning knowledge from one form to another, in a self-transcending process. Four modes of socialization, externalization, combination and internalization provide a cycle of actions that lead to the formation of new knowledge underlying innovative solutions.

The engineering consulting firms begin the knowledge accumulation process for a job as soon as they decide to enter competition, and regardless of whether the firm will eventually be awarded the design contract. Very often construction projects involve a number of participants including the architects, the consultants, the quantity surveyors, the contractors and so forth. In situations where the engineering consultant has control over which firms to partner with, it will of course give priority to the ones with which it has had previous good working relationships. At this early stage of a project, the management of knowledge follows the characteristics of the phase of *socialization*, with an emphasis on the mobilization of tacit knowledge. In the process of formulating bids, interactions among the group of consultants are less formal and constrained though they typically take place in face-to-face meetings. Preliminary requirements of the project are analysed, and inputs and ideas from different members of the team are explored, synthesized and evaluated for aptness of application. In essence, this is the process through which tacit knowledge is mobilized. Knowledge is created and disseminated through personal meetings and networks, frequently in brainstorming meetings where all the possible avenues to developing an appropriate design are explored. In addition to the team that is directly involved in preparing for the project, however, many engineering consultants will try to exploit wider networks of expertise.

Modern construction projects tend to be very sophisticated in that many disciplines are involved. It is therefore essential that an idea be discussed considering all the impacts that it may have on the entire system. Therefore, a phase of *externalization* is frequently initiated, preparing for consultations with partners and clients by means of a more explicit conceptualization of the ideas involved in the project. More innovative firms typically continue the knowledge accumulation process by means of liaison meetings including all the potential project participants such as the engineering designers, the architects, the quantity surveyors and, perhaps, client representatives. At this stage, meetings are not totally formal as the key is to share knowledge and ideas. Information is presented orally, in graphics, or in written formats. At this stage, team members are free to investigate ideas until a consensus is reached.

The knowledge creation cycle thus enters into a phase that usually requires team members to transform tacit knowledge into explicit forms for presentations. However, ideas that have been launched earlier are mixed with new ideas or proposed solutions in a process that does not follow a linear sequence in being transformed into explicit forms. The ideas may have to be bounced around at several different kinds of meetings – pure internal meetings internal design liaison meetings and client meetings. The process of accumulating knowledge and turning tacit knowledge into explicit knowledge is thus often an intermingling process, which may go through several iterations before ideas are finally articulated in their final forms. Once a design contract is awarded, however, the concrete work of refining and testing the concepts is initiated. During the bidding process, consultants may have put in effort to derive a design with innovative features that will promise to deliver good values to the client, and up to this point ideas and innovations are quite high priorities on the agenda. But after a bid has been won, a phase of *combination* emerges, as innovations have to be examined in detail for practical purposes, relying on the synthesis of information and data derived from a wide range of potential sources. Since engineering innovation in Hong Kong is often guided by the demands of construction scale, scope and cost, the innovative efforts usually seek to enhance the construction design from these perspectives. In fact, costs and time-related matters are of utmost importance to the client. Consequently, the consultants are frequently required at the inception of the project to provide justifications for costs and other critical factors related to the preliminary conceptual design. Having to refine the original ideas, after considering every aspect of them, is fairly demanding and will often result in substantial improvements.

Incremental innovation tends to occur throughout the project life cycle of a construction project, and some innovative firms will continue to introduce incremental changes into the design to fit the particular conditions existing at the project site. Although some innovations rely on the development of technology planned well in advance, others will frequently evolve as the project moves along. Innovations that would affect the entire building plan are frequently scrutinized and assessed during the initial stages by means of simulation models. Some important innovations relate to systems that can facilitate the process of assessment of design feasibility by means of advanced simulation. One of the major engineering consultancy firms in Hong Kong, Ove Arup and Partners (HK), has utilized a simulation programme developed for Computational Fluid Dynamics (CFD) to model the air flow around the entire housing complex, thus creating an optimal building layout for micro-climate control. Even within the building, the same technology can be applied to enhance the design of the building plan. Arups has used CFD to generate quantitative models that simulate how air flows inside an apartment. By adjusting the positions of the windows, natural ventilation of the apartments is optimized for maximum energy efficiency. The same concept has been applied to study interior lighting of a building. By adjusting the positioning of the windows and inserting artificial light shelves, the amount of natural daylight entering a room can be maximized. Through the use of in-house expertise and state-of-the-art computer software, concepts are tested and adjusted to fit the situation.

In order to maintain a repertoire of knowledge that can be available for the firm in future projects, it is essential that explicit knowledge generated in a particular project be appropriated through acquisition and integration. Knowledge created in an organization usually requires some kind of process to carry out what Nonaka calls *internalization*. If new knowledge is not transformed into tacit forms embodied in an organization, the natural evolution of the knowledge base will cease. Internalization involves sharing the knowledge with others in the organization. The acquired or derived knowledge is to be embodied in the general practice and procedures in the organization. Usually, internalization relies on a continuity of human resources and capabilities in the firm, but some firms also emphasize the explicit dissemination of information. Large international consulting firms such as Ove Arup and Partners have developed global skill networks on different fields of specialties. Each member within a particular network can request the latest information on specific issues in the field through electronic means from around the world. Global engineering consultancy firms have frequently orchestrated such networks in a way that ensure that members are very keen to participate. They usually focus on linking employees from different offices in the firm, and help individual project teams examine the feasibility of their innovative ideas. If the requested information is available elsewhere in the world, it can be easily obtained within a day or two, a quality that makes such networks a very important resource of the firm.

Patterns of knowledge creation and accumulation in the engineering consultancy sector in Hong Kong exhibit many of the characteristics associated with knowledge-intensive services, such as a strong dependence on human resources, the vital importance of tacit knowledge, and the key role of experience and reputation. Moreover, the processes of knowledge creation involve extensive sharing of both tacit and explicit knowledge that is similar to patterns observed in other business sectors. In Hong Kong, these aspects of knowledge accumulation are reinforced by the need to recruit engineers who can communicate and interact creatively and widely in order to support innovation. Large engineering consultancy firms have succeeded in generating an environment promoting this type of skill, but small firms appear to be struggling to integrate their knowledge management for the purpose of promoting innovation.

## INFORMATION TECHNOLOGY INFRASTRUCTURE

Advanced information and communication technology networks have influenced the organizational structure and management for many engineering companies working at the global level (Kini, 2000). Engineering consulting firms in Hong Kong also appear to have adopted IT at a faster rate than the Hong Kong construction industry as a whole. A survey of information technology usage for a broad range of consultants conducted in 1998 pointed to civil engineering firms as relatively advanced users (Works Bureau, 1998). Facilities such as fax machines were used extensively, and the use of telephones and email for communication within and between offices was ubiquitous. However, much of the communication taking place between project participants still tend to rely on meetings where handwritten notes and minutes are prepared, and the survey indicated that the use of tape recorders, word processors or electronic note boards was negligible at these meetings. A more advanced technology for conducting such meetings is video-conferencing, but the majority of Hong Kong consultants did not use this technology. The short distances and convenience of travel between points in the territory is probably a good reason for the lack of interest in video-conferencing, and only a few firms were using the Internet for video-conferencing as a tool when conducting business with overseas locations.

The majority of the consultants surveyed used computer-aided design (CAD) in their head offices for the production of construction drawings, with civil engineering firms using this technology more extensively than other consultants. However, the distribution of these drawings took place primarily in the form of a hard copy, and to a much lesser extent as electronic files on disk. Few firms distributed construction drawings as electronic files across local area networks (LAN), but a majority of firms appear to regularly distribute such files via the Internet. The hard-copy prints of drawings and design remain the foundation for revisions and checking; the more advanced approach of revising/checking drawings in their electronic form has not yet become popular among Hong Kong firms. The reliance on printed documents and the manual procedures for organizing and filing these shows that Hong Kong firms maintain good practice for process control and document management, even if this fails to exploit some of the advantages of systems based on electronic distribution and sharing of documents.

Email has now become a ubiquitous mode of communication, and the majority of civil engineering consultants use this facility for communication of messages. Less than half the firms in subsectors such as building services consultants and structural engineering consultants use email, however. Within the firms, email is provided mainly for the head office for managerial personnel and professional staff on specific project assignments. These email systems are utilized for exchange and amendment of written messages, and for agreeing on draft texts. Civil engineering consultants also attach written text or drawing files to emails for the purpose of distributing these files. At the time of the survey in 1998, few engineering firms had developed an Internet presence, although staff in many firms would already rely on access to the Internet. The civil engineering consultants in the survey indicated that they were very concerned about the impact of information technology on competition and business strategy, but that an overall role of IT strategies did not attract much attention.

A study prepared as a background for introducing electronic tendering for the Hong Kong government during 2001 provided evidence of a modest utilization of advanced communications infrastructure, with only 30 per cent of the firms operating intranets and 52 per cent using internal email and groupware systems (Works Bureau, 2000b). The IT infrastructure of large firms was considerably better than small firms, to the extent that small engineering consulting firms would have difficulties entering competition under an e-tendering system. These surveys appear to indicate that engineering consultancy firms in Hong Kong have successfully established a basic stand-alone IT infrastructure for production and communication of written documents and drawings. But the majority of firms have yet to exploit the opportunities for more sophisticated networking that advanced information technology offers today, including exchange of drawings, images, multimedia files and documents.

Even if engineering consultancy firms in Hong Kong recognize the significance of the opportunities that information technology and networks such as the Internet can offer to enhance cooperation in the design process, their approach to investment in IT and re-engineering of organizational procedures appears to have been cautious. Small firms, in particular, are held back by their relative shortage of infrastructure (such as networks or Internet servers) and technical systems (such as CAD or project management systems). Efforts to improve productivity in the sector by means of an IT-enabled flow of knowledge and information are therefore also constrained by the existing level of preparedness and organizational inertia.

## CONCLUDING REMARKS

This chapter has sought to explore key contingencies shaping innovation processes in the engineering consulting sector in Hong Kong, based on a taxonomy of four major dimensions of engineering consultancy business: professional culture, institutional framework, knowledge creation and information technology infrastructure.

The study suggests that the professional culture of engineering consultancy in Hong Kong, which has been rooted in Anglo-American traditions of professional autonomy and ethics, has established a framework that seeks to maintain international standards for quality of services and innovation. Thereby the professional culture attempts to distance engineers from the questionable practices of some local Hong Kong contractors and subcontracting entrepreneurs. The institutional context of engineering consultancy in Hong Kong has witnessed a tendency towards greater complexity of project-based services, which in turn has fostered incremental innovation and/or more collaboration with partners in relation to innovative initiatives.

Other aspects of the institutional framework, such as new procurement approaches and building codes have tended to constrain innovative efforts of engineering consultants.

The vital importance of knowledge creation and accumulation in engineering consulting indicates that innovation must rely on recruitment, training and continuous learning by engineering staff. In addition, the most successful firms have adopted knowledge accumulation strategies that mobilize tacit and explicit knowledge in a virtuous cycle. Some phases of this cycle also extend networks of social and technical interaction beyond the project group, to clients, project partners and firm-based networks of expertise. Finally, the study discussed the expansion of the information technology infrastructure for engineering consultancy firms in Hong Kong, and suggested that further opportunities for exploitation of such infrastructure in innovative efforts exist, particularly for small firms.

## NOTE

1.  Funding for the research conducted for the present paper from the Research Grants Council in Hong Kong (HKUST6168/00H) is gratefully acknowledged. Mr. M.A. Kwok Wai has provided extensive and extremely valuable research assistance.

## REFERENCES

Abbott, A. (1988), *The System of Professions*, Chicago: University of Chicago Press.
ACEHK (1999) 'Memorandum and Articles of Association of the Association of Consulting Engineers of Hong Kong' (as amended up to 10 February 1999), Hong Kong, mimeo.
Boxall, P. and M. Steeneveld (1999), 'Human resource strategy and competitive advantage: a longitudinal study of engineering consultancies', *Journal of Management Studies*, **36** (4), 443–63.
Burrage, M. and R. Torstendahl (1990), *Professions in Theory and History*, London: Sage.
Campagnac, E. and G. Winch (1997), 'The social regulation of technical expertise: the corps and profession in France and Great Britain', in R. Whitley and P.H. Kristensen (eds), *Governance at Work: The Social Regulation of Economic Relations*, Oxford: Oxford University Press, pp. 86–103.
Chapman, N.F.S. and G. Grandjean (1991), *The Construction Industry and the European Community*, Oxford: BSP Professional Books.
'Construct for excellence. Report of the Construction Industry Review Committee' (January 2001), Hong Kong, mimeo.
Corrie, R.K. (ed.) (1991), *Project Evaluation*, London: Thomas Telford.
Engineers Registration Board (2000), 'General information', Hong Kong, mimeo.
FIDIC (2001), 'FIDIC Code of Ethics', Lausanne, Switzerland, mimeo.

Friedson, E. (1994), *Professionalism Reborn*, Chicago: University of Chicago Press.

Gann, D. (1994), 'Innovation in the construction sector', in M. Dodgson and R. Rothwell (eds) *The Handbook of Industrial Innovation*, Aldershot, UK and Brookfield, USA: Edward Elgar, pp. 202–12.

Gann, D. and A. Salter (2000), 'Innovation in project-based, service-enhanced firms: the construction of complex products and systems', *Research Policy*, **29** (7–8), 955–72.

Groák, S. (1995), 'Project-related research and development', in D. Dunster (ed.), *Arups on Engineering*, Berlin: Ernst & Sohn.

Hartley, P.M. (2000), *Consulting Engineering: Constructing the Future*, Baldock, Herts: Research Studies Press.

Harvey, R.C. and A. Ashworth (1993), *The Construction Industry of Great Britain*, Oxford: Butterworth-Heinemann.

Henderson, K. (1999), *On Line and On Paper: Visual Representations, Visual Culture, and Computer Graphics in Design Engineering*, Cambridge, MA: MIT Press.

Hobday, M. (2000), 'The project-based organization: an ideal for managing complex products and systems?', *Research Policy*, **29** (7–8), 871–93.

Hough, R. (1996) 'Intuition in engineering design', in D. Dunster (ed.), *Arups on Engineering*, Berlin: Ernst & Sohn, pp. 19–26.

Howells, J. (2000) 'Services and systems of innovation', in B. Andersen, J. Howells, R. Hull, I. Miles and J. Roberts (eds), *Knowledge and Innovation in the New Service Economy*, Cheltenham, UK and Northampton, MA, USA: Edward Elgar, pp. 215–28.

Kao, Charles et al. (1997) *Engineering Hong Kong: 50 Years of Achievements*, Hong Kong: Chinese University Press and Henderson & Associates.

Kini, D.U. (2000), 'Global project management – not business as usual', *Journal of Management in Engineering*, **16** (6), 29–33.

Linder, M. (1994), *Projecting Capitalism: A History of the Internationalization of the Construction Industry*, Westport, CT: Greenwood Press.

Lo, T.W. (1993), *Corruption and Politics in Hong Kong and China*, Buckingham: Open University Press.

Manseau, A. and G. Seaden (eds) (2001), *Innovation in Construction: An International Review of Public Policies*, London and New York: Spon Press.

Metcalfe, J.S. and I. Miles (eds) (2000), *Innovation Systems in the Service Economy*, Boston and London: Kluwer Academic.

Miozzo, M. and C. Ivory (2000), 'Restructuring in the British construction industry: implications of recent changes in project management and technology', *Technology Analysis and Strategic Management*, **12** (4), 513–31.

Nam, C.H. and C.B. Tatum (1988), 'Major characteristics of constructed products and resulting limitations of construction technology', *Construction Management and Economics*, (6), 133–48.

Nonaka, I. and N. Konno (1998), 'The concept of "Ba": building a foundation for knowledge creation', *California Management Review*, **40** (3), 40–54.

Nonaka, I. and H. Takeuchi (1995), *The Knowledge-Creating Company*, New York: Oxford University Press.

Palmier, L. (1985), *The Control of Bureaucratic Corruption: Case Studies in Asia*, New Delhi: Allied Publishers.

Raelin, J.A. (1986), *The Clash of Cultures*, Boston, MA: Harvard Business School Press.

Reynolds, T.S. (1991a), 'Overview: the engineer in 19th century America', in T.S. Reynolds (ed.), *The Engineer in America: A Historical Anthology from Technology and Culture*, Chicago and London: University of Chicago Press.

Reynolds, T.S. (1991b) 'Overview: the engineer in 20th century America', in T.S. Reynolds (ed.), *The Engineer in America: A Historical Anthology from Technology and Culture*, Chicago and London: University of Chicago Press.

Roberts, J., B. Andersen and R. Hull (2000) 'Knowledge and innovation in the new service economy', in B. Andersen, J. Howells, R. Hull, I. Miles and J. Roberts (eds), *Knowledge and Innovation in the New Service Economy*, Cheltenham, UK and Northhampton, MA, USA: Edward Elgar, pp. 10–35.

Rossides, D.W. (1998), *Professions and Disciplines*, Upper Saddle River, NJ: Prentice-Hall.

Rowlinson, S. and P. McDermott (eds) (1999), *Procurement Systems: A Guide to Best Practice in Construction*, London: E. & F.N. Spon.

Slaughter, S. (1993) 'Innovation and learning during implementation: a comparison of user and manufacturer innovations', *Research Policy*, **22**, 81–95.

Smith, N.J. (ed.) (1995), *Engineering Project Management*, Oxford: Blackwell Science.

Stallworthy, E.A. and O.P. Kharbanda (1985), *International Construction and the Role of Project Management*, Aldershot: Gower.

Wearne, S. (1993), *Principles of Engineering Organization*, 2nd edition, London: Thomas Telford.

Vincenti, W.G. (1990), *What Engineers Know and How They Know It*, Baltimore, MD and London: Johns Hopkins University Press.

Winch, G. (1994), *Managing Production: Engineering Change and Stability*, Oxford: Clarendon Press.

Winch, G. (1998), 'Zephyrs of creative destruction: understanding the management of innovation in construction', *Building Research and Information*, **26** (4), 268–79.

Works Bureau (1998), '1998 Works Bureau IT survey of Hong Kong consultants', Hong Kong: mimeo

Works Bureau (2000a), *Policy Objective for Works Bureau*, Hong Kong: Hong Kong Special Administrative Region Government Printing Department.

Works Bureau (2000b), 'Report for questionnaire survey on electronic tendering', Hong Kong: mimeo.

# 4. Scientometrics and the evaluation of European integration

## Koen Frenken and Loet Leydesdorff

## 1. INTRODUCTION

A fascinating facet of the European Union is the multiplicity of meanings that are generated with respect to European integration. Different perceptions among Europeans contest the meaning of integration in general and regarding each social subsystem (economy, politics, science, sports, and so on) in particular. It is therefore both surprising and understandable that relatively few attempts have been reported to measure European integration in a formal way. This is surprising because of the importance of the question, but understandable because of the changing and conflicting meanings of European integration (Leydesdorff, 1992; Luukkonen, 1998).

In this chapter, we elaborate on the topic of European integration in science. We will not deal with questions related to the effects of European integration, but only with the scientometric question of how one can quantitatively indicate integration of the European science system. This research question is in a certain sense a sine qua non for further research. Without indicators of integration, both the determinants and the effects of (European) integration are hard to assess statistically, let alone the question of the effectiveness of European science policies. Admittedly, however, the empiricist approach loses an explicit perspective of multiplicity of local meanings of 'Europe'. In this respect, our study is intended to facilitate and supplement debates rather than to provide a final answer to the questions whether European integration 'exists'.

In this chapter, we first discuss the use of scientometric indicators in research evaluation from a historical perspective in (Section 2). A discussion of European science policy follows (Section 3). Then, we introduce a number of indicators of integration and discuss our empirical results concerning the evolution of the European science system in the 1980s and 1990s (Section 4). We close the chapter with a discussion of possible avenues of future research for enhancing research evaluation (Section 5).

## 2.  SCIENTOMETRICS AND RESEARCH EVALUATION

### The Endless Frontier

The idea that scientific knowledge could be organized deliberately and controlled from a mission perspective can be considered as resulting from experiences in the Second World War. Before that time the intellectual organization of knowledge had largely been left to the internal mechanisms of discipline formation and specialist communications (Bush, 1945; Whitley, 1984). The military impact of science and technology through knowledge-based development and mission-orientated research during the Second World War (for example, the Manhattan project) made it necessary in 1945 to formulate a new science and technology policy under peacetime conditions.

Vannevar Bush's report to the US President, entitled *The Endless Frontier*, contained a plea for a less interventionist science policy (Bush, 1945). Quality control should be left to the internal mechanisms of the scientific elite, for example, through the peer review system. The model of the US National Science Foundation (NSF) (1947)[1] was thereafter followed by other Western countries. For example, the Netherlands created its foundation for Fundamental Scientific Research (ZWO) in 1950. With hindsight, one can consider this period as the institutional phase of science policies: the main policy instrument was the support of science with institutions to control its funding.

Alongside the military coordination by NATO, the Organization for Economic Cooperation and Development (OECD) was created in 1960 in order to organize science and technology policies among its member states. This led in 1963 to the *Frascati Manual for the Measurement of Scientific and Technical Activities*, which can be understood as a response to the increased economic importance of science and technology. This manual defined parameters for the statistical monitoring of science and technology on a comparative basis. One was then able to compare the output performance and resource efficiency of various nation states. This rapidly led to questions concerning 'strengths and weakness' of nations in specific disciplines, and later led to policies based on differential increases in the budgets of particular disciplines. Thus, the focus remained on financial input-indicators, while the system relied on peer review in scientific disciplines for more detailed decision-making at the lower levels of individual scientific disciplines and specialties (Leydesdorff, 2003).

## Output Indicators

The use of scientometric indicators in research evaluation emerged in the 1970s in the USA and somewhat later in European countries. Before that time research evaluation proceeded mainly through the peer review system, on the one hand, and through economic indicators, on the other. The latter types of indicators (for example, percentage of gross national product [GNP] spent on R&D) have been developed by the OECD in Paris, and can be considered as input indicators.

The *Science Citation Index* produced by Eugene Garfield's Institute of Scientific Information came to be recognized as a means to objectify standards using literature-based indicators (Price, 1963). The gradual introduction of output indicators such as number of publications and citations has proven socially legitimated both internally and externally to the science system. Internal use primarily consists of quality control and benchmarking within and across disciplinary frameworks. For example, output records are increasingly used as a tool in the academic labour market. Externally, output indicators are used mainly by policy-makers and science administrators who wish to assess institutions and to evaluate investments in research projects. In the early 1980s, scientometricians developed a fine-grained model that introduced output as a feedback parameter into the finance scheme of departments during the early 1980s (Moed et al., 1985).

In different European countries, very different trajectories in the use of output indicators emerged. In some countries like the UK, the idea of using output indicators to feedback on budgets was rapidly introduced as a tool in the funding of university research. The other European countries did not follow the UK in this extreme rationalization of a budget model for research, but pressures prevailed during the 1990s to make publication and citation rates visible in evaluation exercises. For example, after the German unification in 1990, extensive evaluation of the research portfolio of Eastern Germany was immediately placed on the relevant scientific and policy agendas (Weingart, 1991).

## Methodological Complications

Publication and citation analyses have become standard tools for research evaluation. However, some methodological problems remain unresolved. The consequent uncertainties have been reflected in hesitations to apply these tools as standards in policy-making processes and research management decisions. How shaky is the ground on which the evaluations stand?

First, one can legitimately raise the question of the unit of analysis in scientific knowledge production and control (Collins, 1985). The intellectual organization of the sciences does not coincide with their institutional organization. Scientist self-organize in communities that cross the institutional and national boundaries, while the budgetary organization has remained largely within departments and nation states.

Second, the complex relationship between the intellectual and institutional organization of research is especially problematic when dealing with emerging fields of research. New scientific developments (for example, artificial intelligence) start in very different and unstable institutional settings. This calls for a *cognitive* unit of analysis rather than an institutional unit of analysis. However, cognitions cannot easily be observed or measured though progress in scientometrics is being made. One way to define a cognitive unit of analysis is to cluster journal–journal citations as citing relations reflect cognitive linkages (Leydesdorff and Cozzens, 1993; Van den Besselaar and Leydesdorff, 1996). We return to this issue in the final section of this chapter.

## 3. EUROPEANIZATION AND S&T POLICY

### Subsidiarity

The Single Act of the European Community in 1986 and the Maastricht Treaty of the European Union in 1991 have marked a gradual transition within Europe to a supra-national science, technology and innovation policy. The EU policies continuously referred to science and technology (S&T), because these are considered as the strongholds of the common heritage of the member states. However, the 'subsidiarity' principle prescribes that the European Commission should not intervene in matters that can be left to the nation states. Therefore, a 'federal' research programme of the EU could not be developed without taking the detour of a focus on *science-based innovation* using framework programmes rather than on basic science within a ongoing open-call programme (Narin and Elliott, 1985).

The national orientation on basic science and the European orientation of science-based innovation, explains why by far the largest share of European funding of science is still organized at the national level. Given the primacy of basic science in public funding, the budgets remained nationally organized. At the turn of the century, the member states still account for about 95 per cent of expenditures on public civil research and development in the European Union (Banchoff, 2002). This also explains why European networks often emerged from non-EU intergovernmental programmes. Expenditures in non-EU intergovernmental institutions exceed the current budget of the EU research budget (Banchoff, 2002).

Examples of such institutions are the European Centre for Nuclear Research (CERN) and the European Space Agency (ESA).

Hitherto, the EU level of science policy has centred around thematic frameworks that focus primarily on science-based innovation rather than basic science. It is recognized that European science could also benefit from a tighter coordination of national basic science programmes, for example, by allowing foreign research groups to compete for national resources. However, recent initiatives to coordinate national research programmes and non-EU multilateral programmes through the European Commission have hitherto failed (Banchoff, 2002).

## Internationalization

The failures of the European Commission to integrate national science policy within a comprehensive logic should not be taken to mean that European integration in science is expected to stagnate. In this context, one must carefully distinguish between the integration of science policies (within the political subsystem) and the integration of science itself (within the science subsystem). As part of a more general pattern of 'internationalization' the European research activities may well continue to integrate. An answer to this question can only be provided by empirical research.

The pattern of internationalization is to some extent exogenous to science policy. The rise in the number of international collaborations in science can also be understood as an organizational consequence of the evolutionary dynamic towards ever greater division-of-labour and specialization. Other processes often mentioned as contributing to internationalization are improvements in mobility and ICT, and the emergence of English as a world language in science. All these factors have rendered the costs of collaboration much lower than before.

It is, however, important to recognize at this stage of our discussion that there is no theory of scientific collaboration that explains why the number of international collaborations have gone up so drastically over the past 20 years. Such a theory is badly needed, not only for academic purposes, but also in order to systematize research evaluation. Policies can only be evaluated with some degree of precision when factors exogenous to policy can be accounted for too. As explained in the introduction, we will only deal with empirical indicators in the remainder of the chapter. However, it is important to stress that the development of European indicators is ultimately to be paralleled by the development of theories that explain internationalization as a historical phenomenon (Wagner, 2002).

## 4.   INDICATING INTEGRATION

We will discuss a number of indicators of European integration that have
been developed in earlier works (Frenken, 2002; Leydesdorff, 1992; 2000).
We proceed in three steps. First, we provide descriptive statistics for the
output trends of the European member states. Second, we analyse 'systemness' by testing for the Markov property in the distribution of output
data of European member states. In this context, systemness can be understood as a measure of European integration. Third, we analyse collaboration patterns among European member states as expressed by multiple
addresses in publication data. European integration can then be tested for
by analysing changes in bias of countries to collaborate among each other.

**Descriptive Statistics**

Output trends provide one with very basic information on the 'performance' of the European system vis-à-vis the rest of the world, and of
European member states vis-à-vis each other. Figure 4.1 shows performance in terms of percentage of world share of publications, for the
European Union in comparison with the USA and Japan during the period
1980–98. The European system is indicated for both the European Union
of the 15 current member states (EU) and the European Community of 12
member states.

Figure 4.1 exhibits, among other things, the relative decline of the US
publication system and the advance of the other two major systems. The
second polynominal is used for the curve fitting in the case of the EC set in

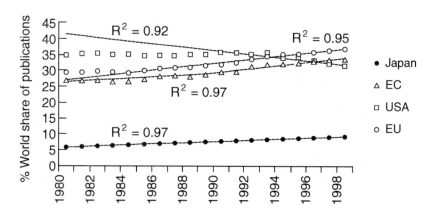

*Figure 4.1    Percentage world share of publications for the USA, Japan and
Europe during the 1980s and 1990s*

order to highlight how the line potentially deviates from a linear trend ($r > 0.98$): the relative changes of the 1980s seem to be enhanced during the 1990s. Since 1990, the USA has lost 0.51 per cent per year in terms of its world share of publications ($r > 0.95$), while the EU has gained 0.56 per cent per year ($r > 0.97$).

The overall increase of the share of the European Union during this period (Figure 4.1) was not caused by the R&D systems of the relatively large shares of the UK, France and Germany. As we can see from Figure 4.2, European nations differ considerably in their participation in this increase.

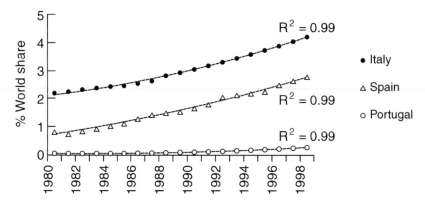

*Figure 4.2   Trend world share of publications for three Southern European countries*

The most spectacular growth rates are exhibited by the Italian and Spanish data. As visible from Figure 4.2, this increase is even gaining momentum in the 1990s compared with the 1980s. During the 1990s, Italy and Spain have grown with 0.14 per cent yearly ($r > 0.95$). Among other countries, depicted in Figure 4.3, some are also increasing their world share of publications, while others like the Netherlands and Sweden have recently witnessed a flattening of output share. The larger countries, shown in Figure 4.4, show no clear trends, though Germany has increased its world share mainly because of the unification in 1991.

**Testing for 'Systemness'**

Following work by one of us (Leydesdorff, 1992; 2000), one approach to analysing European integration in scientific research is to view the European system as a *distribution* of output shares of member states. Time

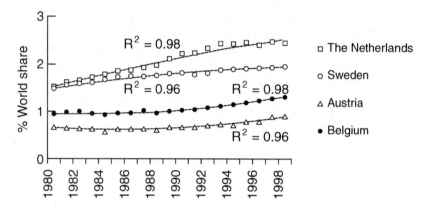

*Figure 4.3    Trend world share of publications for some smaller European countries*

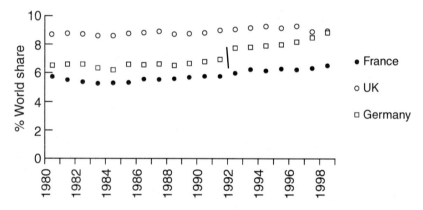

*Figure 4.4    Trend world share of publications for larger European countries*

series on scientific output then gives one an evolving yearly distribution of output shares of member states. Using these distributions, information theory can be applied to analyse some aspects of the nature of the under-lying evolutionary process.

Let $p_i$ be the share of output of country $i$ in year $t$ and let $p'_i$ be the share of output of country $i$ in year $t+1$. The stability of the distribution can then be measured by looking to what extent the a priori distribution at year $t$ $(p_1,\ldots,p_{15})$ corresponds to the a posteriori distribution at year $t+1$ $(p'_1,\ldots, p'_{15})$. This is more widely known as the expected information content $I$ (Frenken and Leydesdorff, 2000; Leydesdorff, 1995; Theil, 1967; 1972):

$$I(p'/p) = \sum_{i=1}^{15} p'i^{\cdot 2}\log\frac{p'_i}{p_i} \qquad (4.1)$$

When the shares of all countries remain unchanged during the transition from year $t$ to year $t+1$, the I-value would equal zero. This would only be the case when the growth rate of the output share of each country during the transition from year $t$ to year $t+1$ is exactly the same. As such, the I-value expresses integration in terms of a convergence of growth rates. For any differences in growth rates of countries, the I-value can be shown to be positive (Theil, 1972). The larger the deviations between the resulting distribution of output shares in year $t+1$ compared with the previous year $t$, the higher the I-value.

Figure 4.5 shows the I-values and the fitting trends for the evolving distribution of the output shares of EU countries and for the evolving distribution of output shares of the EU plus the USA and Japan. The slope in the EU case is negative, while it is slightly positive in the case of the global comparison. This can be considered as an indication of increasing systemness (integration) in the EU data set compared to the global trend since complete integration would mean that $I=0$.

Note that the EU trend is heavily disturbed in 1992. At this time, the effects of the German unification appear in the data as the science system

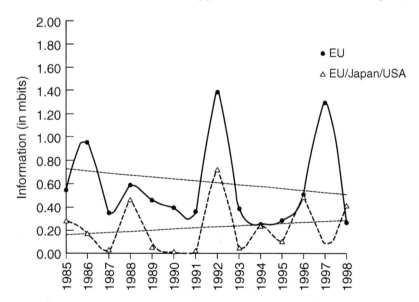

*Figure 4.5*   *Comparison of the Markov prediction of the EU subset with the set of USA + Japan + EU on a year-to-year basis*

of the former East Germany becomes formally integrated with the data on the former West Germany. Obviously, leaving out the historical event would yield a new fit of the trend line for the EU, which is both smoother and decreasing at a faster rate.

Also note that the I-measure of the expected information content that indicates the stability of an evolving distribution is in itself content-free. It can thus be applied to other social subsystems in the European system and can be expressed in a distribution of countries' shares (Leydesdorff and Oomes, 1999).

## Inter-institutional Collaboration in Research

The second integration indicator is not based on output shares but on the frequencies of collaborations within and among each European member state. Frenken (2002) defined an inter-institutional collaboration as a pair of different institutional addresses occurring in a publication contained in the *Science Citation Index* that covers all natural and life sciences (Katz and Martin, 1997).[2] Counting the number of inter-institutional collaborations within and among each country in the European Union, generates a (symmetric) $15 \times 15$ matrix containing both intra-national and international collaborations. The number of inter-institutional collaborations between two European member states $i$ ($i = 1,...,15$) and $j$ ($j = 1,...,15$) as a share of the total number of collaborations is denoted as $q_{ij}$.

As shown in Frenken (2002), the degree of bilateral integration of country $i$ with respect to country $j$ can then be measured as the difference between the observed share of collaborations $q_{ij}$ and what would be expected from the product of the individual shares $q_{i.}$ and $q_{.j}$. The difference between the observed share and the expected share is measured by the natural logarithm of the division of $q_{ij}$ by the products of $q_{i.}$ and $q_{.j}$:

$$T_{ij} = \ln \frac{q_{ij}}{q_{i.} \cdot q_{.j}} \tag{4.2}$$

The $T_{ij}$-value is a measure of *bias*. The value is positive when country $i$ is collaborating with country $j$ more than is expected from the shares of both countries in all output. The $T_{ij}$-measure is negative when country $i$ is collaborating with country $j$ less than what was expected from their shares. When $i = j$, the measure indicates the bias to collaborate nationally.[3]

Formula (4.2) gives us a new matrix with all bilateral bias values among each pair of countries. To obtain a single comprehensive integration measure for all 15 countries, one can use the dependency measure $T$ known as the 'mutual information' of a matrix distribution (Frenken, 2000; Langton, 1990; Theil, 1967; 1972):

$$T = \sum_{i=1}^{15} \sum_{j=1}^{15} q_{ij} \cdot \ln \frac{q_{ij}}{q_{i.} \cdot q_{.j}} \qquad (4.3)[4]$$

(Alternatively, one can take the two base logarithm instead of the natural logarithms as to express the indicator in bits as in formula 1; see Theil, 1972).

This measure is thus a weighted sum of the bilateral bias-values obtained by formula 4.2. The larger shares $q_{ij}$ have a correspondingly higher weight in the summation.

It can be shown that the mutual information value $T$ is non-negative for any frequency distribution (Theil, 1967; 1972). When all pairs of countries would collaborate exactly to the extent as expected from the product of their individual shares, all bias values equal zero and the T-value consequently adds up to zero. This would indicate total independency in the matrix distribution, and in our context, perfect integration of the European system. In any other case, the mutual information value will be positive, and the higher the value, the less the countries are integrated in a system. A higher degree of dependency in a matrix distribution thus indicates a lower degree of integration.

What is important to note is that the indicator proposed by Frenken (2002) differs from other integration indicators in that the indicator takes into account both intra-national ($i=j$) and international ($i \neq j$) interactions. In this way, the measure adjusts for size of countries, that is, for the higher probability of scientists in larger countries to interact with fellow national citizens compared to scientists in smaller countries. Other measures typically lack this property and thus often indicate that small countries are more internationalized (Frenken, 2002).

The mutual information measure has been applied to the period 1993–2000 and the results are exhibited in Figure 4.6. Clearly, the European Union is integrating as the mutual information falls over time indicating a fall in bias among European member states.

Further analysis has shown that the fall in mutual information indicating European integration is due to a fall in biases among European member states and not a fall in bias to collaborate nationally (Frenken, 2002). This means that the degree of 'geographical localization' does not seem to have decreased. What has changed in the process is that, in so far as Europeans collaborate within Europe, they have increasingly lost their bias in their choice of partner.

A second observation that has come out of the further analysis is that the largest countries are best integrated. The UK, France and Germany have on average the lowest bias values vis-à-vis other European countries, while smaller countries typically favour collaboration with authors in the larger countries (Frenken, 2002). This result calls for further research into the

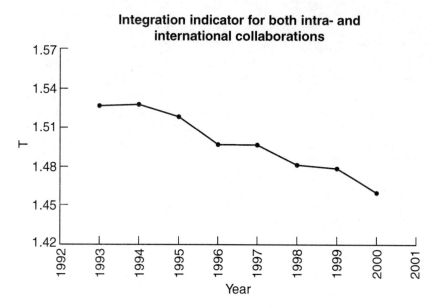

*Figure 4.6    T-values indicating the level of integration of all EU countries*

different 'roles' which small and large countries play within the European science system. The outcome at least suggests that some sort of scale advantages of large countries attract scientists from smaller countries to collaborate with scientists from larger countries. These scale advantages could well be associated with a larger extent of specialization and a higher budget to invest in expensive research infrastructures.

## 5.   DISCUSSION

The integration of the network of co-authorship relations among authors with addresses in European member states does not preclude the conclusion that international coauthorship relations also increase continuously between authors in Europe and authors with addresses outside the EU. However, we could show that the European system exhibits an increasing tendency towards systemness when compared with the relations among Europe, the USA and Japan (Figure 4.5), and that an integration measure applied to the European data shows a steady increase in the internal integration among the EU countries (Figure 4.6). In addition to this 'Europeanization', 'internationalization' could be shown in Figures 4.2, 4.3 and 4.4 as a development in its own right. A spectacular increase of the visibility of Southern European countries in the international databases during the 1990s (Figure 4.2) followed upon a similar effect for the smaller countries of Northern Europe during the 1980s (Figure 4.3). The larger countries (Figure 4.4) have been mainly stable, with the exception of Germany after its unification in 1991. Germany has become more important as a partner in international collaboration during the 1990s to the extent that at the global level it has taken over functions from the former Soviet Union (Wagner and Leydesdorff, 2002).

The higher and increasing density of network relations among EU countries can perhaps be compared with trade relations. The network of co-authorship relations is most tightly knit at the national levels, but the European level is an increasingly relevant level. The European programmes have been successful by contributing resources to the (nationally integrated) R&D systems which have been in transition towards internationalization to a variable degree.

A first extension of the scientometric studies reported here could be to focus more systematically on the linkages between European science policy, economic competitiveness and social developments. Note that the beneficial effects of the European integration on scientific knowledge production can be expected *within* the European and national science and higher education systems. It has been shown that international co-authored papers receive significantly more citations than other papers, while it has also been found that international collaboration increases the research productivity of individual scientists (Katz and Martin, 1997). Collaboration not only increases the rate of knowledge production, but also provides a greater diffusion of results and transfer of research skills within the research community. These effects spill over to students through higher education (Katz and Martin, 1997).

These direct effects of European integration in science are important in their own right. Science policy should always first be assessed on meeting the objective to strengthen the scientific knowledge base. However, this conclusion leaves open the question to what extent European networking in science has also contributed to economic and social objectives. These objectives have explicitly been included in European science policies as selection criteria for funding, in particular within the various framework programmes. However, the economic and social impacts remain uncertain as long as European science and technology policies are not supplemented with systematic policy evaluation *ex post*. An important research question within this context would be to investigate scientific disciplines and technological sectors in terms of their sensitivity to European funding and in terms of their effects on science-based innovation and social policies. Also note that, even within disciplines and sectors, variation may arise along geographical lines, rendering some type of policies more effective in particular types of European regions. If science is indeed going through a process of Europeanization, the realization of its potential impacts on economic and social domains may require (supplementary) local policies to account for regional varieties.

A second extension of the scientometric programme could be to analyse networking behaviour among researchers in more detail. In this study we addressed the question of European integration from the perspective of the science system as a whole using the *Science Citation Index* data on all disciplines in natural and life sciences. By doing so, we provided a macro-analysis of European integration and found evidence that this integration process is actually taking place. In science, however, different disciplines are organized in different ways at the meso-level. Science evolves mainly through self-organizing processes of communication and collaboration within 'invisible colleges' that form disciplines and specialities at national and international levels. Therefore, explanatory research should go beyond indicator analysis and replace the institutional unit of analysis (for example, national addresses) with an intellectual unit of analysis (for example, journal sets). Can a European level of self-organization be made visible in the case of techno-sciences like 'biotechnology' (Leydesdorff and Heimeriks, 2001)? Can information and communication technology be considered a relevant (European) unit of analysis? Theorizing about the determinants and effects of collaboration should begin at delineating scientific disciplines and to take into account their specificities. A research programme with a focus on rationales and dynamics of collaboration in different disciplines is currently under way (Wagner, 2002).

## NOTES

1.  Actually, President Truman vetoed the first NSF act of 1947. The creation was then postponed until 1950.
2.  This definition takes the institutional address as the unit of analysis and not the author. This means that inter-institutional collaboration does not correspond to co-authorship. There are two differences. One person can be associated with more than one institution, which would yield two addresses with only one author in an SCI-record. And, two or more persons can be co-authors associated with the same institution, which would yield one address and two or more authors in an SCI-record. The measurement of scientific collaboration is covered more thoroughly by Katz and Martin (1997).
3.  An important property of the measure is symmetry of positive and negative bias: that a country collaborating $x$ times more than expected yields value $\ln(x)$ while a country collaborating $x$ times less than expected with another country yields $\ln(1/x)$. The symmetry of the indicator follows from: $\ln(x) = -\ln(1/x)$.
4.  For $x = 0$; $x \cdot \ln x = 0$.

# REFERENCES

Banchoff, T. (2002), 'Institutions, inertia and European Union research policy', *Journal of Common Market Studies*, **40** (1), 1–21.

Bush, V. (1945), *The Endless Frontier: A Report to the President*, reprinted 1980, New York: Arno Press.

Collins, H.M. (1985), 'The possibilities of science policy', *Social Studies of Science*, **15**, 554–8.

Frenken, K. (2000), 'A complexity approach to innovation networks: the case of the aircraft industry (1909–1997)', *Research Policy*, **29** (2), 257–72.

Frenken, K. (2002), 'A new indicator of European integration and an application to collaboration in scientific research', *Economic Systems Research*, **14** (4), 345–61.

Frenken, K. and L. Leydesdorff (2000), 'Scaling trajectories in civil aircraft (1913–1997)', *Research Policy*, **29** (3), 331–48.

Katz, S. and B.R. Martin (1997), 'What is research collaboration?', *Research Policy*, **26** (1), 1–18.

Langton, C.G. (1990), 'Computation at the edge of chaos: phase-transitions and emergent computation', *Physica D*, **42** (1–3), 12–37.

Leydesdorff, L. (1992), 'The impact of EC science policies on the transnational publication system', *Technology Analysis and Strategic Management*, **4**, 279–98.

Leydesdorff, L. (1995), *The Challenge of Scientometrics: The Development, Measurement, and Self-Organization of Scientific Communications*, Leiden: DSWO Press, Leiden University.

Leydesdorff, L. (2000), 'Is the European Union becoming a single publication system?', *Scientometrics*, **47** (2), 265–80.

Leydesdorff, L. (2003), 'Scientometrics indicators and the evaluation of research', *La Revue pour l'Histoire de la Recherche*, forthcoming.

Leydesdorff, L. and S.E. Cozzens (1993), 'The delineation of specialities in terms of journals using the dynamic journal set of the SCI', *Scientometrics*, **26** (1), 135–56.

Leydesdorff, L. and G. Heimeriks (2001), 'The self-organization of the European information society: the case of "biotechnology"', *Journal of the American Society for Information Science and Technology*, **52** (14), 1262–74.

Leydesdorff, L. and N. Oomes (1999), 'Is the Europeaqn monetary system converging to integration?', *Social Science Information*, **38** (1), 57–86.

Luukkonen, T. (1998), 'The difficulties in assessing the impact of EU framework programmes', *Research Policy*, **27** (6), 599–610.

Moed, H.F., W.J.M. Burger, J.G. Frankfort and A.F.J. Van Raan (1985), 'The use of bibliometric data for the measurement of university research performance', *Research Policy*, **14**, 131–49.

Narin, F. and N. Elliott (1985), 'Is technology becoming science?', *Scientometrics*, **7**, 369–81.

Price, D.d.S. (1963), *Little Science, Big Science*, New York: Columbia University Press.

Theil, H. (1967), *Economics and Information Theory*, Amsterdam: North-Holland.

Theil, H. (1972), *Statistical Decomposition Analysis*, Amsterdam: North-Holland.

Van den Besselaar, P. and L. Leydesdorff (1996), 'Mapping change in scientific specialties: a scientometric reconstruction of the development of artificial intelligence', *Journal of the American Society for Information Science*, **47** (6), 415–36.

Wagner, C.S. (2002), 'International linkages: is collaboration creating a new dynamic for knowledge creation in science?', manuscript, Amsterdam School of Communications Research, University of Amsterdam.

Wagner, C.S. and L. Leydesdorff (2002), 'Mapping the global network using international co-authorships: a comparison of 1990 and 2000', manuscript, Amsterdam School of Communications Research, University of Amsterdam.

Weingart, P. (1991), *Die Wissenschaft in osteuropäischen Ländern im internationalen Vergleich-eine quantitative Analyse auf der Grundlage wissenschaftsmetrischer Indikatoren*, Bielefeld: Kleine Verlag.

Whitley, R.R. (1984), *The Intellectual and Social Organization of the Sciences*, Oxford: Oxford University Press.

# 5. Schumpeter's theory of economic development revisited

**Robbin Te Velde**

## INTRODUCTION

It has been more than 90 years since Joseph Schumpeter published his *Theorie der wirtschaftlichen Entwicklung* (1911). Give and take a few often cited passages it seems to be forgotten altogether. The most obvious reason to discard the work as a sin of youth is the overly romantic thesis of the entrepreneurial 'act of will' on which the greater part of the theory rests. Moreover, the conventional reading of Schumpeter stresses the difference between his early work (Schumpeter Mark I) and his later work (Schumpeter Mark II, especially referring to *Capitalism, Socialism, and Democracy*) which seems to suggest that Schumpeter dissociated himself from the central thesis of *The Theory of Economic Development*.

Closer reading, though, shows that Schumpeter's vision during his entire career was in fact completely consistent (Langlois, 1987). He has never abandoned his initial model of the entrepreneur as the agent of technological and economical change (Csontos, 1987). Furthermore, his stress on the individualism of the entrepreneur is only romantic with hindsight from the current stage of industrial capitalism. In the waning years of the Austro-Hungarian empire, during which *The Theory of Economic Development* was written, the typical entrepreneur was his[1] own manager, engaged in activities ranging from invention to finance to direct supervision of his factory (Chandler, 1977; 1990). Hence if we glance back from a distant entrepreneurship at the end of the twentieth century it *was* a 'romantic activity' centred on heroic individuals.

The merit of Schumpeter's early work is, however, not that it gives such an accurate description of a particular historical context but, rather, that it seems to go beyond history. The image of the entrepreneur as a wheeler-dealer or wheedling dealer will be recognized by most present-day practitioners (*sic!*) of business. It is only the context in which he operates that has been changed.

Alas, in the intervening decades mainstream economic theory has paid little attention to the micro-level of the individual entrepreneur. Even the collective of the firm has been considered as an empty point in an infinite space of demand and supply (Blaug, 1998; Smelser and Swedberg, 1994). The Theory of Economic Development rightfully puts the activities of the individual entrepreneur at the centre of the analysis.

The major contribution from the work, though, is that it connects those activities with the overall dynamics of economic development. The image of radical change that Schumpeter evokes is often contrasted with the tranquil gradual functioning of the Walrasian framework. The introduction of so-called 'new combinations' – the major responsibility of the entrepreneur – is, however, part and parcel of the functioning of the economic systems as a whole. *The Theory of Economic Development* is not a treatise on entrepreneurial activity, it is a *general* theory of economic development. I will elaborate the symbiotic relationship between the 'dynamic' entrepreneur and the 'static' economic system in the first section.

The central issue that pervades all of Schumpeter's work is the dichotomy between continuity and change in economic systems. Although the focus of his work is on the latter, he is not so much interested in change per se but in the relationship between change and continuity. With regard to the role of the entrepreneur in the overall process of economic development, he seems to be caught between describing the entrepreneur as an active external agent of change, a generator of novelty *de novo*, or merely as a passive 'bearer of the mechanisms of change'. The grail of Schumpeter was to explain economic development as a process of 'revolutionary evolution' – a tension which he was never able to solve. Intuitively, though, he seems to have taken the right direction by taking the interplay between the individual action and the ever-changing environment as the determining factor. This is the issue that is covered in the second section.

The third section deals with the actual functioning of the entrepreneur as the active bearer of the mechanisms of change. It follows the description of Elam (1993) of the entrepreneur as a 'virtuous leader'. During the modern industrial era the capability of the entrepreneur to build and especially maintain extensive social networks has become increasingly important. As a 'virtuous leader' the entrepreneur has two basic functions. One is to 'share commitment' among the members of the innovation network. The second is to 'guarantee certainty'. In other words, the entrepreneur not only has to generate a feeling of enthusiasm that 'something great is going on' but also that it 'can really be done'.

The issue of virtuous leadership is further elaborated in the final section. It builds on the notion of Rip and Te Velde (1987), Rip and Kemp (1998) and van Lente (1993) that the materialization of innovation involves both the management of the physical development of the innovation and the management of the expectations that surround the innovation. The heart of the matter, and the art of entrepreneurship, is to align the actual development trajectory and the evolution of expectations in such a way that they reinforce each other. The section concludes with two examples of such alignment processes – one which has not been really successful so far (UMTS) and one which seems to have worked out quite well (digital experiment case).

## THE THEORY OF ECONOMIC DEVELOPMENT

Capitalism is by nature characterized by eternal change. It never is and cannot even be stationary (Schumpeter, 1943). The neoclassical theory of equilibrium cannot deal with such change because it only investigates the new – theoretical – equilibrium *after* the changes have occurred (Schumpeter, 1934). But before the new equilibrium is reached – if it is reached at all – a great many positive or negative discrepancies between cost and receipt in the economic system occur. As a theory on its own the static Walrasian framework therefore has little or no empirical relevance.

Despite this harsh criticism Schumpeter does not reject the theory of equilibrium. On the contrary, the static description of economic systems – economic life from the standpoint of a 'circular flow' – is the underlying base for his own dynamic model of economic development. But the introduction of so-called 'new combinations', which set and keep the capitalist engine in motion, cannot be explained by the neoclassical theory because it simply cannot deal with discontinuous changes. Schumpeter does not deny the existence of autonomous growth in economic systems (for instance, due to a quasi-automatic increase in population and capital *à la* Rostow). He just argues that the disruptive processes of 'creative destruction' account for the greater part of economic growth. Hence the description of the steady state of economic systems needs to be complemented by the description of the dynamics of economic change. This is reflected by the basic structure of Schumpeter's model of economic development that also has two complementary spheres (Figure 5.1).

The first sphere in Figure 5.1 is the system of the 'circular flow', that is either in equilibrium or striving for it.[2] Schumpeter's description of the 'circular flow' starts from the assumptions that commodities without complements do not exist in the system, and that somewhere there is always a demand readily awaiting every supply. Under these conditions, all goods find a market, and the circular flow of economic life is closed. In a steady state, costs in the closed system are the price totals of the services of the production factors and prices obtained for the products must equal these

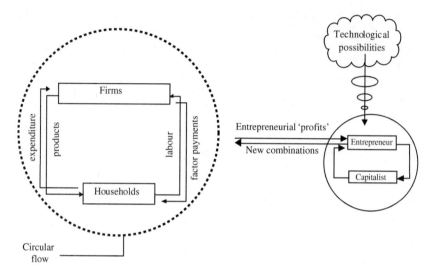

*Figure 5.1    Schumpeter's model of economic development*

price totals. Although Schumpeter makes the naughty remark that in this static framework profits are a symptom of *im*perfection, he basically repeats the mantra of neoclassical economy here that, under conditions of perfect competition, marginal costs equal marginal revenues.

A much more interesting observation is that in such a steady state all behaviour from actors in the model, be it producers or consumers, is based on merely routines. The sellers of all commodities appear again as buyers in sufficient measure to acquire those goods that will maintain their consumption and their productive equipment in the next economic period at the level so far attained, and vice versa. Consequently, the individual household or firm acts according to empirically given data and in an equally empirically determined manner. Data may change, but everyone will cling as tightly as possible to habitual economic methods and only submit to the pressure of circumstances as it becomes necessary. The ultimate consequence of this mechanical way of combining the original factors of production is that there is 'no class of people in the economic system whose characteristics is that they possess produced means of production or consumption goods'. That is, people that Schumpeter would define as entrepreneurs are completely absent in the 'circular flow'.[3]

The second sphere is the symbiotic pair of the entrepreneur and the capitalist that is always looking for ways to induce change in the peaceful yet boring routine-life of the circular flow. While consumers' wants are the fundamental force in the circular flow, in the second sphere producers take the leading role.[4] Schumpeter defines production as the combinations of materials and forces that are *within our reach*. The producer is not an inventor (Schumpeter, 1947). All components that he needs for his product or service, whether physical or immaterial, already exist and are in most cases also readily available. The basic driving force behind structural economic growth is the *introduction* of new combinations of materials and forces, *not the creation* of new possibilities:

> They [new combinations] are always present, abundantly accumulated by all sorts of people. Often they are also generally known and being discussed by scientific or literary writers. In other cases, there is nothing to discover about them, because they are quite obvious ... it is this 'doing the thing', without which possibilities are dead, of which leader's function consists ... It is, therefore, more by will than by intellect that the leaders fulfil their function, more by 'authority', 'personal weight', and so forth than by original ideas. Economic leadership in particular must hence be distinguished from 'invention'. As long as they are not carried into practise, inventions are economically irrelevant. And to carry any improvement into effect is a task entirely different from the invention of it, and a task, moreover, requiring entirely different kinds of aptitudes ... It is, therefore, not advisable, and it may be downright misleading, to stress the element of invention as much as many writers do. (Ibid. pp. 88–9)

Development in the Schumpeterian sense is then defined by the carrying out of new combinations. This concept covers the following well-known cases:

1. The introduction of a new good – that is, one with which consumers are not yet familiar – or a new quality of a good (for example, using remote access to mainframes for personal point-to-point communication).
2. The introduction of a new method of production, that is, one not yet tested by experience in the branch of manufacture concerned, which needs by no means to be founded upon a discovery scientifically new, and can also exist in a new way of handling a commodity commercially (for example, the use of palmtops in hospitals for immediate digital storage of patient records).
3. The opening of a new market, that is a market into which the country in question has not previously entered, whether or not this market has existed before (for example, selling game consoles to the elderly).
4. The conquest of a new source of supply of raw materials or half-manufactured goods, again irrespective of whether this source already exists or whether it has first to be created (for example, selling ice cubes from Greenland – 'pure pre-historical stuff, with natural bubbles' – to trendy bars in New York).

5.  The carrying out of the new organization of any industry, like the crea-
    tion of a monopoly position (for example, through trustification) or
    the breaking up of a monopoly position (for example, the Ministry of
    Justice response to Microsoft's bloody conquest of the browser
    market).

We would consider most of these cases as marketing activities. The contribution of science and technology to such activities can only be modest.[5]
The essence of entrepreneurship is rather the 'education of consumers [to
teach them] to want new things'.[6] In the last part of this chapter we will see
that this is not a process without any resistance, hence the emphasis of
Schumpeter on the 'act of will' of the entrepreneur. He is, however, realistic enough to notice that the carrying out of new combinations involves
more than just a strong 'act of will': command over means of production
is necessary. In most of the cases, the entrepreneur or producer-to-be must
resort to credit, especially since most new ventures that start do not have
returns from previous production. Consequently, if someone wants to
become an entrepreneur at all, she or he must succeed in raising funds, that
is, in finding – and convincing – some kind of sponsor.

   The provision of credit comes from a second hero in the dramatic play
of economic change, the 'capitalist'. Schumpeter argues that these capitalists are entrepreneurs in their own right. First, it is they who bear the financial risk (the entrepreneur only risks his reputation – but this is a grave issue
in certain cultural settings). Secondly, because capital is nothing but the
diversion of the factors of established production to new uses, the venture
capitalist needs to be a bold and outspoken person too. He needs to *dictate*
a new direction to production.

   In fact Schumpeter already anticipates the rise of venture capitalists here.
Because most of the money that goes around in the circular flows in definite established channels, by far the greater part of the funds of the capitalist consists of funds which are themselves the result of successful
innovation and 'entrepreneurial profit'. This is an interesting sociological
perspective on the actual (*sic!*) functioning of an industry, which could have
enriched the rather sterile body of mainstream economic research.[7] The
crucial point here is that the two poles in the model of economic development really are two separate social and cultural domains (which is why I
choose to use the term 'sphere'). The difference between the two spheres is
what drives the dynamics of the overall system. There will be a constant
pressure from the circular flow to assimilate the maverick entrepreneurial
sphere, but without potential difference there will be no innovative power.
It is for this reason that Schumpeter is very strict on the distinction between
the two spheres. As soon as entrepreneurs start to build up their businesses

and settle down to 'running it as other people [from the circular flow] run their businesses' they lose their entrepreneurial character.

The key difference between the two spheres is the way in which the people in those spheres deal with risk or, more precisely, behavioural uncertainty. In the circular flow, all behaviour is based on rigid routines. The entrepreneur, on the other hand, does not have any fixed patterns or structure to rely on when he tries to introduce new combinations.[8] Quoting Schumpeter at length:

> While in the accustomed circular flow every individual can act promptly and rationally because he is sure of his ground and is supported by the conduct ... he cannot simply do this when he is confronted by a new task ... While he swims with the stream in the circular flow which is familiar to him, he swims against the stream if he wished to change its channel. What was formerly a help becomes a hindrance. What was a familiar datum becomes an unknown. Where the boundaries of routine stop, many people can go no further and the rest can only do so in a highly variable manner ... (Schumpeter, 1934, p. 80)

Hence it takes a considerable amount of courage (or stubbornness) to operate outside the safe haven of the circular flow:

> In particular with the ordinary routine there is no need for leadership ... This is so because all knowledge and habit once acquired becomes as firmly rooted in ourselves as a railway embankment in the earth. It does not require to be continually renewed and consciously reproduced, but sinks into the strata of subconsciousness ... from this it follows also for economic life that every step outside the boundary of routine has difficulties and involves a new element. It is this element that constitutes the phenomenon of leadership ... Here the success of everything depends upon intuition, the capacity of seeing things in a way which afterwards proves to be true, even though it cannot be established at the moment, and of grasping the essential fact, discarding the unessential, even though one can give no account of the principles by which this is done ... (Ibid. 85)

One of the great ironies of entrepreneurship is that once an innovation becomes successful – that is, once it becomes established in the circular flow – the activity stops being entrepreneurial. This implies that the entrepreneurial sphere needs constant replenishment of entrepreneurial cannon fodder. There are two theoretical options to embody new initiatives: either getting new people in or recycling the already established ones. In the last case, the task of the entrepreneur is strictly limited to the recurrent initiation of new routines, for if he hangs on too long to the original idea he will be assimilated by the circular flow and lose his entrepreneurial ability.[9] Schumpeter seems to incline towards the second theoretical possibility when he suggests that the carrying out of new combinations is a special function and the privilege of a relatively small special class of people. This would suggest that it is usually the same people that reappear as entrepreneurs.

Whether entrepreneurship is also the privilege of a limited number of cultures or localities is another question. Schumpeter is not particularly clear on this point. On the one hand, he argues that people in pre-industrial societies (in this case, Central Europe *anno* 1900) cannot step out of the beaten path of the circular flow because their economy has not changed at all for centuries. On the other hand, he presumes that entrepreneurial aptitudes are distributed in a statistically normal way. There is no reason to believe why this presumption should not hold on a global scale. In the example of Central Europe Schumpeter seems to confuse cause and effect. The first and foremost reason for a lack of economic change is the particular structuring of the society concerned, which smothers the entrepreneurial function, not the lack of entrepreneurial aptitude per se.[10] Answers will usually be found in the structural traits of the circular flow, not in the cultural characteristics of the other sphere.

The limited task of the entrepreneur, which is bound to the recurrent introduction of new routines, underlies the dynamic character of Schumpeter's model of economic development. The (dis)ability of the entrepreneur to deal with specific kinds of uncertainty is the key to understand the dynamics of the model. One of the distinguishing traits of an entrepreneur is that he can deal relatively well with (behavioural) uncertainty in the originating entrepreneurial sphere but *not* with uncertainty in the circular flow. This is because a perverse effect appears once a new combination is introduced into the circular flow. The new combination alters the hitherto stable data of the closed system and upsets the equilibrium. Routines that could always be trusted blindfolded suddenly do not work anymore. This makes accurate calculation in general impossible, but that the negative impact is felt most strongly in the planning of new enterprises.[11] Thus successful entrepreneurs cannot deal very well with uncertainty in the circular flow. What they are relatively good at is in foreseeing what kind of improvement a new (but existing and known) combination will bring to the established structure of the circular flow, not in the actual realization of these improvements.[12] That is, how to combine technology push and market pull into 'technology pull' (Allen, 1984; 1997).

## THE ORIGIN OF INNOVATIONS

In the preface of *The Theory of Economic Development* Schumpeter contrasts his model with the mainstream theory of equilibrium. One of his major criticisms is that innovation is merely treated as an exogenous variable whereas it is precisely this variable that should be explained. Yet his description of science and technology as a readily available pool of knowledge and of the heroic entrepreneurs as *dei ex machina* seems to suggest that he treats the variable in a similar way.

The problem Schumpeter faced was how to explain that novelty (for example, new combinations, structural changes) could arise out of existing structures and processes. The conventional solution in evolutionary theory is to adopt the gradualist dictum *natura not facit saltum* – nature does not make jumps. Structural changes then can only be explained by some external cause (for example, technological change). Schumpeter could have chosen the gradualist camp as many others did. It would have saved him from the problem of having to explain the very occurrence of novelty. But it would also have turned technological change into an exogenous variable – a fate that has haunted the neoclassical heirs of the gradualist Marshall). Instead Schumpeter chooses the opposite saltationist standpoint: nature *does* make jumps.[13] He insists on several occasions that shock-wise changes in economic life are not forced upon it from without but arise, by its own initiative, from within. Economic evolution is in a certain sense endogenous and changes in the circular flow are not just mere adaptations of economic life to changing data.

What Schumpeter is after is to encapsulate the shock-wise, structural changes that set his model apart from the classical theory of equilibrium in an overall evolutionary process of economic development.[14] What he tries to describe is a process of 'revolutionary evolution'. This is a contradiction in terms and Schumpeter has never been able to solve the tension between continuity and change. The explicit role he ascribes to entrepreneurs as the sources of innovation does not seem to be in accordance with his emphasis on endogenous evolutionary change. But Schumpeter's arguments are really more subtle than that of '[a] dramatist who would like to write the epic of the heroic entrepreneur' (Andersen, 1991, p. 33). As he himself stressed in the later editions of *The Theory of Economic Development*, Schumpeter was not so much interested in the individuality of entrepreneurs and in the concrete factors of change, but with the method by which these work, with the mechanism of change. He sees the 'entrepreneur' merely as the *bearer of the mechanism of change* (Schumpeter, 1934, p. 61f). These changes (for example, the appearance of new markers, new scientific findings) are generated by the evolution of the socio-economic system and would have occurred anyway but they have to be effectuated by an acting individual: the entrepreneur.

Schumpeter did not have the mathematical tools at his disposal that could explain how small incremental steps could cumulate to big radical changes. He therefore had to present the entrepreneur as the external generator of novelty, which contradicts his argument that the entrepreneur is 'merely the bearer of [endogenous] evolutionary change'. Just as gradualists need a meteorite to explain the sudden extinction of dinosaurs, so Schumpeter needed an entrepreneur to explain the jump from stagecoaches to railways.

Recent developments in mathematical theory might, however, support Schumpeter's initial intuition that radical changes might occur from within. The theory of self-organization describes the behaviour of systems that are neither stable nor chaotic but something in between. Such systems, of which economic systems are prime examples, are constantly at the edge of chaos but self-organize themselves into this critical state, with no external tuning or organization required (Bak, 1997). One feature of such systems is a power law distribution of the characteristic events (for example, radical socio-technological innovation) (Bak and Sneppen, 1993). Although large events are comparatively rare, events can and do happen on all scales, with no different mechanism needed to explain the rare large events than that which explains the smaller, more common ones.

Economic systems are, however, not fully deterministic systems – contingency occurs. This means that there is at least some space for voluntaristic action from agents. But they are bound to the ongoing endogenous changes of the system as a whole. Entrepreneurs are neither 'merely' bearers of change nor autonomous agents. It is the interplay between the individual action and the ever-changing environment that determines the final outcome.

In short, the entrepreneur does not have to be depicted as a generator of novelty *de novo*. Economic systems, just like any self-organized systems, naturally have infrequent large events. However, these events have to be set in motion by the 'acts of will' of the entrepreneur. Hence, the crucial role from the entrepreneur within the overall evolution of an economic system is to introduce those new combinations that have an avalanche effect throughout the system (Figure 5.2). Once a certain critical mass has been reached the influence of the entrepreneur on the innovation trajectory becomes limited. If the innovation trajectory does not ride on the wave of an emergent broader societal event, the capturing of every additional audience or market niche has to be initiated by the acts of the entrepreneur himself. In most of these cases the entrepreneur will soon run out of resources and his constituency will fall apart.

## THE PERPETUAL ENTREPRENEURIAL FUNCTION

In the explanation above, which is primarily based on the earlier work of Schumpeter, the entrepreneur plays a small yet essential role in the overall

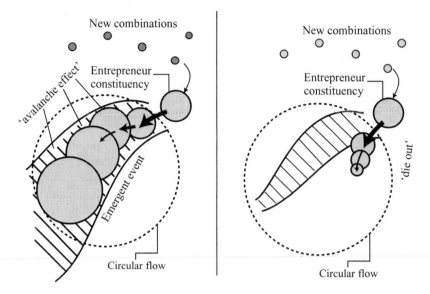

*Figure 5.2     New combinations*

process of economic development. In his later work, Schumpeter seems to contribute much less importance to the entrepreneur. He envisaged his demise and replacement by a new mode of economic development (Freeman, 1982; Philips, 1971). This new mode, which is characterized by the growth of the great combines (Schumpeter, 1934) and the rise of trustification, is the final stage of capitalism. After that, it would inevitably resolve itself into socialism (Schumpeter, 1943).[15]

Schumpeter explicitly tackles the diminishing importance of the entrepreneur in Chapter XII of *Capitalism, Socialism, and Democracy*, 'The obsolescence of the entrepreneurial function'. His core argument is that the social function of the entrepreneur, of 'getting things done', is already losing importance and is bound to lose it at an accelerating rate in the future even if the economic process itself of which entrepreneurship was the prime mover went on unabated. In so far as the empirical observation that the role of the entrepreneur is changing is correct, it does not render the theoretical argument invalid that the entrepreneurial *function* loses its importance. In fact, the central conclusion of *Capitalism, Socialism, and Democracy* rests on the argument that the very disappearance of the entrepreneur is the reason why the process of economic development comes to a halt and capitalism gives way to socialism. We are, however, still awaiting the conversion to socialism and capitalism, which is nowadays truly global in character, hardened in its goals and much more flexible than any of its predecessors, and has not disappeared but has rather regenerated itself in a more virulent form (cf. Castels, 1996; 1997; 1998). It seems that Schumpeter has grossly overrated the obsolescence of the entrepreneurial function. The two arguments he advances to support his thesis are also not particularly rock solid.

The first argument is that the 'routinization of technological progress' which he saw unfolding around him in the laboratories of the giant corporations would lessen the need for entrepreneurial initiative.[16] This does not follow from Schumpeter's own model of economic development, in which invention and innovation really are two separate things.[17] An institutionalization of the invention process would probably have an impact on the practice of innovation but it does not render it irrelevant. From an empirical point of view we could contrast Schumpeter's first argument with one of the most frequently recurrent themes in cultural history, that the ever-increasing rate of scientific and technological developments has only *increased* general feelings of uncertainty.[18] Paradoxically, by striving to reduce uncertainty and complexity at a particular level today we only introduce higher uncertainty and complexity to deal with tomorrow. Stated differently, as the complexity of the knowledge base of the economy continues to grow, so does the relative ignorance of each individual within this economy (Beck, 1992). In an era of high technology, industrial production has never been riskier (Elam, 1993). If there ever was a need for entrepreneurial leadership, it is in the age of high technology and high uncertainty.

Schumpeter's second argument is that due to the incessant stream of new products, consumers have so much become accustomed to economic change that they accept it as a matter of course. Under such circumstances the personality and willpower of the entrepreneur needed to 'educate consumers' and to 'teach them to want new things' become less important. This argument can be criticized along similar lines as the first argument. Consumers might have become used to constant change, but the seemingly meek absorption of yet another technology could also be an indication that people are pounded into apathy by the forceful rhythm of technological change. If there are so many new products and services appearing every year, it becomes increasingly difficult for a firm to give a distinctive edge or profile to its specific products.

Schumpeter mentions a third kind of resistance to innovation which he thinks has *not* decreased in importance: the established interests of those producers who are threatened by the innovation in the productive process. Whereas he has overstated the relevance of the first two kinds of resistance, he seems to underestimate the range of the third kind of resistance. Not only will the existing producers resist changes to the present situation, but so also will a much wider range of groups that make up the 'maintenance constituency' of the dominant established technology. These are all individuals and groups that have come to depend on the technology (cum market) and have adapted to its constraints. This group includes both the conventional category of consumers and a whole range of individuals and groups whose primary function is to keep the system going (Granovetter and McGuire, 1998; Staudenmaier, 1988).

Schumpeter is correct, then, in the observation that economic development tends to become depersonalized and atomized – individual action tends to become replaced by bureau and committee work – but this does not mean that the entrepreneurial function as such has lost importance over time. What has happened instead is that the function no longer resides in individuals but in collectives. However, given the immanence of the third kind of resistance to innovation, there is still considerable need for '*personal* force and *personal* responsibility for success' (Schumpeter, 1942, p. 133, emphasis added) because innovation is primarily about constructing, maintaining, and extending social networks. Furthermore, in the present post-industrial era of high technology, high complexity and high uncertainty, the role of 'virtuous leadership' in managing such networks might have become even more important (Elam, 1993).

The ubiquitous presence of information and communication technologies might lead one astray in a similar way as the rise of corporate R&D made Schumpeter believe that the entrepreneurial function had become obsolete. But in so far as ICT has facilitated the managing of social networks, the essence of the entrepreneurial function is still the management of people, not of information. Innovation does require substantial quantities of the latter, but information has no meaning unless it is being complemented by personal knowledge and experience. Information is (literally) 'empty talk' unless it is brought to life and lived in and out by skilled individuals (Dosi et al., 1988; Elam, 1993; Tsoukas, 1996).

Information is in the end always anchored in somebody's personal knowledge. The more complex the particular piece of information becomes, the more we need to rely on people who have experienced and learnt things we have not (cf. Hayek, 1949; Knight, 1921). Information alone is never going to be enough to successfully tame the uncertainties that invade our minds – it always has to be complemented by trust:

> If your information does not come from a reliable source it will not matter how accurate it is, you will still not be able to use it. If you cannot place enough trust in the probity and technical competence of a particular worker, it will not matter how honest or talented she actually is, you will still not be able to employ her … [as] industrial production becomes more knowledge-based and skill-intensive it must also become more virtuous. As technological ambitions grow so does the challenge of managing the 'non-contractual elements in contract'. Therefore, if

innovative power is too low to take on a new productive challenge the first thing
we should look for is an absence of virtue rather than a shortage of information
or skill. (Elam, 1993, p. 92)

The entrepreneur has two important functions within the innovation process
in his capacity of 'virtuous leader'. First, while joining forces in the new
enterprise, he has to commit not only himself but also the other actors to a
broad programme of collective learning.[19] It is not possible to arrive at such
a situation by blunt exercise of formal hierarchical power – mutual binding
is only effective when it is done on a voluntary base. Effective, informal, collaboration only occurs when personal interests and social obligations are
perceived by each participant as more or less the same thing, in other words,
when there is 'freedom in commitment' (Ulijn and Weggeman, 2001):

> [The other actors] will have to be able to share his 'vision' and feel comfortable
> about being a party to it. The entrepreneur will also need to be able to success-
> fully detach and partially free the people he depends on from the other compet-
> ing commitments they have (no doubt including personal ones) and bind them
> tightly to his own enterprise. Therefore, rather than effective communication; the
> pattern of innovation as interactive learning ... can be conceived as primarily
> hinging on 'shared commitments' and the ability of all people implicated to
> award each other enough 'credit'. Or, in other words, new combinations in a
> world of high technology are, in the last analysis, best conceived as founded of
> nothing more solid or reliable than so much trust. (Elam, 1993, p. 111)

Secondly, the entrepreneur acts as a 'guarantor' for certainty and as a focal
point of trust. Thus, whereas the first function boils down to building and
sharing a dream that 'something great is going on', the second function is
basically to convince all actors involved that these great things 'can really
be done'. By virtue of his virtue, the entrepreneur assures the individual
participants that all other agents – both human ('he will stick to his
promises') and non-human ('this site can handle over 100000 visitors a
day') are to be trusted.

Schumpeter's treatment of 'personal weight' – in some way comparable
with Elam's notion of 'virtue' – in *The Theory of Economic Development* is
rather ambiguous. One the one hand, all the entrepreneur has to do is to convince the banker who is to finance him.[20] On the other hand, he has to
'impress the social group [that is adjoined to the new combination]' and
'educate the consumers' and teach them 'to want new things, or things which
differ in some respect or other from those which they have been in the habit
of using' (Schumpeter, 1934, p. 65). In the age of 'perfect competitive capitalism', from which Schumpeter already noted in *Theorie der wirtschaflichen
Entwickling* that it was coming to an end, one could argue that the carrying
out of new combinations was a low-trust affair. It could be depicted, albeit

in a fairly romantic and superficial way, as a feat of the exceptional will-power of a single entrepreneur. That image was no longer valid in the Fordist industrial era, when the capability of the entrepreneur to build and maintain extensive social networks – its ability to 'woo support' and 'to negotiate with and handle men with consummate skills' (Schumpeter, 1927) and to 'interfere to a serious extent with others' (Schumpeter, 1949) – had become much more important.

## MATERIALIZING INNOVATION

Schumpeter's lofty theoretical notion of the entrepreneur as the 'bearer of the mechanisms of change' especially refers to the first stages of the inno-vation journey – the recognition of the window of opportunity in the cir-cular flow, and the actual initiation of the innovation process. Schumpeter pays less attention to the later stages of the journey, probably because he does not count the activities in these stages to 'true entrepreneurship'. The pain in the innovation process comes, however, usually in the later stage. Although building an initial niche for the new combination does take con-siderable efforts, the most difficult part is in the scaling up from niche to mainstream project (see Brown, Chapter 6 in this book). Schumpeter does describe the transition from the micro (a single innovation journey) to the meso level (the emergence of a new industry) but this is merely an *ex post* explanation of the occurrence of business cycles.[21] He does not explain why some particular new combinations induce an avalanche effect in the circu-lar flow, and why so many others just seem to peter out.

The issue at stake here is the sociology of the introduction of new com-binations, which is especially covered by the field of technology dynamics.[22] Given the predominant role of 'marketing activities' in Schumpeter's theory, he seems to be keenly aware of the importance of 'social construc-tion' in the process of innovation. What is underexposed in his analyses is the crucial role of *expectations* as the missing link between the 'marketing activities' of the individual entrepreneur and the reception of the collective environment.

New combinations do not drop like manna from heaven – their realiza-tion requires considerable resources. This is especially valid for complex technological innovations that often require massive amounts of (high-skilled) labour and capital. The crucial challenge for any entrepreneur is to acquire these necessary resources while there is yet little to offer in return to the sponsors. The establishment of shared positive expectations about the innovation-to-be is part and parcel of the implementation of any new combination. The entrepreneur – who is initially on his own – always has to operate within a given 'cultural matrix of expectations' (van de Belt and Rip, 1987) – a set of expectations that are shared and stabilized at a certain level and are *embedded* in an organization, a professional community, or in society as a whole (van Lente, 1993, p. 49). This matrix depicts the conceptual side of the established 'ways of doing' in the circular flow. It is nearly impossible for an entrepreneur to deviate too much from the established matrix. This is the third kind of resistance against innovation that was mentioned before. Yet the fact that expectations are naturally rather diffuse and vague leaves the entrepreneur considerable moving space to align others into his plans. In other words, the entrepreneur is not a Darwinian slave of the selection environment but can, at least to a certain extent, change the selection environment so that it better fits its variation – he is thus not merely a 'bearer of the mechanisms of change'.

If expectations were just conceptual soap bubbles they would be of very limited interest. Yet the evolution of expectations has a very material side. When expectations become to some extent shared and stabilized, they can force the actors involved to join the bandwagon (van Lente, 1993, p. 50). How strong such pressures can be is witnessed by the present sorry state of several European telecom giants who have spent billions on UMTS[23] frequencies, pushed by the 'animal spirits' at the stock markets. The diffuse promise of wireless Internet access was in fact so powerful that any decision *not* to invest in this technological trajectory would probably have resulted in a sharp drop in value at the stock markets.

Promises alone will not be enough to sustain the support for a certain innovation – rhetoric can buy the entrepreneur some much needed time but at the end of the day expectations have to be grounded into the material reality, that is, at least some empirical evidence should be constructed to support the claims being made. This is the 'guarantor' task of the entrepreneur. The rhetorical (evolution of expectations) and material (actual material development) dimension of innovation trajectories each have their own distinctive dynamics. When these two tracks support each other, expectations can turn into self-fulfilling prophecies. If these two tracks grow too much apart, the entire operation might fall apart (see Brown, Chapter 6 in this book). The inherent qualities of a product are not *automatically* linked to the perception of the product. While most entrepreneurs (and especially the more technically orientated ones) focus on the first issue (that is, the material track) the 'management' of the rhetorical track is an important task on its own. Expectations have certain dynamics on their own. They are generated, coupled with other expectations, transformed from a general to a specific level, stabilized and destabilized (van Lente, 1993, p. 58). Most dynamics occur when expectations are exported outside the current support community. This is because the shape of dynamics heavily depends on the characteristics of the bearer. Hence, when other actors with different backgrounds are getting involved, the original expectation (or set of expectations) might be considerably transformed. The tragedy of the entrepreneur is that he needs a certain critical mass to get his innovation going but that he often loses control when more and more people are getting involved. This is the perverse effect of the introduction of a new combination into the circular flow that has been noted before.

Skilful management of expectations involves talking to the right kind of people at the right moment in time using the right dose of expectations. You should capture your audience but do not disappoint them afterwards. The introduction of any new combination or radical innovation is necessarily surrounded by a hype of overly optimistic expectations. The *thesis* is brought forward that this particular technology holds great promises. Hence, in 1999, at the first presentation of the UMTS consortium, manufacturers and operators proudly stated that the technology had a bandwidth of 2 Mbps – ample speed for broadband applications such as two-way video-conferencing. In the following year, Siemens launched television commercials which suggested that such applications were already feasible (van Bentum, Bogaarts and Croonenberg, 2001). The rhetorical track is now much further advanced than the material track. This is not a sustainable situation: if the two tracks are not better aligned, the introduction of the new technology will lose momentum. Hence, the focus now shifts to the material track. The observation of the actual state of the technology and the disenchantment of the original illusion of radical progress is the *antithesis* in the dialectical process of innovation. A vivid example of such an antithesis is the statement of the Marketing President of Ericsson made at the beginning of 2001 that '[as] a private person [he] would already be satisfied if [he] would have 25kpbs permanently available' (van Bentum, Bogaarts and Croonenberg, 2001). Note that this is a factor 80 less bandwidth than was initially promised.

The contrast between the thesis and antithesis can be interpreted in two ways. If the rhetorical and material track have grown widely apart the most obvious conclusion is the *negative synthesis* that the technology can not fulfil the initial high expectations and that no more money should be thrown down the drain. Given the wide gap between dreams and reality in the case of UMTS some commentators indeed soon reached the conclusion that the innovation was 'the worst thing which has ever happened to the telecom industry' (ibid.). On the other hand, if the differences between the two tracks still seem to be surmountable the very deficiency of the material track can be rhetorically used to attract extra resources. This is the *positive synthesis*: *if only* additional investments are made the technology will be able to fulfil its promises. Skilful entrepreneurship requires the timely formulation of antitheses in such a way that the additional resources are geared towards the resolution of the critical problems – the 'reverse salients' that hamper further diffusion of the innovation (cf. Hughes, 1983). It is against this light that the Ericsson's President of Internet Applications argues that the telecom industry should radically alter the way in which it attempts to attract users: '[It's] all about services, not the technology. We have great opportunity here, but we should stop talking to the user about WAP and GPRS. Communication should always be service-oriented. They shouldn't have to care about the technology' (Springham, 2001). In other words, the problem is not so much in the mismatch between theory and practice but in the specific rhetorical strategy that has been chosen. Later on, though, the same spokesperson does explicitly acknowledge the danger of inflating expectations too much:

> As one of the few companies to have started talk of 4G, I wonder exactly what services we can expect, and whether the market runs the risk of falling into the same trap as before and promising more than it can realistically deliver? The answer is straightforward, namely that for every new technology and generation that you want to introduce, you have to start planning ten years in advance. (Ibid.)

So much for UMTS, but planning is one of the least important things in the introduction of new combinations. Most successful innovation trajectories seem to have a rather spontaneous and ad hoc character instead (cf. Rip and Te Velde, 1997). There is, however, just a thin red line between success and failure. But it is exactly because of this reason that the concrete actions of the entrepreneur at the micro-level still matter – a right dose of 'personal weight' can really make the difference.

This point is illustrated by an innovation trajectory described in detail by Te Velde (2000), which involved the migration of a paper-based information service firm to the Internet. The heroic entrepreneur in this story is the regional manager who supervised a number of country branches. He wanted to establish a digital-delivery experiment in one of the local branches to see whether subscribers wanted information faster and whether they were prepared to pay a premium for on-line access to the archives of the firm. The perceived emerging trend in the circular flow was that more and more people in that particular country were using the Internet. More importantly, though – and this was the 'flash of geniality' of the regional manager – these people were getting used to another conception of time and speed. They wanted news on an instant basis and not to wait another week for printed reports.

The innovation journey was initiated by looking for technology that could provide an instant access solution and that was available off the shelf.

No R&D was involved. Even the application that would run on top of the standard software was already available to the company. Hence it did not take much effort and 'personal weight' of the manager to get his digital-delivery experiment going. Alas, then the negotiations with Oracle failed and the top management wanted to drop the experiment altogether. The regional manager did not want to rest his case. He contacted a friend of his abroad who worked on his PhD at a technical university and offered him the opportunity to do field research in the company – in return for building a pilot system.[24] The engineer said he could built a system which would offer similar functionalities as the original design but for a fraction of the costs. This was the thesis of the innovation. It was built on shaky foundations because the engineer had no background in designing such systems and was not particularly versed in the specific software that would be needed to implement the system. For this he relied on one of his students who had advised him to use that particular piece of software – one of the crucial non-human actors in the play. By virtue of his virtue the regional manager, in turn, had to assure the top management that his friend and the student could do the job, and that these amateurs could be trusted.

The core social network now consisted of the regional manager, the engineer and the student. The manager organized a niche for the experiment which also involved the setting-up of a physically protected space for the 'IT department' – the isolated attic in his own office. The development of the system was concentrated at this attic and from there spread from the office into the other branches and the consumers elsewhere on the continent. In terms of power this shifted the centre of gravity from the head office of the company to the office of the regional manager. When the system grew bigger the strategic question would be, where would the project be further developed? This phase in which the experiment would be transitioned to corporate mainstream was of crucial importance to the regional manager since it basically involved the question who would control the IT infrastructure of the company. He would, of course, rather see the IT department remain located at his office. When the chief executive officer (CEO) of the company came over from the head office to see the much hailed system, he saw, in fact, just an embryonic network of one server and one local client – truly an antithesis of promising innovation. The IT people nevertheless managed duly to impress the CEO and this enabled the regional manager to forge a positive synthesis: with some more additional resources the experiment could be scaled up to the entire office and from there (and not from the head office) to the rest of the company. And so it happened.[25]

The next step was to convince the employees in the office to start using the system, to 'want them to want the new thing'. The new system forced the employees to work in a much more rigid and prescribed way. It took a considerable amount of 'personal weight' from the regional manager to get them used to the new routines but he was a good communicator and could really 'handle his people with consummate skill'. Timing was of crucial importance here. If the system were to be launched when it was still too much in a testing phase it would take considerable efforts from the users to adjust to it. Too much disturbance of the daily work would lower productivity and the top management would start to complain – and intervene. Resistance of the employees in the local office – another part of the maintenance constituency – was partly overcome by riding on the rather diffuse and vague expectation of the coming of the 'information age'[26] and by offering them the possibility to 'personalize' the graphical user interface of the remote clients. While the employees were changing the appearance of their screens, a system was put in place that rigidly organized the work flows and made remote control possible from almost every part of their work.[27]

The original innovation ended with the successful launch of the interactive website of the company (which was, in fact, nothing else than the 'public mirror' of the intranet). Thousands of subscribers migrated from the paper to the digital edition of the information services. The top management now followed stock and joined the bandwagon of the first entrepreneur. They decided to have a fancy portal built in imitation of comparable sites in the USA. The second innovation project turned out to be a disaster and almost brought the company to the verge of ruin. The major reasons for this were the enormous gap between the promise of the thesis and the grim reality of the antithesis, and the ill-structured social network that supported the innovation. The project was driven by the latent promise of the dotcom economy that web-based services would soon generate substantial streams of revenues. This promise was not based on any ongoing trend in the circular flow. The customer was ill-defined – if defined at all. The antithesis of the project was a bad-functioning portal with severe security loopholes which had cost several millions of dollars and which did not manage to attract any users. The obvious negative synthesis was that no more money should be spent on it. The social network that the top management had constructed around the project did not include any of the persons that had been involved in the first project. The initial business plan on which the second project was founded (which embodied the local thesis of the innovation) had been drafted by an external expert who, in sharp contrast to the regional manager, had no personal experience of the daily operations of the firm. Based on this business plan, the building and construction of the portal was outsourced to a firm that was hitherto completely unknown to the management. Oversight of the innovation trajectory was further complicated by the fact that the actual production site of the portal was located on the other side of the world. But the most important difference with the first innovation trajectory was that there was no special 'hands-on leader' (see Brown, Chapter 6 in this book) who personally managed the innovation network. Despite the relatively abundant resources and the strong support of the top management, the absence of a heroic entrepreneur might have made the difference here.

## CONCLUDING REMARKS

It was not just out of sheer romanticism that Schumpeter put the entrepreneur on a pedestal. Although he is only a cog in the machine of economic development, the contingent actions of the entrepreneur can lead to an avalanche effect – or a gale of creative destruction – throughout the economic system. For this to happen a lot of individual wheedling and dealing and pushing and pulling is involved, even more so in the current times of high technology and high uncertainty than in the past days of romantic entrepreneurship.

There is no such thing as a manual for 'true Schumpeterian entrepreneurship'. Nevertheless the following concrete recommendations can be distilled from the previous analysis.

The first characteristic of a successful entrepreneur is that he is able to discern emergent societal trends at an early stage. Hence entrepreneurship requires a considerable degree of 'social intelligence'.

Secondly, the entrepreneur should be able conceptually to connect these trends with existing new combinations. He should therefore be able to have enough imagination and empathy to see how these combinations can change the established routines in the circular flow (cf. Allen, 1984).

Thirdly, the entrepreneur should spin a social network around the innovation with the right kind of people and the right kind of non-human actors (Hoogma, 2000). There is no static optimum here: each phase in the innovation journey requires another optimal mix of talents (see Brown, Chapter 6 in this book). The expansion and the maintenance of the network involves the active sharing of commitments and the skilful balancing of promises and material truths. It is of the utmost importance to keep momentum, that is, to 'keep the process going' (Nicholson, 1998). The people in the network are in a sense caught in a beautiful dream. They should not wake up too early.

Fourthly, the productivity of the social network is greatly enhanced by the creation of a protected niche in which the entrepreneur serves as a gatekeeper to the outside world (see Brown, Chapter 6 in this book). This niche should also be a protected space in physical terms, that is, the members of the development team should preferably be concentrated at the same location.[28]

Last but certainly not least, the entrepreneur should take due care of the up-scaling of the niche (see Brown, Chapter 6 in this book). In this difficult process he will usually lose control over the development of the innovation (Nicholson, 1998). Rather than convulsively trying to cling to the original innovation, he should retreat in grace and concentrate his skills and efforts on the introduction of another new combination. This is Schumpeter's ideal of the 'true entrepreneur' as a recurrent generator of change. It is in the general interest of economic development if the entrepreneur does not settle down, builds his own business and ultimately ends up as one of the many managers in the circular flow. Of course, people are in general not interested in the general interest. But there are nevertheless some people who do not seem to be in the business game primarily for money but rather for the joy of creating novel ways of doing established things.

If we can draw one conclusion from Schumpeter's work it is that these people should be nurtured and not be assimilated in the routinized world of the circular flow.

## NOTES

1. 'The entrepreneur' might also be a woman, of course. Although the vast majority of entrepreneurs in the developed world are male, when the business is about things that really matter it is usually woman that is the entrepreneur.
2. This is a tricky assumption: how can we know whether a system is striving for equilibrium if it never reaches that point?
3. Schumpeter does not regard the 'managers' (or *apparatchik*, if one wishes) in the circular flow as entrepreneurs because they have '[neither] a special function nor income of a special kind'. He actually borrows this quote from Walras ('*[un] entrepreneur faisant ne bénéfice ni perte*') and diverts slightly from the literal translation ('[he would be] an entrepreneur [who] does not make benefits nor losses').
4. [Yet] innovations in the economic system do not as a rule take place in such a way that first new wants arise spontaneously in consumers and then the productive apparatus swings around through their pressure. We do not deny the presence of this nexus. It is, however, the producer who as a rule initiates economic change, and consumers are educated by him if necessary; they are, as it were, taught to want new things, or things which differ in some respect from those they have been in the habit of using (Schumpeter, 1934, p. 65)
5. Compare the observation of Terrence Brown (in Chapter 6) that micro-innovation networks ('skunk works') may be most effective in product-orientated companies that understand that you have not really created a product, if you have no market for it.
6. There is a deep yet sad conclusion we can derive from Schumpeter's observation here and that is that economic development is based on the ever-existing discontent of man with its present material conditions. Animals cannot imagine another world than the physical world they are living in. Man, on the other hand, is continuously constructing mental images of better worlds in which to live. Well-being – not bare being – is the fundamental necessity of man. Hence man is the animal that considers necessary only the objec-

tively superfluous and he invented technology to produce these superfluities (Ortega y Gasset, 1962). If we consider progress synonymous to economic development it is the continuous effectuation of our dreams and the production of superfluous things which we call progress. If we rather define progress as any reduction in the difference between what we have and what we want, a down-scaling of our grandiose dreams could also be considered as progress.

7. For a recent elaboration of such a view see Granovetter and McGuire (1998).
8. Compare the distinction Takahiro Fujimoto (2001) makes between 'routinized manufacturing capabilities' and 'evolutionary learning capabilities'.
9. This brings up an interesting psychological issue. Since bringing an initiative to full stature will usually be more rewarding from a financial point of view than the recurrent initiation of new initiatives, Schumpeter's 'genuine' entrepreneurs are not primarily in the game for money. Instead they are mainly driven by the kick of creating something new.
10. This is an important ideological point as well. One should be very careful with cultural explanations for a presumed lack of entrepreneurship.
11. Just as in the case of Schumpeter's observation that in the circular flow (which seems to resemble the ideal model of the clearing market) production must flow on essentially profitless, the observation he makes should not really surprise economists. It is a well-known fact that genuine uncertainty cannot be analysed within the framework of mainstream economic theories. At most risk (in Knight's sense) is that assumed but behavioural uncertainty cannot be included since in most cases it would not yield a market equilibrium (see, for instance, Diederen, 1993, on this point).
12. Compare for instance Arthur (1996): '[above all,] the rewards go to the players who are first to make sense of new games looming out of technological fog, to see their shape, to cognise them. Bill Gates is not so much a wizard of technology as a wizard of precognition, of discerning the shape of the next game'. For a theoretical (epistemological) foundation of this argument, see Te Velde (1999; 2002).
13. 'Natura non facit saltum – diesen Satz hat Marshall als motto seinem Werke vorangestellt, und in der Tat drückt er treffend den Character desselben aus. Aber ich möchte ihm entgegenhalten, dass die Entwicklung der menschlichen Kultur wenistens, und namentlich die des Wissens, gerade sprunggeweise vor sich geht. Gewaltige Anläufe und Perioden der Stagnation, überschwengliche Hoffnungen und bittere Enttäuschungen wechseln sich ab und mag das Neue auf dem Alten fussen, so ist der Fortschritt doch kein stetiger. Unsere Wissenschaft weiss davon zu berichten' (*Bemerkungen über das Zurechnungproblem*, 1909, reprinted in *Aufsätze zur ökonomischen Theorie*, 1952, quoted in Andersen, 1991).
14. It is here that Schumpeter gives his famous stagecoach–railway example: 'The author begs to add another more exact definition, which he is in the habit of using: what we are about to consider is that kind of change arising from within the system which so displaces its equilibrium point that the new one cannot be reached from the old one by infinitesimal steps. Add successively as many mail coaches as you please, you will never get a railway thereby' (Schumpeter, 1934, p. 64f).
15. The final argument was not only highly politically incorrect in the specific setting in which it was introduced, it also proved to be plainly wrong. This might explain why Schumpeter has mainly figured as a 'footnote economist' in post-war economic theory – often mentioned but hardly taken seriously (Andersen, 1991; Freeman, 1994).
16. '[For, on the one hand,] it is much easier now than it has been in the past to do things that lie outside the familiar routine – innovation itself is being reduced to routine. Technological progress is increasingly becoming the business of teams of trained specialists who turn out what is required and make it work in predictable ways. The romance of earlier commercial venture is rapidly wearing away, because so many more things can be strictly calculated that had of old to be visualised in a flash of genius' (Schumpeter, 1943, p. 132).
17. See the first quote in this chapter.
18. See the massive two volumes of Johannes van de Pot on the evaluation of technical

progress (van de Pot, 1994). For the specific theme of cultural change lagging behind technological change, see Chapters 200–202.

19. Compare the construction of 'mutual consensus' between people as closed self-organizing ('autopoietic') systems (Te Velde, 1999; 2002).

20. '[The entrepreneurial kind of leadership] has none of that glamour which characterises other kinds of leadership. It consists in fulfilling a very special task which only in rare cases appeals to the imagination of the public. For its success, keenness and vigor are not more essential than a certain narrowness which seizes the immediate change and nothing else. "Personal weight" is, to be sure, not without importance. Yet the personality of the capitalist entrepreneur need not, and generally does not, answer to the idea most of us have of what a "leader" looks like, so much that there is some difficulty in realizing that he comes within the sociological category of leader at all. He "leads" the means of production into new channels. But this he does, not by convincing people of the desirability of carrying out his plan or by creating confidence in his leading in the manner of a political leader – the only man he has to convince or to impress is the banker who is to finance them – but by buying them or their services, and then using them as he sees fit' (Schumpeter, 1934, p. 89).

21. '[The] carrying out of new combinations is difficult and only accessible to people with certain qualities ... However, if one or a few have advanced with success many of the difficulties disappear. Others can then follow these pioneers, as they will clearly do under the stimulus of the success now attainable. Their success again makes it easier, through the increasingly complete removal of the obstacles ... for more people to follow suit, until finally the innovation becomes familiar and the acceptance of it a matter of free choice ... [every] normal boom starts in one or a few branches of industry, and it derives its character from the innovations in the industry where it begins. But the pioneers remove the obstacles for the others not only in the branch of production in which they first appear, but, owing to the nature of these obstacles, *ipso facto* in other branches too' (Schumpeter, 1934, p. 229).

22. See the extensive overview of the field in Rip and Kemp (1998). In this chapter I draw primarily from the work of Harro van Lente, one of the students of Rip.

23. UMTS (Universal Mobile Telecommunications System) is a so-called 'third-generation' (3G), broadband, packet-based transmission of text, digitized voice, video, and multimedia at data rates up to and possibly higher than 2 megabits per second (Mbps), offering a consistent set of services to mobile computer and phone users no matter where they are located in the world. Based on the Global System for Mobile (GSM) communication standard, UMTS, endorsed by major standards bodies and manufacturers, is the planned standard for mobile users around the world by 2002, that is, the present year.

24. Compare the observation of Terrence Brown (Chapter 6 in this book) that 'skunk works' (see note 5) can often emerge rather than being mandated by top management directive. Individuals somewhere in the organization begin working on solutions to problems they believe are important. They generally use the 'beg, borrow and steal' method of acquiring resources to further their work.

25. This strategic decision was not without consequences. The more the 'digital new combination' became the backbone of the firm the more the paper-based activities at the head office moved to the periphery of the business. Some people were transferred from the head office to the office of the regional manager but eventually the entire head office was closed down.

26. The employees in that particular office did not show a blind faith in technology but they just seemed to think that the coming of the information age was something inevitable and that one should better adapt to 'stay ahead': 'Using the computer, to me, makes my work seem more professional. In terms of communication, we've started emailing each other now. That's good, I guess, because it just goes to show that we're moving towards technology. But it makes the relationship more impersonal and I am a people person, I prefer more personal touches. I don't like it but I have to live with it because I have to move forward with the masses. That's the way to succeed, I guess' (personal communication).

27. All employees from the company (which had several offices spread around the continent)

were connected to the same central database. There was no local storage and the system was entirely web based. Employees used their browsers to directly connect to the central database. From a management point of view this had the advantage that from any Internet host in the world the production of the employees could be followed on-line, in real time. The authorization rights of the employees – and with it the access to functioning of the applications on their local computer – could also be changed over the Internet (provided, of course, that one had the highest authorization rights). Hence from any hotel room in the world the regional manager could get an instant overview of the production of employee X at branch Y and could, in case of emergency, take remote action and change the authorization rights of the employee.

28.  An intriguing example of this lesson it the fact that the high-tech Dutch multinational Philips – despite the promise of ICT-mediated distant collaboration – has recently started the construction of an 'R&D campus' near their headquarters at Eindhoven.

# REFERENCES

Allen, Thomas J. (1984), *Managing the Flow of Technology*, Cambridge, MA: MIT Press.

Allen, T.J. (1997). 'Managing technical communication and technology transfer: distinguishing science from technology', in R. Katz (ed.), *The Human Side of Managing Technological Innovation*, New York: Oxford University Press, pp. 307–19.

Andersen, E.S. (1991), *The Core of Schumpeter's Work* (Smaskrift 68), IKE/Aalborg University.

Arthur, W.B. (1996), 'Increasing returns and the new world of business', *Harvard Business Review*, **74** (4), July–August, pp. 100–109.

Bak, P. (1997), *How Nature Works: The Science of Self-Organized Criticality*, Oxford: Oxford University Press.

Bak, P. and K. Sneppen (1993), 'Punctuated equilibrium and criticality in a simple model of evolution', *Physical Review Letters*, **71**, 4083–6.

Beck, U. (1992), *Risk Society: Towards a New Modernity*, London: Sage.

Belt, H. van der and A. Rip (1987), 'The Nelson-Winter-Dosi model and synthetic dye chemistry', in W.E. Bijker, T.P. Hughes and T.J. Pinch (eds), *The Social Construction of Technological Systems. New Directions in the Sociology and History of Technology*, Cambridge, MA: MIT Press, pp. 187–99.

Bentum, J. van, R. Bogaarts and E. Croonenberg (2001), 'Verspilde miljarden', *FEM/De Week*.

Blaug, M. (1998), 'The state of modern economics', *Challenge*, **4** (3), 11–34.

Castells, M. (1996), *The Rise of the Network Society*, Oxford: Blackwell.

Castells, M. (1997), *The Power of Identity*, Oxford: Blackwell.

Castells, M. (1998), *End of Millenium*, Oxford: Blackwell.

Chandler, A.D. (1977), *The Visible Hand: The Managerial Revolution in American Business*, Cambridge, MA: Harvard University Press.

Chandler, A.D. (1990), *Scale and Scope: The Dynamics of Industrial Capitalism*, Cambridge, MA: Belknap Press of Harvard University Press.

Csontos, L. (1987), 'Wieser's influence on Schumpeter' (appendix to Richard N. Langlois, 'Schumpeter and the obsolescence of the entrepreneur'), paper presented at the History of Economics Society Annual Meeting, Boston.

Diederen, P. (1993), 'Technological progress in enterprises and diffusion of innovations', PhD thesis, University of Maastricht.

Dosi, G., C. Freeman, R. Nelson, G. Silverberg and L. Soete (1988), *Technical Change and Economic Theory*, London: Pinter.

Elam, M. (1993), 'Innovation as the craft of combination: perspectives on technology and economy in the spirit of Schumpeter', PhD thesis, Linkoping University.

Freeman, C. (1982), *The Economics of Industrial Innovation*, Cambridge, MA: MIT Press.

Freeman, C. (1994), 'The economics of technical change', *Cambridge Journal of Economics*, **18**, 463–514.

Fujimoto, T. (2001), 'Multi-Path system emergence – an evolutionary framework to analyze process innovation', paper presented at the Future of Innovation Studies Conference, ECIS/Eindhoven.

Granovetter, M. and P. McGuire (1998), 'The making of an industry: electricity in the United States', in M. Callon (ed.), *The Laws of the Markets*, Oxford: Blackwell, pp. 147–73.

Hayek, F.A. (1949), 'The use of knowledge in society', in F.A. Hayek (ed.), *Individualism and Economic Order*, London: Routledge and Kegan Paul.

Hoogma, R. (2000), 'Exploiting technological niches: strategies for experimental introduction of electrical vehicles', PhD thesis, Twente University.

Hughes, T.P. (1983), *Networks of Power: Electrification in Western Society, 1880–1930*, Baltimore, MD: Johns Hopkins University Press.

Knight, F. (1921), *Risk, Uncertainty and Profit*, Boston, MD: Houghton Mifflin.

Langlois, R.N. (1987), 'Schumpeter and the obsolescence of the entrepreneur', paper presented at the History of Economics Society Annual Meeting, Boston.

Lente, H. van (1993), 'Promising technology: the dynamics of expectations in technological developments', PhD thesis, Twente University.

Nicholson, G.C. (1998), 'Keeping innovation alive', *Research Technology Management*, **41** (3), 34–40.

Ortega y Gasset, J. (1962), *History as a System and Other Essays Towards a Philosophy of History*, New York: Norton (original Spanish text from 1940).

Philips, A. (1971), *Technology and Market Structure: A Study of the Aircraft Industry*, Lexington, MA: D.C. Heath.

Pot, J.H.J., van de (1994), *Steward or Sorcerer's Apprentice? The Evolution of Technical Progress: A Systematic Overview of Theories and Opinions*, Delft: Eburon.

Rip, A. and R. Kemp (1998), 'Technological change', in S. Rayner and E.L. Mayone (eds), *Human Choice and Climate Change*, Columbus, OH: Batelle Press (Volume 2: Resources and Technology).

Rip, A. and R. Te Velde (1997), *The Dynamics of Innovation in Bio-Engineering Catalysis: Cases and Analysis*, Seville: JRC/IPTS.

Schumpeter, J.A. (1911), *Theorie der Wirtschaftlichen Entwicklung. Eine Untersuchung ueber Unternehmergewinn, Kaptial, Kredit, Zins und den Konjunkturzyklus*, Berlin: Duncker & Humblot (8th edition, 1993).

Schumpeter, J.A. (1927), 'Social classes in an ethnically homogeneous environment', in J.A. Schumpeter (ed.), *Two Essays*, New York: Meridian Press.

Schumpeter, J.A. (1934), *The Theory of Economic Development: An Inquiry into Profits, Capital, Credit, Interest, and the Business Cycle*, Cambridge, MA: Harvard University Press.

Schumpeter, J.A. (1943), *Capitalism, Socialism and Democracy*, London: Allen and Unwin.

Schumpeter, J.A. (1947), 'The creative response in economic history', in R.

Clemence (ed.), *Essays: Joseph A. Schumpeter*, New Brunswick, NJ: Transaction Publishers.

Schumpeter, J.A. (1949), 'Economic history and entrepreneurial history', in R. Clemence (ed.), *Essays: Joseph A. Schumpeter*, New Brunswick, NJ: Transaction Publishers.

Smelser, N.J. and R. Swedberg (1994), 'The sociological perspective on the economy', in N.J. Smelser and R. Swedberg (eds), *The Handbook of Economic Sociology,* Princeton, NJ: Princeton University Press, pp. 3–26.

Springham, J. (2001), 'Creating new value at Ericsson', *Mobile Commerce World*, 15–17.

Staudenmaier, J.M. (1988), 'The politics of successful technologies', in S. Cutcliffe and R. Post (eds), *In Context: History and History of Technology – Essays in Honour of Melvin Kranzberg*, Bethlehem, PA: Lehigh University Press, pp. 151–72.

Tsoukas, H. (1996), 'The firm as a distributed knowledge system: a constructionist approach', *Strategic Management Journal*, **17** Winter special issue, 11–25.

Ulijn, J. and M. Weggeman (2001), 'Towards an innovation culture: what are its national, corporate, marketing and engineering aspects', in C.L. Cooper, S. Cartwright and P.C. Early (eds), *Handbook of Organisational Culture and Climate*, London: Wiley, pp. 487–517.

Velde, R. Te. (1999). 'Markets for knowledge: where minds do meet?', paper presented at Annual conference of European Association of Evolutionary and Political Economists, Prague, November.

Velde, R. Te (2000), 'Building on the Internet: been there. Done it. Seen it?', paper presented at the Virtual Society/Get Real conference, Berkhamshire, May.

Velde, R. Te (2002), 'To know or not to know', in P.M. van Baalen, M. Weggeman and A. Witteveen (eds), *Knowledge and Management: New and Critical Perspectives*, Dordrecht: Kluwer Academic.

# 6. Skunk works: a sign of failure, a sign of hope?

## Terrence E. Brown

## INTRODUCTION

Organizing for innovation has become a key business objective. Of the many organizational innovations to emerge, one of the most well known is the *skunk works*. The evidence, at least anecdotally, is that great innovations are often the result. Skunk works are seen as business at its most innovative. However, this chapter begins by taking a slightly different view that the creation of a skunk works is often a signal of management dysfunction. Furthermore, not only does the creation of a skunk works signal management dysfunction, but also may even accelerate the dysfunction.

However, the chapter does not stop there. The skunk works concept and practice is actually confused, complex and misunderstood. The term 'skunk works' covers a wide range of innovation entities. As a result, this chapter attempts to begin to define, clarify and structure the concept.

I use the term *skunk works-like* as a generic term to represent the widely used and (well?-) known management of innovation concept, especially through most of the beginning of the chapter. However as the chapter develops, some clarifying distinctions are made.

## HISTORY OF THE NAME

The confusion over the skunk works concept starts right at the beginning with misunderstanding of origins of the name.

### The Wrong Story

Harry Newton (2001) of the Newton's Telecom Dictionary claims that because the skunk works team work so much or so intensely that they see neither sunshine nor soap, hence the name 'skunk', the night-time active, stench-squirting animal. He further claims that the term for the animal is derived from American settlers from the Algonquin Indian term *seganku*.

### The Right Story

In 1943 the US intelligence system reported that the Germans were gearing up production for a new propellerless *jet* fighter. This threw the War Department into a panic. They turned to aeronautical whizz, Clarence 'Kelly' Johnson. Johnson was the designer of the best Allied airplane, the 400-mph P-38. They recruited him to design a new plane that could fly at least 200 mph faster (Gywnne, 1997; Rich, 1994; Wilson, 1999).

Officially called the Lockheed Advanced Development Project; it was housed literally in a large circus tent pitched outside Lockheed's main facility in Burbank, California. Very quickly the stench from a nearby plastic factory led engineer, Irven Culver, to begin calling it the 'skonk works' after the smelly, backwoods moonshine still that produced 'kick-apoo joy juice' from old shoes and skunks in the (then) popular (and still running) US comic strip *Li'l Abner* (Gwynne, 1997; Rich, 1994).

It took Johnson and his team of 43 engineers (and 30 shop mechanics) just 43 days to create Lulu Belle, the prototype for the P-80 Shooting Star, the first US fighter to fly over 500 mph (Gwynne, 1997; Wilson, 1999). The war ended before the plane was built. Renamed the F-80, Lockheed ultimately built 9000 for the Korean War and a host of other legendary aircraft. These successes led Johnson's team to be moved to a permanaent facility, a windowless production hangar. Although this was now protected from the smells emanating from the plastic factory, the name stuck. However, just a short time later, trademark lawyers from the *Li'l Abner* comic strip came knocking (Wilson, 1999). As a result the 'skonk works' was formally christened 'skunk works', a name then actually trademarked by Lockheed. After its merger with Martin Marietta, Lockheed Martin spun off the skunk works as a separate operation. It continues to develop primarily 'black projects' – military secret projects (Rich, 1994).

## REASON FOR EXISTENCE

The primary reason that a skunk works was ever created was because of the war. It was a life or death, wartime effort. It was a heavily mandated effort to compress the time it took to research/develop innovative military (aircraft) projects and prototypes. Given that speed was essential, it was taken out of the regular organization to shield it from the bureaucratic, formal procedures and generally slow processes of corporate R&D programmes.

Why do skunk works-like programmes exist today? Are today's objectives different? No, not really. Skunk works-like programmes today are used to accelerate the research and development cycle. Is there a different type of war effort? Yes, the war is for market share, market leadership and profits. During recent times, large corporations have been losing the innovation battle against smaller, more entrepreneurial firms. As we move to even more dynamic business environments, innovation has become a survival issue. As a result, of the many organizational innovations to emerge, one of the most well known is the skunk works.

### Success

Especially since management guru, Tom Peters, made them fashionable during the late 1970s and 1980s, there are countless examples of larger corporations using what they call skunk works. Today, skunk works are basically special teams of passionate intrapreneurs, who are isolated from the rest of their business, given resources and relatively free reign to innovate and develop. The evidence, at least anecdotally, is that great innovations are often the result. Although skunk works may in fact be important tools for innovation, I take a slightly different perspective on why skunk works are typically created by large corporations.

### Management Failure and the Secondary Effects

My view is rooted in Schrage's (1999) perspective that the creation of a skunk works is a signal of management dysfunction. The formation of a skunk works is a signal that the *regular* organization's structure, systems, process, and so on is no longer able to handle innovation or radical change so, as a result, must form a new, separate organization, built on exclusivity, in order to innovative. Furthermore, not only does the creation of a skunk works signal management dysfunction, but also may even accelerate the dysfunction. Shielding the skunk works from the *rest* of the organization has an implied and an unstated element, which is that the parent organization is a bad environment for innovation, creativity, and so on. So just the creation itself is an admission of failure (Schrage, 1999). However, this does not have to be the case, nor is it always the case.

Failure to be innovative within the existing organization coupled with general competitive threats has caused management itself to start innovating (that is, administratively). However, this innovating is not driven by a search of competitive advantage directly, it is driven by desperation. In their desperation many managers have attempted to create skunk works-like programmes without fully understanding the requirements, commit-

ment or further ramifications. This move to establish skunk works-like programmes is also driven by institutional pressures and benchmarking.
Managers create these programmes, because other companies are doing it
(DiMaggio and Powell, 1983). This 'me to-ism' is rarely a good management strategy. Therefore, the creation of many skunk works-like programmes is driven by the surrendering of management, first to desperation
and second to institutional forces. This is certainly not the best way to start
an innovation programme.

Now, once they have established these skunk works-like programmes, the
secondary effects begin. For example, to build the programme, management must select certain employees, supply them with plenty of resources
and free them from the constraints of most company rules, regulations and
policies. Managers, who do not see the potential problems with this set of
decisions, probably deserve the outcome. Selecting out certain people and
freeing them from the bureaucratic and the resource constraints that the
remaining organization still has to face, it is asking for trouble.

The preferential treatment accorded the members of the skunk works-
like programmes (for example, the separate facilities, the resources, the
special attention, and so on) raises additional questions. If the efforts are
public, which most are these days, can the organizational culture of the
parent organization take it? Furthermore, skunk works-like programmes
invariably have reintegration problems. First, the new product/service must
face 'not invented here' problems, when and if the products are reintegrated
into the mainstream. This is additionally difficult without company wide
support. Second, the skunk works-like members often face problems as
*they* attempt to reintegrate back into the mainstream organization. With
feelings of jealousy by those left out, on one hand, and the possible expec-
tant attitude among the former members on the other, reintegration tends
to be problematic

In the past Xerox had a skunk works-like programme, which they defined
as 'internally sequestered groups of people who simulate being separate
organizations' for the purpose of innovation (Gwynne, 1997, p. 21).
However, they discontinued the programme because they could never get
the support and acceptance from the organization as a whole. They produced great inventions, but never could create value.

It does seem that many corporations that create skunk works-like projects do so without a complete understanding of what this type of programme is, what is required to successfully accomplish it and what the
organizational implications are. Despite that, skunk works-like projects
may still have value, if used properly. However, a consultant revealed that
more Fortune 200 companies had skunk works-like programmes than had
advanced technology groups, *but these works were kept going by having them*

*work on simple projects* (Gwynne, 1997). This is a misuse of the concept. The story of the skunk works is actually more complex than it appears on the surface. The rest of this chapter discusses some of this complexity and raises additional questions.

## WHAT IS A TRUE SKUNK WORKS?

It is unclear whether or not Kelly Johnson ever gave his precise definition of a skunk works, but he did give a set of 14 operating rules, which really only apply to special types of military projects (Astech-engineering.com, 2001). However, consultant Neal Goldsmith defines it this way, 'A skunk works is a protected and culturally antithetical body for the purpose of innovation' (Gwynne, 1997, p. 19).

Single and Spurgeon (1996, p. 39) define it as a 'method of managing the innovation process, characterized by extremely efficient use of time by a small group of creative engineers'. The information technology dictionary defines it this way:

> A skunkworks [author's spelling] is a group of people who, in order to achieve unusual results, work on a project in a way that is outside the usual rules. A skunkwork is often a small team that assumes or is given responsibility for developing something in a short time with minimal management constraints. Typically, a skunkwork has a small number of members to reduce communications overhead. A skunkwork is sometimes used to spearhead a product design that therefore will be developed according to the usual process. A skunkwork project may be secret. (Whatis.com, 2001)

For the purposes of this chapter, a skunk works is defined in this manner: a true skunk works is an isolated and highly skilled team designed to accelerate the research, but especially the development of innovative product/ services. This team typically works outside the bounds of the parent's rules and regulations and under time pressure.

Another way to look at the skunk works concept is to examine it across two dimensions: the level of management support and the level of secrecy.

### Mandated

It is generally the case today that most skunk work-like programmes in large firms are mandated and created by top management. In establishing these programmes *good* management take the responsibility to make sure that they have adequate resources, especially human and financial.

However, if top management is going to manage any programme, one can be assured that they are going to pay close attention to the activities. On the one hand, management's close attention should ensure that the programmes not only have sufficient resources but the attention should also ensure that the programmes have strong management support. On the other hand, top management has all of the incentive and what they believe, the right, to interfere with the programmes. If asked, you can be certain that the managers would say that they were just observing and giving suggestions. However, it is clear that top management's reputation would be on the line as well. Given this, they interfere. Now, this interference can take many forms, but one of the most damaging is the constraint they can put on creativity and innovation. How? Well, given their experience, knowledge of the market and who knows what else, they may intentionally or unintentionally limit innovation. This is problematic because it tends to limit how new, cutting-edge products/services are developed.

In addition, occasionally top management sees the skunk works programme as a pool of resources that they can use outside of the skunk works mandate. Given these reasons, many mandated programmes fall short of their intended goal.

**Emergent**

Instead of being mandated by top management directive, skunk works can often emerge. Individuals or teams somewhere in the organization begin working on solutions to problems they believe are important. They generally use the 'beg, borrow and steal' method of acquiring resources to further their work. While corporations (for example, IBM) may sometimes have unspecified resources that are available for unspecified projects, most gain resource including human and financial, as the project gains attention and support, albeit usually quietly (Gwynne, 1997).

Since non-company sanctioned projects take place, especially in the beginning, under the radar screen, there can be a few advantages. One, they may have greater flexibility to take certain action, given that their actions are unofficial. Two, top management may unofficially allow them to take on projects that are high risk, offbeat and unsanctionable. If they succeed, management can help claim some credit, if they fail, at best no one finds out and worse, they can disavow it. However, the team participants may not be as lucky, if the project fails.

For example, in a recent story described by Field (2001) a group of rogue engineers at Compaq thought that they could develop a high-density computer by reducing some of the extra features and by using mostly parts from their current AlphaServer DS10. Although top management seemingly liked the idea, the funding request was turned down, because 'unfortunately' the DS10 was the company's top focus and hope for the future. Although the 'rogue' engineers continued to work on the high-density server on their own time and unofficially, top management did not discourage the project. In a short time, the group was successful and their persistence resulted in a multimillion dollar global business for Compaq. One interesting aspect of this and other emergent skunk works is that they occurred inside the organization, which runs counter to the recommended and usual pattern. This implies that this kind of innovative activity can, under the right circumstances, exist within the organization.

**Secret**

The original Lockheed skunk works was, of course, an ultra-secret, wartime military operation. Since then it has been assumed that skunk works activity should be secret; if not the entire skunk works, certainly the nature of the specific projects. It is important to note that, when secrecy is discussed, it is generally meant to mean that the appropriate top managers are aware, but generally not the entire organization. However, most emergent projects start small and are carried out in near or total secrecy, and, as a result, top managers generally do *not* become aware of these projects until they become too big, too successful or big failures. Secrecy provides short-term protection.

The first question is, is secrecy inherent in the skunk works concept? I think the answer to this one is yes. Secrecy is an integral part of the origin of the concept. Also, while you can certainly have successful innovation in a public environment, there are clear advantages of working in secret. For example, fewer distractions, fewer compromises and a greater ability to fail, which leads to more creativity. There are many more reasons. However, there are disadvantages as well. For example, it may be more difficult to reintegrate the resulting products, because the rest of the organization may be less prepared. It may also cause greater organizational problems since secrecy often leads to suspicion. There are others disadvantages as well.

The second question is, are secret skunk works more effective? This is an empirical question that cannot be answered at this time. However, those successful secret skunk works will be the ones that can best maximize the advantages while minimizing the disadvantages.

**Public**

On the flip side, you have what can be characterized as public skunk works. These are the skunk works that are usually mandated by top management.

They are public in that it is organizationally known that this special research/development programme exists, but this is not known by the general public (or competition). The rest of the organization may or may not know the specific projects or products under research and/or development. As such, the level of public awareness as well as the manner in which the rest of the organization is informed varies greatly. In one example, a manager created what he called a skunk works-like programme and published a regular newsletter to highlight its progress. After he did not gain, in his view, 'management support' he abandoned it (Gwynne, 1997).

If secrecy is an inherent part of the skunk works process, than a public skunk works is sort of an oxymoron. This is not to say that public skunk works cannot be effective. There often are. In fact, it does seem that many, if not most, corporate skunk works are relatively public, herein lies some of the problems. The organizational problems and resentment that often accompanies skunk works programmes are more likely to affect the more public skunk works.

## SKUNK WORKS MATRIX

Although there are many ways in which to analyse skunk works, one is to look across the two dimensions: level of secrecy and level of management support (see Figure 6.1).

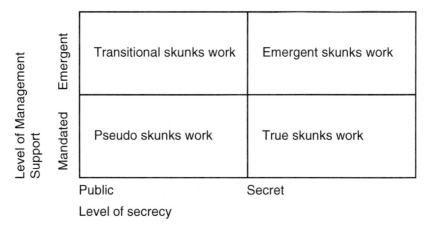

*Figure 6.1    The skunk works matrix*

**True Skunk Works**

A skunk works that is both secret and mandated should be referred to as a *true skunk works*. Given this, the original Lockheed version would be represented by the dot at the intersection of 100 per cent mandated and 100 per cent secret. A true skunk works is an isolated and highly skilled team designed to accelerate the research, but especially the development of innovative product/services. True skunk works today are the exception, often limited to military projects, government projects and the rare sheath start-up. Given that top management has their full support (and resources), these cases are likely to be more successful than many other innovation programmes. Also with that support the reintegration tends to be less problematic because top management can use its influence and power to make sure it is accepted and supported organizationally (if possible). The success of the true skunk work also stems from the interpersonal relationships, the informality and the interaction of the highly skilled participants.

**Pseudo-Skunk Works**

Skunk works-like programmes that are public and mandated by top management can be called *pseudo-skunk works*. Most corporate skunk works-like programmes today are of the pseudo type. As a result, most of the problems associated with what is called skunk works are really problems of pseudo-skunk works. In fact as discussed above, the fact that the programme is known throughout the organization tends to lead to some of the organization's dysfunctions and problems.

**Emergent Skunk Works**

Skunk works-like programmes that are secret and emergent can be called *emergent skunk works*. Emergent skunk works generally begin small and secret. As a result, even top management can be in the dark. However, if they grow beyond the ability of the team to acquire resources on their own, or they grow too large or make too much *organizational noise*, they will cease to be secret. At that time emergent skunk works are forced to migrate to the next type of skunk works-like programmes.

**Transitional Skunk Works**

Skunk works-like programmes that are both public and emergent can be called *transition skunk works*. Transition skunk works are typically in a state of flux. It is difficult to be both emergent and public without management consent. It is a place of active limbo, where many decisions need to be made. More specifically, management must decide whether or not to mandate the programme (that is, give support and mandate) or to kill the programme. If management decides to give its consent, it can be seen as a cooptation. When this occurs the programme is forced to migrate down to a pseudo-skunk works. On the other hand, management can kill the programme. However, truly renegade transitional skunk workers sometimes sneak back to an emergent skunk works. Here they work even more secretly and more unofficially than previously. This, of course, may be a career-risking activity.

## RESEARCH ACTIVITY CONTINUUMS

Another way of looking at skunk works and skunk works-like programmes is by simply looking at them as a continuum of research and development programmes. Figures 6.2 and 6.3 are just to serve as rough guides, because different organizations have different names and use their research organizations differently. It is more important to note the start/end points and what is between them. First, one can look at the degree of counterculture or how aberrant is the culture from the overall corporate culture norm.

Independent     R&D team     Corporate R&D   Advanced research facility    skunk works

*Figure 6.2    Research activity continuum: degree of counterculture*

Theoretical research   Pure research     Corporate R&D    Applied research     skunk works

*Figure 6.3    Research activity continuum: degree of market awareness*

The individual researcher is most closely aligned with the general organizational culture. Although the norms and practices of his/her specific discipline will have some effect on his thoughts and behaviour (DiMaggio and Powell, 1983), it is likely that the organization culture will dominant. On the other hand, the skunk works' culture is expected to be completely different. Given the mix of people, the sense of urgency, the task, the resources, separate location and the fact that they are not bound by the regular rules and regulations of the parent organization, and so on, it is very likely to develop its own culture, norms, rules, practices, and so on. Corporate research laboratories and advanced research facilities fall somewhere in the middle.

Secondly, one can look at the degree of market awareness or at how much the market is taken into account during the research and/or development. On the one hand you have theoretical research, which I define as the research precursor to pure research. It takes place in the minds and on the notepads and computers of researchers. It has absolutely no direct linkage to any invention, innovation or product. On the other hand, the skunk works is specifically designed to create an innovative solution (that is, a product). Pure research, general corporate R&D and applied research fall somewhere in the middle.

## KEY TRANSITIONS

There are at least two transitions that the successful true skunk works or pseudo-skunk works must experience. They are the market transition and the organization transition.

### The Market Transition

Successful true skunk works and pseudo-skunk works will continue to be the ones that recognize that their output has to be a product and not just an invention. The true skunk works and pseudo-skunk works that may be most effective are in product-orientated companies that understand that you have not really created a *product* if you have no market for it.

As mentioned previously, Xerox had what they called a skunk works programme. One of the reasons for its failure is also common among true skunk works and pseudo-skunk works. It was too technologically orientated, in that it created great new advances and inventions, but not innovations. Innovation has two sides that must work in tandem – invention (technology) and market orientation. The *new* product/service must have market orientation or a business orientation. Being too technologically orientated is a common point of failure and is a common misconception. Skunk works of all types are *not* just about creating next generation products; it is about satisfying next generation customers.

Although there is no clear empirical evidence at this time, it may be the case that true skunk works and pseudo-skunk works projects that are 'market pulled' instead of 'technology pushed' are more successful (Single and Spurgeon, 1996).

The solution may be to have a marketing person involved early in the process (Single and Spurgeon, 1996). This is to make sure that the development has the market in mind. This marketing person also has a role near the end of the process in that he/she can assist in preparing the actual marketing group for the acceptance and support of the new product/service.

## The Organization Transition

Having the right team members is key, but it is also vital for the creation of any competitive advantage. However, an internal study by American Express found that 85 per cent of their problems with their skunk works-like projects resulted from not including the correct people in the project team (Gwynne, 1997). If one looks a little deeper, one can discover that, while having the right mix of talent is important, applying the right talent during specific critical stages is just as important or more so.

Perhaps no point is more critical than when the formerly closed, small product development project moves to a high-profile company-wide project. I call this transition point – *the organizational acceptance inflection point*. This process exists for all new products/services, but is not as extreme or as important as in the case with a skunk works-like programme. Not only is this a symbolic and organizational issue, it is an operational issue as well. The new product must be integrated into the production cycle, the marketing cycle, the financial cycle, and so on.

In addition, there is an ownership transfer (Gwynne, 1997; Single and Spurgeon, 1996). Up to this point, the entire project belongs solely to the development team; however, at the acceptance inflection point ownership must be relinquished and turned over to the mainstream organization. This transfer can be a difficult and an emotional one, but it needs to be a successful one, in order for the process to continue.

The solution may be to have an organizational transition person involved early in the (true or pseudo-) skunk works' process. This is to make sure that the development team has the organization in mind. This person has a tricky role as he/she must move back and forth between the team and the organization, especially as the product nears completion. The programme champion can also be helpful in assisting in this transition as well (see below).

A successful traversing of these transition points can make the difference between success and failure of the entire true skunk works or pseudo-skunk works effort, independent of the value of the new innovation itself. In addition to the successful navigation of these transition points, there are also other factors that can help lead to success.

# KEYS TO SUCCESS

Gwynne has pointed out the 'basic incongruity' of skunk works-like programmes (Gwynne, 1997, p. 19): the fact that for maximum effectiveness skunk works need to operate in secrecy, but concurrently new technologies, innovations, new products, and so on must get rapid corporate acceptance and significant market exposure and publicity. Is this a paradox or just a management challenge?

Analysis has led to the development of a list of success factors. It is not the first list, nor, hopefully, will it be the last. This list is not complete, nor is it inclusive; however, it does further the discussion.

### Success Factors

1. The corporation needs to have a *special* culture that allows the existence of a counterculture entity associated with it (Gwynne, 1997). Not every organization will allow a *foreign* entity to exist within it. It is analogous to a body allowing a virus to exist without trying to destroy it. The successful organization must not only allow the skunk works to exist and flourish, it must sometime create the entity itself.
2. There needs to be a strong sense of urgency. The Second World War drove the urgency of the original skunk works. The successful skunk works must also be driven by a sense of urgency. Threat of competition can be useful.
3. The skunk works should have a powerful top management supporter, sponsor or champion. This champion has an important multi-functional role. First, the champion must protect the skunk works from the rest of the organization. Second, the champion must make sure that the required resources are available. Finally, the champion may play a role in transitioning the project to the corporate mainstream.
4. The skunk works must have freedom from the regular organizational processes and bureaucracy.
5. The skunk works need a *special* hands-on leader, who is not only respected for his/her technical skills and intellect, but can also be charismatic, although perhaps not in the traditional sense of the word.
6. A successful skunk works is one characterized by informal processes with close personal interaction. One task of the hands-on leader is to spur the creation of this type of environment.
7. There must be a strategy for commercializing the skunk works output (Single and Spurgeon, 1996). Commercialization is crucial. The first skunk works was also driven by customer satisfaction; it had only one rather demanding client, the US War Department. Accordingly,

     skunk works needs to be customer and product orientated. The more well defined the customer, the better.

8.   The organization and the skunk works must have the ability to understand and handle the important transitions: the market and the organization.

9.   Innovations fail more often than they succeed, as a result skunk works that are designed on a 'one shot deal' basis face huge odds. Successful skunk works should be long-term programmes with the portfolio approach in mind (Gwynne, 1997).

10.  The skunk works should not only be culturally distant from the rest of the organization, but physically/geographically distant as well. The distance is in part symbolic, but it has other effects. For example, the distance (and isolation) helps among other things rapidly to create group cohesiveness, which can be instrumental in group dynamics and performance.

## IS THE SKUNK WORKS SALVAGEABLE?

As stated above, the establishment of a skunk works-like programme is typically an admission by management that their organization is no longer capable of competing with other organizations, especially smaller, entrepreneurial ones, in the production of innovations. As stated above, skunk works-like programmes can be symptomatic of organizational and management dysfunction instead of organizational and management success. Furthermore the establishment of skunk works-like programmes often tends to create additional organizational dysfunctions.

Given this, can the skunk works as organizational tool of rapid innovation, be salvaged? The answer is, probably, yes. There is evidence, especially anecdotally, that large corporations are having success with what *they* call skunk works. Where exactly these programmes would be categorized under the skunk works matrix, is still an empirical question.

One thing is clear, to create a successful skunk works-like programme the organization as a whole must be prepared, must be committed and must understand and be sensitive to the secondary effects that might result. If that is not enough, these organizations must also be aware of the key success factors.

One potential solution for reducing some secondary effects is the emergent skunk works. The emergent skunk works may be the method that allows large corporations to create radical product innovations inside the organization without some of the negatives that may come along with the establishment of a true skunk works. How? This type of skunk works develops from the bottom up, which allows it to gain some organizational support early. It is a project of the *people*. Secondly, as it migrates to a transitional skunk works, management then can make the support/not support decision.

There are two partially related organizational challenges here. First, in order for this to occur on a frequent basis, the organizations need to foster a special type of culture, that allows independent creative action as well as tolerance/acceptance of failure. Secondly, virtually all true skunk works and pseudo-skunk works require isolation and a counterculture environment, which are hard enough to maintain within the reach of the large corporation. How difficult is that to maintain actually within the regular organization? How can you have a group inside the organization that has its own set of rules? Assuming it can be done, are the resulting innovations radical or just evolutionary? These are difficult questions with which management may have to deal.

A possible solution would be the rapid migration from emergent skunk works to transitional skunk works. This way management can make the support/not support decision as early as possible, while the project is still small. If they decide to support it, it would then migrate to a pseudo-skunk works, which is generally isolated from the mainstream. This would cause minimum disruptions to the regular organization, while allowing the development process to continue in a skunk works-like manner.

### Skunk Works for Hire

Another indication that skunk works-like programmes are here to stay is by watching what is just beginning to occur. This current business environment characterized by rapid change and uncertainty is helping spur the move to increased outsourcing of all parts of the value-added chain. This movement has now begun to take root in the corporate research area. There are now skunk works for hire. These new organizations can take a kernel of an idea and fully develop it or can take a fully developed product and test or evaluate it and any task in between (Fjelstad, 2000). Although special attention must be given to issues of ownership of the intellectual property, this option can help reduce some of the organizational fallout due to the creation of skunk works-like programmes within the organization. However, what does it say about organization's failure or the lack of ability to innovate?

## FUTURE RESEARCH QUESTIONS

There are many open questions surrounding skunk works-like programmes. Examining the skunk works matrix can be useful here. For example, which are more effective, programmes that emerge or ones that are mandated? Which are more effective, secret programmes or public one? Which are more effective, true skunk works or the pseudo-skunk works? Which is more effective the established pseudo-skunk works or the one that migrates from an emergent skunk works? Given all this, which is more efficient? How do you foster an environment that allows for emergent skunk works?

A successful skunk works-like programme is one characterized by informal processes with close personal interaction. Can this be formalized, institutionalized or must it just be encouraged? As one can see there are countless questions that need to be researched.

## CONCLUSION

As we move to even more dynamic business environments, it has become increasingly important for business to be innovative, not just to gain a competitive advantage, but to survive. Often technological innovations must be preceded by administrative innovations. In other words, management innovations as well as organizational innovations are often required to enable product/service innovations and creativity. Large corporations have turned to skunk works-like programmes as solutions, which may in fact indicate current organization problems as well as future problems. Despite the fact that many skunk works-like programmes are created under less than ideal conditions for less than ideal reasons, use of skunk works of all types by large corporations seem to be accelerating. However, there may be hope.

This chapter certainly raises more questions than it answers. If you believe that to be so, then this chapter has been successful. In fact, a chapter that completely answers questions is a dead end, a discussion killer, rather than a provocation to more discussion, more debate and more research. Hopefully, this chapter, by not answering many questions, has succeeded in spurring the dialogue.

## REFERENCES

Astech-engineering.com (2001).

DiMaggio, P.J. and W. Powell (1983). 'The iron cage revisited: Institutional isomorphism and collective rationality in organizational fields', *American Sociological Review*, **48**, 147–60.

Field, K.F. (2001), 'Working outside the box', *Design News*, www.designnews.com, 26 February.

Fjelstad, J. (2000), 'Manager/innovator gun for hire: the next step in outsourcing', *Electronic News*, September 18, p. 76.

Gwynne, P. (1997), 'Skunk works, 1990s style', *Research Technology Management*, **40** (4), 18–23.

Newton, H. (2001), *Newton's Telecom Dictionary: The Official Dictionary of Telecommunications, Networking and the Internet*, 17th edition, New York: CPM Books.

Rich, B. (1994), 'Inside the skunk works', *Popular Science*, **245** (4), 52–9.

Schrage, M. (1999), 'What's the bad odor at the innovation skunkworks', *Fortune*, December 20, p. 338.

Single, A. and W. Spurgeon (1996), 'Creating and commercializing innovation inside a skunk works', *Research Technology Management*, **39** (1), 38–41.

Wilson, J. (1999), 'Skunk works magic', *Popular Mechanics*, **176** (9), 60–67.

Whatis.com (2001).

# 7. Entrepreneurship and the design process: the paradox of innovation in a routine design process

**Jérémy Legardeur, Jean François Boujut and Henri Tiger**

## 1. INTRODUCTION

The problematic of innovation has been extensively studied both in the social sciences and in the engineering design fields. In this chapter our aim is not to address this question in a theoretical and general way. Rather, we prefer to go deeper in a case study to understand the detailed workings of a specific design situation when a new technology is introduced. In our case, we have witnessed the introduction of a new material (a composite material called SMC[1]) in a design department of an industrial company. In the following we will call it the 'composite project'. The aim of this project was twofold: testing the capacity of this material in a semi-structural application, and changing the design practices and organization through the introduction of a new material. The challenge was on the two aspects: moving the technical limits of the technology and making the organization and the actors evolve in the same time. This chapter deals with the second aspect.

After presenting the context of this study we will analyse the different aspects of this innovation process in this particular design situation. We observed that design habits were deeply rooted in the history of the product and especially they were shaped by the underlying technology used in this industry since the beginning, that is, the steel and its related manufacturing processes. In that context the composite material forced implicit knowledge to elicit and introduce new participants in the design process. Furthermore, the design organization itself was modified since the composite project was not a regular project related to a specific range of product; it was an upstream project that had no clear aim and allocated resources. The challenge then was to make this project co-exist with normal business; all in all a classical situation innovation faces. Otherwise one could not call it innovation.

Before going further in the case study, it is important to present our

research methodology since the results are deeply linked to our methodological premises. An interdisciplinary research team composed of social scientists and engineering design researchers has carried out this study. We
practise an ethnographic-style research, spending long periods of time in
companies, involved in design projects as full-time participants. A PhD
student, a graduate from a mechanical engineering school, was involved in
the development project as an engineer. Over a period of one year, he has
been one of the main actors of the composite project, and therefore one of
the main actors of the innovative process we analyse in the following.
Eventually he will be regarded as an entrepreneur. This particular and difficult position, however, produces very fruitful results on the understanding
of the real design activity. In fact, we share with the social sciences the
action research position. But the main difference lies in the outcome of our
work. Although we present here a stand-alone analysis of a design situation, our aim is to develop methodologies and tools that could provide significant change and help to design organizations.

## 2.   INITIAL CONTEXT: A ROUTINE DESIGN PROCESS

In this section we will expose what we mean by 'routine design', and
describe the main characteristics of the situation we observed. This will
give us the opportunity to introduce the context of this study.

In the autumn of 1998 we entered the design office of an industrial
company. This office's job was to produce designs of structural parts.
During our early investigations we found a relatively stable situation in the
following aspects:

- Product stability: we found a strongly standardized product, where
  the product breakdown structure and parts families were seldom
  revised. This rigid product standardization is not propitious to a
  global reasoning, leading to the redefinition of the different functions' perimeters.
- Initially, the involved participants formed a relatively stable network
  of actors. The involved actors represented mainly technical trades
  such as product engineering, simulation and process engineering.
  The industrial designers and marketing or materials specialists were
  seldom consulted.
- The stability of the organization was based on the pre-eminence of
  the design office over the other participants. The design office was
  classically organized and we did not find any teamwork.

- The stability of the design process was based on a predefined schema (input data collection, specification lists, requests for offer, and so on) and framed by project development planning and the design process seemed to be quite stable. Nevertheless, at the level of our observation, the participants seemed to be in a constant agitation where the management attitude was more reactive than proactive.
- A particular view over the 'product–process' integration: a deep knowledge of the technical possibilities of steel, its related forming and assembly processes, led the designers to draw parts that were implicitly optimized for that technology. Again implicitly, participants were involved in a prescriptive top-down scheme where non-explicit choices were orientating the downstream processes.

All these points show that there is a great pattern of constancy in the total product development system, including the technical solutions, the technologies, the organization and the involved trades. The product is the result of a constant optimization over many years. It has reached a degree of achievement that hardly prohibits significant gains in terms of cost, weight or performance and thereby prohibits any major product evolution too.

## 3.   THE SMC TECHNOLOGY WITHIN THE DESIGN OFFICE: THE STORY OF AN UNFULFILLED INNOVATION

The SMC technology shows us, throughout the process of its introduction in a design office, that beyond the technical problem lies all the complexity of an industrial situation. We will show in this section how the SMC technology acts as an instrument or a medium for innovation, including organizational changes, attitudes, learning processes, and so on.

Also, the SMC technology is not new; it has been industrially transformed for more than 30 years and in that sense it is not an innovation. Nevertheless the material itself and its related manufacturing technology has a particular interest in our case: it is rather unknown and poorly employed in the design office. Furthermore the SMC technology is victim of persistent prejudices. Besides, the deep interrelation between the material, the part shape and the process characteristics is a major difference compared with steel. This is why every SMC solution has its own particular material formulation, process parameters and part shape (ribs position, thickness, and so on). It is merely impossible to anticipate a shape without having precise information about the process and the material. This character disables many design habits and rules of thumb based on the knowledge of the manufacturing processes of steel parts. Designing an industrial composite solution involves new actors, new practices and, finally, leads to knowledge creation. All these characteristics led us to consider that we are faced with an innovative process.

The results presented here are drawn from fieldwork by a PhD student who had been in charge of the SMC project during a period of one year within the industrial company. We will be relating this case considering it as an innovative process, and mostly using Callon, Latour et al.'s concepts to analyse the situation (Akrich, Callon and Latour, 1988a; 1988b; Callon, 1986; Latour, 1987). Extending Callon and Latour's theory, we consider the concept of entrepreneur as being a result of social interactions rather than being a figure that would exist prior to the process itself. While describing the different steps of the process, we will meet new actors, witness the creation of a network and observe the evolution of the design problem. It is the description of this movement, made of alliances and shifts of either things or persons, that one can qualify as innovative or not.

### 3.1  First Step: Concept versus Solution – a Required Step in Order to Move from the 'Steel Culture' towards the 'SMC Culture'

At the beginning of the project, the company's material laboratory was trying to introduce organic materials within design offices which were traditionally more inclined to use steel as a 'natural' material in their designs. The material laboratory and the research team then proposed to the design office a joint development of an application using an SMC-type composite material. The head of the design office accepted this offer, although they had expressed no clear need of it. For the design office representatives this project was perceived as an opportunity for testing a new technology.

This first entry in the field led us to engage in a prospective phase aimed at investigating the potential applications in the subsystem the design office was in charge of. In order to bring out the potential orientation of the study, this phase began with a set of meetings involving the engineers responsible for the development of the various functions.

It is interesting to notice that all the propositions we elicited from the interviews were related to existing parts. The engineers obviously lacked knowledge of the SMC technology, and their propositions mainly relied on their former experience in the design of steel parts and did not integrate the actual potential of the new technology. But this attitude also reflects a bias and a lack of confidence in a technology that is poorly mastered. Besides, we would like to point out that if the mechanical strength criteria were very often put forward by the engineers, it was used paradoxically. Engineers either imagined low-stressed applications such as body panels, or proposed to replace steel in highly stressed applications according to the image carried by aeronautic or space applications.

In order to open the game and enlarge the field of possible applications, the research team suggested consulting the composite supplier, which was one of the partners of the research programme. This composite supplier has a great experience in the field of SMC development, but in our case it is the knowledge of the industrial process that will enlarge the set of selection criteria. Then, following the suggestions of the supplier and the researchers, a new selection is made among the potential applications taking into account the new process characteristics and, above all, the possibility to integrate various functions within a same part.

This new criterion, together with the knowledge brought by this new actor of the network, shifted the initial question from a material substitution problem to a real design issue. For the research team the problem was no longer to replace steel parts by composite ones, but to imagine new possibilities integrating different functions. We observe here an evolution of the studied perimeter and a shift in the level of abstraction (that is, from part to functions). The attention of the team is drawn by the specific and limited part of the product, a concept of SMC part is therefore imagined (see Figure 7.1).

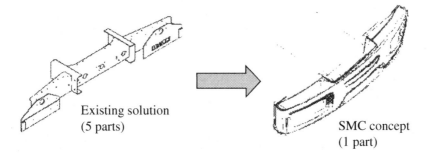

Existing solution
(5 parts)

SMC concept
(1 part)

*Figure 7.1   The SMC concept*

We propose characterizing the step described above as the result of the construction of a shared and explicit problematic. During this stage, a debate occurred among the partners that led to the extension of the network, introducing a new actor (composite supplier) and that allowed the construction of the actors' identities, mainly based on their respective competencies. We pointed out that the new problematic is coherent with each other's interests. The supplier seized the opportunity to open new markets, and its competency is indirectly recognized as a specialist of the SMC technology. The material laboratory had the opportunity to disseminate its expertise throughout the company. The design office seized the opportunity for testing a new technology, and the researchers began to validate their hypothesis on the efficiency of product and process integration through the creation of a network of actors.

### 3.2   Second Step: Network Extension and the Validation of the Concept

In this section we will see how the various alliances between the actors can be presented as a 'system of alliances' which is connected to the network of actors. We also will see how actors and their 'representatives' (various product representations or objects) interact in the process of creating the system of alliances.

The first informal proposition of the SMC concept raised little enthusiasm from the designers. They were expecting a list of technical requirements for each part of the subsystem (Figure 7.1). However, the situation that will perceptibly evolve after various events will modify the context and allow the adoption of the proposition. In this step the PhD student plays the role of an interface actor facilitating the information flow and knowledge-building within the network.

Originally four alternative configurations were considered from the initial SMC concept, each of them corresponding to a specific level of integration. The four propositions were presented to the project engineer using comparison tables. These tables put forward specific composite criteria such as the integration of functions that are mixed with other traditional criteria (cost, weight, and so on). Other objects such as sketches of solutions were used as support to evaluate the four propositions. The project engineer chooses the solution he rejected a few weeks ago, selecting the alternative that involved the maximum of integration (five parts replaced by a single one).

During this step the role of the PhD student evolved towards the stabilization of the network he had progressively constituted in the previous step. He, first, remained an interface between the various actors, but in a different way. Whereas in the previous step the problem was to create the network, the problem now is to collect and disseminate information throughout the network. Second, he imagined new instruments, examples include the tables described above, in order to empower the propositions and give them some objectivity compared to an abstract 'SMC concept'. Following Akrich, Callon and Latour (1988a and b) we argue that this table operates as a representative (or a spokesperson) of the composite actor in the selection process. In this way it is an intermediary object in the design process (Jeantet, 1998; Vinck and Jeantet, 1995). Indeed, this table is, first, a representation of the SMC solution, secondly, the translation of the process capabilities (cost, production rates, accuracy, and so on), and, finally, it behaves as a mediator between the composite actor and the design actor.

However, the network keeps evolving continuously and a new actor, seldom present at this step, will come into the network, namely the industrial designer. Soon after the SMC concept has been validated, the project engineer came to a meeting of a new larger project that involved an industrial designer. The latter presented some rushes of the new product among which was one corresponding to the same specific part of the composite project. The project engineer was stricken by the similarity between the SMC concept and the rush presented by the industrial designer. In the mean time the project engineer was consulted for alternative composite solutions in his field. The PhD student was then asked to contact the industrial designer in order to work on a finer description of the shape of what still remains a SMC concept.

This example shows how the work of the PhD student led to the enrolment of a new actor, the enlargement of the network and the increase in legitimacy of the SMC concept. We argue that he was at the centre of a socio-technical device aiming at increasing the actor's impact upon the SMC concept. This socio-technical device mixed human beings and things in a complex network of interactions. The rushes, sketches and tables were not involved in the process as solutions to the problem; rather, they were intermediary objects that mediated the interactions. In that sense they were also representations giving more credibility and substance to the SMC concept, it only needs a reminder of the impact of the designer's rushes on the project engineer's attitude toward the SMC concept, to be convinced that the various representations and objects play a key role in the design process.

### 3.3   Third Step: Involvement of New Actors – a Twofold Objective for the SMC Project

The rushes made by the industrial designer showed a realistic view of the solution which gave a good idea of the shape of the future part. It represented a translation of the SMC concept into a shape, representing a solution to the problem. This solution was presented to the different participants to the project, including the department in charge of the industrial property, in order to find similar applications developed by the competitors. Our application seemed to be unique in this product area. We must remember that the part had a semi-structural function, which is quite unusual for such a material.

Then, new criteria appeared during a meeting with the marketing department. The marketing department is concerned with the maintenance problems and the volumes of products to be manufactured, two criteria that are not in the favour of the SMC technology. Indeed, the skills and competencies for repairing SMC parts are not yet generally available among the different agents. In the meantime, the PhD student was invited to present the designer's rushes to a meeting of the different participants in the project of the new product. The solution was welcomed positively. After that the aim of the project became clearer: the SMC project should provide a solution to a specific range of existing products, while remaining adaptable to the future product. We see here how the involvement of new actors together with the implication in a new project led to the evolution of the problem itself, shifting from the question of the functional integration to the choice of a possible field of application for the SMC part.

The SMC project was now orientated towards two specific products. The economical dimension was then considered more precisely. The supplier was informally consulted in order to validate the technical choice, and to provide information on the minimum production rates profitable for such an application. It appeared that the application was at the lower limit of profitability, leading to a reconsideration of the solution. Work with the standardization department led to a reconsideration of the design in order to widen the perimeter of the application.

At this stage, a first geometric model was built, following some specific building principles provided by the supplier. These are mainly orientated towards the manufacturing process of the tools; when in the design office of the buyer company, the modelling principles are more orientated toward the mechanical simulation of a steel part (see Section 4.3). The PhD student then built a Finite Element Analysis (FEA) model, meshing the surface and using material data provided by experts of the domain (mainly external). A static evaluation of the part's strength proved satisfactory, followed by a dynamic simulation showing some weakness of the part. An optimization of structural rib positions led to an acceptable configuration, after more than 20 successive versions. Besides, one of the first versions of the part model had provided the input data for a first price evaluation made by the supplier.

This pre-project phase had lasted ten months. It allowed the setting of a composite solution within the design office. We saw how the SMC concept progressively imposed its evidence compared with initial propositions stuck in single-parts reasoning schemes. We also witnessed the enrolment of new actors that paradoxically made the problem more complex when improving its credibility among the existing actors of the company. In the next section we will see how the project came to be unexpectedly frozen, and the innovation partly invalidated.

### 3.4 Fourth Step: When the Rationale of the Project is Contradictory to Innovation

The offer made by the supplier shows an important overestimation of the price compared with the actual solution. This objective element (in that sense it is an intermediary object), which is merely a first estimation, will contribute to the disqualification of the solution. We see here how the risk represented by the higher price of the composite solution inhibits further developments. It is an important limitation of projects regarding innovation. The risk was, in our case, overestimated by a project engineer who had little experience (and therefore confidence) in the composite technology. The purchaser related to the design office had little experience in the field of composite material and it was the first time he received a price offer from this particular supplier. After receiving the supplier's estimation, he asked the PhD student for more explanation concerning several technical points. He wanted to have more information on a supplier with whom he had never worked in order to estimate the credibility of the proposition. He came to the conclusion that he needed to meet the supplier in order to negotiate this offer. Unfortunately this meeting was delayed several times and finally cancelled: at the time the project strategy had changed and the negotiation was no longer a priority. What would have been a classical negotiation starting point – the original price offer – turned out to be a breakpoint in the project.

Moreover, in the meantime, the orientation of the new product project showed an evolution in the development strategy. The design team had decided to develop parts with a high level of modularity in order to increase the standardization and the volume of production for each part.

This second event added to the supplier's price offer, and led to a reconsideration of the concept of functional integration, which was at the centre of the SMC project. These events and the underlying conflicts in the design rationale led the network to split up. The problem of function integration thereafter lost all its support and, finally, the project ceased.

## 4. EPILOGUE: SOME KEY ELEMENTS TO FOSTER INNOVATION

Our observations reveal the weakness of an innovative project before it has reached the price negotiation phase. Moreover, this case study shows the antagonism between the everyday project constraints (lead time, costs, risks, and so on) and the uncertainty underlying any innovative project. The price offer combined with the evolution in the development strategy show that an innovative process is weak till the end, that is, before the solution has reached the level of the production. In this section we will come back to the case using specific viewpoints related to our current research questions.

### 4.1 Product Functional Breakdown Structure: Changing the Level of Abstraction

One of the main advantages of the composite parts lies in the ability to integrate different functions within the same structure. This goal can only be reached if the designer can consider a relatively wide perimeter on the product. In our case, the steel-based technology led to a product breakdown that was very difficult to better integrate. Furthermore, the concept of integration is contradictory to the concept of standardization that led to defining a large amount of small interchangeable parts. Thinking in terms of function and function integration represents a breakthrough in design habits. Our study began with a prospective phase in order to determine the potential applications for the SMC technology. Every engineer we interviewed was thinking in terms of existing parts, trying to imagine which part could fit to the SMC material. The result was quite poor. We claim that the introduction of the SMC material requires a design phase where people must reconsider the product breakdown structure and get a higher level of abstraction over the product. In that way designers can be helped by methods such as functional analysis, brainstorming and quality functional deployment.

### 4.2 The Network of Actors and the Role of the Intermediary Objects

Innovation entails new organization and the creation of a network: in a design environment where the steel material and its related processes are a reference technology, it is not obvious that a composite alternative be implemented. At a first glance we could imagine that the virtues and the advantages of the composite material (that is, lightness, shapes, corrosion, function integration, and so on) would impose by themselves, even faced with the technical arguments of the steel. In fact things are not so simple. The acceptability criteria are embedded in a more complex process that requires reopening a debate which was rather stabilized as we saw in Section 2. During our study we observed the introduction of new actors (for example, industrial designers, composite experts), putting on the table new sets of constraints (for example, aesthetic, economic, part maintainability) as shown in Figure 7.2. Moreover, what was described above allows the interface actor to be presented as a kind of entrepreneur, in that he is at the centre of the creation of the network of actors.

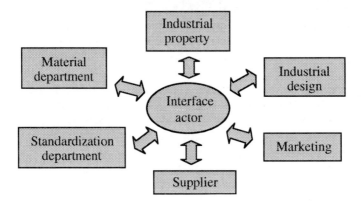

*Figure 7.2 Network of actors*

We also observed the emergence of new media and objects as a partial materialization of the different points of view. All this led to the progressive evolution of the design setting. We paid particular attention to those objects we have called intermediary objects in previous works (Vinck and Jeantet, 1995).

Of course, objects do not tell much outside their context of use, but what is interesting to observe is the process leading the design actors to collectively redefine the objects and the product evaluation criteria. In fact, we observed (see Section 3) that those evaluation criteria were not prior to the process, they were unstable and, finally, as a first hypothesis, we claim that they are one of the outputs of the process. A second hypothesis is related to the opposition between two movements or two tendencies we observed in the design office. The first movement tends to impose the composite solution, while the second one tends to reject it. The position of the different actors may evolve throughout the whole process and, therefore, the criteria and the argumentation also evolve with the actors. This gives the process a dynamic character where the game of argumentation occurs within the boundaries of a constantly evolving arena. Here the design game leads to a new network of competencies with – last but not least – strategy.

### 4.3 Developing Specific Knowledge for SMC Design: Confronting Product and Process Knowledge

For new technologies, the lack of knowledge in the design offices is a great limitation. But this situation is not unique; today most organizations' strategies lead to the externalization of large parts of their activities including development (Kesseler, 1998). In that context, a new technology can only be introduced via an industrial partnership with a supplier expert in that technology (Boujut and Jeantet, 1999; Kesseler, 1998). Furthermore, in our case the application was at the limit of the known capacities of the material and process: few SMC applications have semi-structural functions. The supplier was also in a learner position. The designers had to integrate into the subsystem an SMC part while the supplier holds the knowledge about the process and material possibilities. But the success of the implementation relied also on a thorough knowledge of the product (part's environment, mechanical solicitations, and so on). We observed information exchanges on the technical, economical and strategic levels. As we saw above (Section 3.2), the PhD student played the role of an interface actor between the two companies. He 'translated' the participants' respective constraints and built a clear and broad view of the situation in order to help the two partners (which were not yet bounded by an agreement). Some adjustments were necessary between the participants. For us, it represents a specific learning process of the same nature of Schön's organizational learning process (Schön, 1991). We underline here the importance of the entrepreneur in the creation of such knowledge.

For example, during the simulation phase, the designer was faced with two alternative modelling methods, corresponding to the two methods used in the respectively involved companies (that is, the buyer and the supplier). The designer chose the method of the supplier because it was orientated toward the modelling of the SMC part including process anticipation (ribs positions, outer skin, and so on). The modelling sequence can be summarized as shown in Figure 7.3. The use of such a sequence allowed the designer to anticipate the simulation phase by positioning the elements necessary for eventually stiffening the structure. Another key point is related to the yield criteria. We observed that both the supplier and the design office were using different yield criteria. For historical reasons the supplier used a Von Mises criterion when the design office considered a maximum normal stress criterion. On the other hand, they agreed to consider an isotropic behaviour as a first estimation. The goal of the simulation was twofold: it had to provide information on the global mechanical resistance and should help to detect potential critical zones.

### 4.4   Beyond Top-down Prescriptions towards a Collaborative Product–Process Integration

In Section 2, we saw that a product–process integration movement already existed in the design office. However, it is a top-down prescriptive product–process integration. The design office imagines parts whose shapes and materials involve a specific knowledge of a particular manufacturing

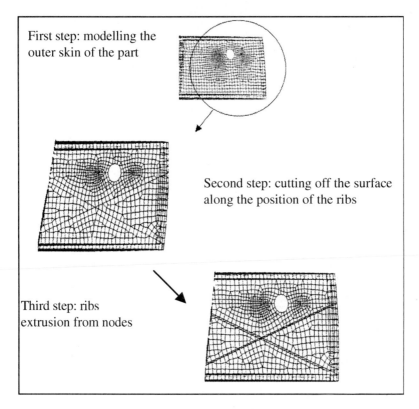

First step: modelling the outer skin of the part

Second step: cutting off the surface along the position of the ribs

Third step: ribs extrusion from nodes

*Figure 7.3    The SMC part modelling method*

process. It is important here to notice that this is most of the time an implicit choice made by habit. Even if people are ready to change, not every evolution is possible.

This prescriptive attitude is deeply rooted in the industrial history and needs long-term efforts to evolve. To achieve a proper innovation process we think that the participants must change their attitude toward product–process integration. We saw in Section 4.3 the importance of the learning process. After Hatchuel (1994) we think that the concept of pre-scription is at the centre of the design process. In our case, we saw how the composite process participants, with the assistance of our PhD student imposed specific constraints on the product. Where the constraints are explicit, then a real negotiation can occur between the design office (product side) and the 'composite actor' (material and process side). We can remember the debate around the choice of the yield criterion.

### 4.5 Towards Adaptive Product Evaluation Procedures

Product evaluation is one of the main activities carried out during a design phase; this has been shown by many studies in the field of cognitive psychology, among which is Bonnardel (1992). In the case of innovation, the former evaluation procedures developed by the designers are insufficient or partially obsolete. They must be modified or even changed to fit the new context. This necessitates a continuous process of redefining the evaluation procedures. In order to compare the composite solution with the traditional ones, we have proposed tables summarizing the pertinent evaluation criteria for both alternative technologies. The participants had to change their evaluation procedures and new criteria came up as well.

## 5. FUTURE WORKS

After more than one year of observation we can elicit important characteristics of the design situation. The observation and participation phase is not yet over, but it already shows that the innovative process is a complex process, fragile and uncertain. Innovation cannot win in a single dimension; to succeed the SMC technology must be robust at the level of the organization, the design practices and the technology. In that sense we call it a product–process innovation. One dimension cannot exist without the others. In order to further the research, the second phase will consist of the development of recommendations we will be carrying out in the field. We are now analysing more specifically the function of the material experts within project teams and, particularly from our first results, the means to introduce more innovation in the design process.

### NOTE

1.  SMC: Sheet Molding Compound is a fibre-reinforced composite used in the car and truck industry mainly for class A applications. It is a thermosetting resin, with glass fibre reinforcement that has relatively poor mechanical properties compared with carbon or Kevlar fibre composites, but with a low price and a high production rate. This is nearly the only composite material used in mass production industry. The production rate can reach 700 to 1000 parts per day.

### REFERENCES

Akrich M., M. Callon and B. Latour (1988a), 'A quoi tient le succès des innovations: 1. L'art de l'intéressement', série Gérer et Comprendre, *Annales des Mines*, **11**, 4–17.

Akrich, M., M. Callon and B. Latour (1988b), 'A quoi tient le succès des innovations? 2. Le choix des porte-parole', série Gérer et Comprendre, *Annales des Mines*, **12**, 14–29.

Bonnardel, N. (1992), 'Le rôle de l'évaluation dans les activités de conception', thèse de psychologie cognitive université d'Aix en provence.

Boujut, J-F. and A. Jeantet (1999), 'Involving suppliers in early product development: a challenge for the purchasing and engineering functions', *ICED 99*, **2**, 1001–7.

Callon, M. (1986), 'Some elements of a sociology of translation: domestication of the scallops and the fishermen', in J. Law (ed.), *Power, Action and Belief: A New Sociology of Knowledge*, London: Routledge and Kegan Paul, pp. 196–233.

Hatchuel, A. (1994), 'Apprentissages collectifs et activité de conception', *Revue française de gestion*, **99**, 109–20.

Jeantet A. (1998), 'Les objets intermédiaires dans la conception. Eléments pour une sociologie des processus de conception', *Sociologie du travail*, **3**, 291–316.

Kesseler A. (1998), 'The creative supplier', PhD dissertation, Ecole polytechnique, Paris.

Latour, B. (1987), *Science in Action*, Maidenhead: Open University Press.

Schön, D.A. (1991), *The Reflexive Practitioner: How Professionals Think in Action*, Aldershot: Ashgate.

Vinck D. and A. Jeantet (1995), 'Mediating and commissioning objects in the sociotechnical process of product design: a conceptual approach', *Management and New Technology: Design, Networks, Strategy*, COST Social Sciences Seri, CCE, 111–29.

# 8. Culture's role in entrepreneurship: self-employment out of dissatisfaction

## Geert Hofstede, Niels G. Noorderhaven, A. Roy Thurik, Lorraine M. Uhlaner, Alexander R.M. Wennekers and Ralph E. Wildeman

## 1. INTRODUCTION

### Importance of Entrepreneurship

In the late twentieth century, entrepreneurship re-emerged as a key agenda item of economic policy-makers across Europe, both for specific nations as well as for the European Union as a whole (Brock and Evans, 1989; Carree and Thurik, 2003; European Commission, 1999; EZ, 1999; OECD, 1998a). Moderate economic growth coupled with persistently high levels of unemployment-stimulated expectations of entrepreneurship's potential as a source of job creation and economic growth (Acs, 1992; Audretsch and Thurik, 2000; Thurik, 1996). This has not always been the case. For instance, in the early and mid-twentieth century – in fact until the 1980s – a focus on entrepreneurship was absent from the European economic policy agenda. The exploitation of economies of scale and scope was thought to be at the heart of modern economies (Teece, 1993). Audretsch and Thurik (2001) characterize this period as one where stability, continuity and homogeneity were the cornerstones and thus label it the 'managed economy'. Small businesses were considered to be a vanishing breed.

The late twentieth century witnessed massive downsizing and restructuring of many large firms as well as the decline of the centrally led economies in Central and Eastern Europe built on certainty and the virtues of scale. By the 1980s evidence mounted to demonstrate that this move away from large firms towards small, predominantly young firms was a sea change, not just a temporary aberration of the 1990s. Audretsch and Thurik (2001) label this new economic period, based less on the traditional inputs of natural resources, labour and capital, and more on the input of knowledge and ideas, as the 'entrepreneurial economy'. Paradoxically, the increased degree of uncertainty creates opportunities for small and young firms, and hence leads to higher rates of entrepreneurship. Further study shows that this change does not take place in all developed economies at the same time or to the same degree (Audretsch et al., 2002). Hence comparative research may explain these variations (Reynolds et al., 2000; Wennekers, Uhlaner and Thurik, 2002).

Although much of the recent comparative research concentrates primarily on economic factors, a different strand of research includes sociological indicators such as culture and institutions (Uhlaner, Thurik and Hutjes, 2002; Wennekers, Uhlaner and Thurik, 2002). This chapter addresses the influence of cultural, social and economic variables on rate of entrepreneurship across more than 20 Western nations and Japan for the period 1974 to 1994.

In most OECD countries the first decades after the Second World War showed historically high rates of economic growth. In the 1960s and 1970s, academic and political interest in many Western countries gradually turned to matters of demand management and income equality, whereas the interest in the causes of economic growth waned. Following the first oil crisis in 1973, a period of stagflation set in, characterized by a combination of inflation and slow growth. Neoclassical theory explained economic growth by accumulation of production factors and by exogenous technological change. Mainstream economics, however, did not show great interest in the ultimate causes underlying long-term factor accumulation and technological development.

After the mid-1980s, economic growth in most countries picked up again, but on the whole at a rate too slow to guarantee an acceptable level of unemployment. Stagflation and high unemployment caused a renewed interest in supply-side economics and, simultaneously, in underlying factors, including cultural and institutional factors (van de Klundert, 1997; North and Thomas, 1973; Olson, 1982). This research focuses attention on factors such as incentives, regulation of markets and social rigidities. Somewhat unclear in such analysis, however, is the primal role of the economic agents (entrepreneurs) who link the institutions at the micro-level to the economic outcome at the macro-level (see, for instance, Wennekers and Thurik, 1999). In spite of a growing attention in research, currently still little is known about entrepreneurship. How and why for instance do individuals decide to start an enterprise themselves? Which role do institutional and cultural factors play in this decision process? And how exactly do these factors frame the decisions of the millions of business owners and of entrepreneurial managers working within large companies? Today, in spite of the fact that the products of scientific discovery represent the major force of culture change, significant differences across cultures remain (Hofstede, 2001; Huntington, 1996). Thus, although it is recognized that different countries in the world are exposed to the same technological break-throughs, we continue to observe variation across cultures that requires another basis for explanation. Huntington (1996) argues that the civiliza-tions upon which these national cultures are based pre-date modern tech-nological advances, thus providing lasting variations between cultures in spite of shared technologies. This variation, in turn, may help to explain differences in level of entrepreneurship across cultures.

## Determinants of Entrepreneurship

The determinants stimulating or hampering entrepreneurship can be inves-tigated at many levels. At an individual level, one can examine the motives of people for turning to business ownership for employment. Furthermore, one can investigate how the market, regulatory and organizational environ-ment fosters entrepreneurial activity. One can also consider differences between countries and examine whether cultural factors are involved. The latter is the main focus of this chapter.

In particular this chapter seeks to address the following research ques-tion: '*Why do some countries have more entrepreneurs than others?*' Many researchers have addressed this question and most of them have focused on economic explanations, thereby underexposing the role of culture. Some references in the literature have made attempts to study culture's influence, but mostly without much empirical foundation.

In this chapter we aim at supplementing the research of the determinants of entrepreneurship at the country level by linking three bodies of litera-ture. First, we consider the traditional economic explanation for level of entrepreneurship. In particular, we consider factors such as per capita income, unemployment and profit opportunities. Second, we embed our study in the literature on the role of cultural traits such as individualism, power distance and uncertainty avoidance in explaining people's motives and actions within the economic arena (see Hofstede, 1980; 2001). Finally, from the literature on the examination of motives for entrepreneurship, we derive dissatisfaction as a major driving force.

To identify the determinants of entrepreneurship, we include data points across countries and different periods of time between 1974 and 1994. First, we examine the bivariate relationships between level of entrepreneur-ship and a number of economic factors, cultural traits and dissatisfaction variables. Subsequently, we carry out regressions on time-series data, using various economic and dissatisfaction variables as independent variables to predict level of entrepreneurship.[1] Thus we can distinguish the role of each independent variable, and see which variable explains national differences in entrepreneurial activity best. Finally, we repeat the regressions for several country clusters, based on cultural traits, to examine whether in different cultural clusters the economic and dissatisfaction variables influence level of entrepreneurship in different ways.

In colloquial speech the terms entrepreneurs, self-employed, and business people are often used as synonyms. In the management and economic literature, however, entrepreneurship is a behavioural characteristic related to perceiving and creating new economic opportunities (see also Wennekers and Thurik, 1999). Within the population of self-employed, some are economically marginal; others run their business in a managerial manner, and only a subset are intrinsically entrepreneurial. For practical reasons of measurement, we will equate entrepreneurs and self-employed in our empirical research. For the purpose of the present exploratory study, entrepreneurial activity is defined as the percentage of a country's population that is self-employed, using a broad definition that also includes chief executive officers (CEOs) of multi-employee establishments. Though not an ideal measure of entrepreneurship, self-employment has the advantage that it is readily available as a comparable measure across a large number of countries and a long period of time (Wennekers and Thurik, 1999). However, in formulating our hypotheses and in interpreting our results we will occasionally distinguish the marginal, managerial and entrepreneurial dimensions.

This chapter is structured as follows. In Section 2, we review past research on the level of entrepreneurship at the aggregated societal level. Then we derive hypotheses about the influence of several economic, cultural, and attitudinal phenomena on national differences in level of entrepreneurship. Subsequently, in Section 3 we present the research method. In Section 4, we present initial results, including descriptive statistics for the dependent variable and initial tests of bivariate relationships. We also include multiple regressions for economic and attitudinal variables on level of entrepreneurship. In Section 5, we present further results, controlling for differences in culture by means of a cluster technique. In Section 6, we discuss results. Finally, in Section 7, we draw our conclusions.

## 2. PAST RESEARCH ON LEVEL OF ENTREPRENEURSHIP AT THE AGGREGATED SOCIETAL LEVEL

The rate or level of entrepreneurship at the societal level depends upon the opportunities provided by the environment as well as the capabilities and preferences of the population. These aspects in turn are influenced by available technology, level of economic development, culture, institutions and the demography of a society. The focus of this section will be primarily on the economic and cultural factors. A further elaboration of these issues is also discussed in an 'eclectic' theory of entrepreneurship proposed by Verheul et al. (2002) and by Wennekers, Uhlaner and Thurik (2002).

### Historically Based Interpretations of Entrepreneurship

Historical analysis forms the basis for some of the earliest and best-known comparative research on entrepreneurship and economic growth, including that of Weber (1904), Schumpeter (1934), McClelland (1976) and Wiener (1981). In the oldest of these theories, Weber proposes a link between the rise of the Protestant work ethic and economic growth. He observes that in the later Middle Ages, the most economically advanced European societies were Venice and the other city-states of Northern Italy, Spain, Portugal and France. At this time, the Northern European countries lagged behind in economic development. But after the Reformation, a distinct change took place. From this time onwards, the countries of Northern Europe drew ahead of those of Southern Europe. Weber suggests that there may be a causal relationship between economic growth and the value system of Protestantism, better known as the Protestant work ethic, which emphasizes personal responsibility for one's actions, and in some sects, further interprets worldly success as a sign of grace (Lynn, 1991; Weber, 1904).

Other theories of economic development also link economic growth to people's attitudes toward work. Schumpeter stresses the importance of the individual entrepreneur as a prime mover in economic growth, and speculates about the psychology of the entrepreneur (Lynn, 1991). In particular, Schumpeter surmises that strong feelings of competitiveness are probably the principal motivation of entrepreneurs, consistently striving to prove themselves better than other people (Lynn, 1991; Schumpeter, 1934). The relationship between competitiveness of a culture and economic growth is validated by more recent research by Lynn (1991).

David McClelland (1976), also searching for a psychological basis for the entrepreneur's success, identifies achievement motivation, that is, the motive to do a job well and to achieve a standard of excellence, as the main driving force of the entrepreneur (McClelland, 1976). He further proposed that strength of achievement motivation in the population was a major factor responsible for economic growth in a number of societies between the sixteenth and twentieth centuries.

Finally, Wiener also proposes a link between the status of the entrepreneur and economic growth. In his book, *English Culture and the Decline of the Industrial Spirit, 1850–1980*, he argues that economic weakness in

England during certain historical periods can be explained by the comparatively low status of making money and choosing a career in business rather than in a profession such as law or medicine, or of that of the country gentleman (Wiener, 1981).

## Push versus Pull Factors as Influences on Entrepreneurship

Applicable to both economic and cultural factors is the notion of push and pull factors for business start-up and entrepreneurship in general (Stanworth and Curran, 1973; Wennekers et al., 2001). Pull factors are concerned with the expectation of being better off as an entrepreneur. Thus, individuals are often attracted to self-employment with the expectation that it will provide greater material and/or non-material benefits. Push factors take into account the conflict between one's current and one's desired state. Push factors are often associated with some level of dissatisfaction. Huisman and de Ridder (1984) report that frustrations with previous wage-employment, unemployment and personal crises are among the most cited motives of a large sample of entrepreneurs in 11 different countries. Van Uxem and Bais (1996) find that 50 per cent of almost 2000 new Dutch entrepreneurs mention dissatisfaction with their previous job among their motives to start for themselves. At the macro-level, Wennekers et al. (2001) also find support for push factors of entrepreneurship, as measured by self-employment as a percentage of the labour force. In particular, they find higher self-employment in countries with less prosperity (lower per capita gross domestic product [GDP]), greater dissatisfaction with society and lower life satisfaction. Some of this latter research is elaborated in this chapter.

## Economic Influences on Level of Entrepreneurship

Early comparative models focus primarily on economic factors to explain differences in entrepreneurship across nations. Blau (1987) uses data on the American labour force to identify which factors caused this growth. He highlights two key factors: changes in technology and industrial structure. He suggests that these structural changes diminished the comparative advantage of larger firms (scale advantages) and created better opportunities for small firms as their survival became less dependent on their scale based on economic factors alone. In his general equilibrium model of self-employment he assumes that workers try to maximize the utility of income.

In the economic literature, other explanations for the rebound in entrepreneurship in the late twentieth century are based on supply factors such as tax rates, unemployment, competition and female labour participation (Acs, Audretsch and Evans, 1994; Audretsch et al., 2002; Blau, 1987; Evans and Leighton, 1989; Meager, 1992). Acs, Audretsch and Evans (1994), for instance, conclude that self-employment decreases with an increase in per capita gross national product (GNP), female labour force participation and the relative importance of manufacturing. They also conclude that self-employment increases with an increase in the relative importance of the service sector. Audretsch, Carree and Thurik (2001) assume a two-way causation between changes in the level of entrepreneurship and that of unemployment – a 'Schumpeter' effect of entrepreneurship reducing unemployment and a 'refugee' or 'shopkeeper' effect of unemployment stimulating entrepreneurship. They try to reconcile the ambiguities found in the relationship between unemployment and entrepreneurship by introducing a two-equation model where changes in unemployment and in the number of business owners are linked to subsequent changes in those variables for a panel of 23 OECD countries over the period 1974–98. More recent research by Wennekers and Thurik (1999), Audretsch, Carree and Thurik (2001) and Carree et al. (2002) provides further background regarding the relationship between the relationship of entrepreneurship and economic development at the country level.

This rest of this section describes more specifically those economic variables thought to determine level of entrepreneurship. In particular, we identify the following economic variables, prosperity, female labour share, labour income quota, unemployment and population density, as economic factors predicting level of entrepreneurship.

### Prosperity (level of per capita income)

Recent research suggests a U-shaped curve between level of entrepreneurship and the stage of economic development, first declining and later rising again over time (Audretsch et al., 2002; Carree et al., 2002). The reversal of the trend towards lower levels of entrepreneurship is described as the transition from the managed to the entrepreneurial economy (Audretsch and Thurik, 2000; 2001). A low level of prosperity usually coincides with a low wage level, implying little pressure to increase efficiency or the average scale of enterprise. Small firms in crafts and the retail trade are therefore dominant in such an economy. A major route for ambitious wage earners to increase their income, then, is to set up a shop and become an entrepreneur. Economic development subsequently leads to a rise in wages, which stimulates enterprises to work more efficiently. Lucas (1978) shows that firm size is positively related to the development of national income when labour and capital are substitutes. Economies of scale set in, especially in manufacturing, and the number of small firms (including many marginal entrepreneurs) decreases.

In a later stage of economic development, services become more important and a new rise in entrepreneurship will occur. The advent of information technology, the availability of capital and the differentiation of markets (niches) lead to the occurrence of dis-economies of scale. An increased emphasis on subcontracting may strengthen this process (Acs, Audretsch and Evans, 1994; Bais, van der Hoeven and Verhoeven, 1995). This may partly explain the present resurgence of entrepreneurship in some of the most highly developed economies. We assume that relatively many of these business owners are highly educated and entrepreneurial.

### Female labour share
In the last few decades, the participation rate of women in the labour market has increased substantially in most countries in the Western world (OECD, 1998b; 2000). This can be attributed to changing values and attitudes toward working women and resulting changes in behaviour of working women. However, an increase in the participation rate does not necessarily imply an increase in the number of female entrepreneurs. When focusing on the female participation rate relative to the labour force, it can be said that the increase in participation rate of women has a negative impact on the level of entrepreneurship (Verheul et al., 2002). In most Western countries, working women show substantially lower self-employment rates than working men (Bais, van der Hoeven and Verhoeven, 1995). Thus, in general, under the assumption of lagging female self-employment rates compared with males, over time, a growing participation of women in the labour market typically implies a decreasing share of overall self-employed (of both genders) in the labour force (Acs, Audretsch and Evans, 1994).

There may be a number of factors that explain the fact that a smaller proportion of working women start their own firms (although this pattern may again be changing in some of the most economically advanced societies). Evans and Leighton (1989) point out that people who become entrepreneurs have a long employment history. In many Western countries, married women have a shorter employment history than men, most often due to a break to raise a family, thus reducing the chance they will become self-employed. Furthermore, the life style for entrepreneurs often requires longer working days, which women cannot easily combine with their family obligations. Finally, the direction of causality may also be reversed, in that a high percentage of (male) self-employment ties down many women in a supportive role of paid (or unpaid) family worker. Combining these arguments, we predict female labour share to be negatively related to level of entrepreneurship.

### Earning differentials
Countries vary in the distribution of income over wages and all other income categories. Based on expectancy theory and other psychological

theories of motivation, we might reasonably assume that individuals compare expected profits and wages when weighing the possibilities of future self-employment or wage-employment. They probably also consider the risks they will take with either choice. Relatively high business profits are thus seen as a pull factor for entrepreneurship (Foti and Vivarelli, 1994; Santarelli and Sterlacchini, 1994).

A pragmatic proxy for the earning differential on the country level is the 'labour income quota', which measures the share of labour income (including the compensation of the self-employed for their labour contribution) in the net national income. A high labour income quota indicates that a large share of the national income is taken up by wage earners, leaving less room for income out of company profits. Hence, labour income quota is expected to correlate negatively with the overall level of entrepreneurship.

**Unemployment**
The relationship between entrepreneurship and unemployment is complex. On the individual level, unemployment (or the threat of it) primarily acts as a push factor for entrepreneurship (Acs, Audretsch and Evans, 1994; Evans and Leighton, 1990; Foti and Vivarelli, 1994). Since the opportunity costs for unemployed persons to become self-employed are relatively low, they will make their choice for self-employment sooner.

On the other hand, (high) unemployment may be connected with an economic decline, which makes prospects for self-employment less profitable. Consistent with past research, we expect to find an inverse U-shaped relationship between unemployment and level of entrepreneurship: first a positive relationship, then changing over to a negative relationship when unemployment gets beyond a critical level and people get discouraged from starting their own firms, due to the overall weakness in the economy (Hamilton, 1989; Meager, 1992).

**Population density**
Every region needs a minimum supply of facilities regarding trade and craft for their population to survive in these areas. Therefore, thinly populated areas with many dispersed small villages will often have many small retail outlets and workshops. Conversely, urban areas will give rise to economies of scale, through which small trade and craft firms come under competitive pressure (Bais, van der Hoeven and Verhoeven, 1995). This logic suggests a negative relationship between population density and level of entrepreneurship.

On the other hand, Reynolds, Storey and Westhead (1994) state that beyond a certain point, a very high population density in urban areas explains the birth of new firms in the services sector. The presence of networks attracts other new firms in an urban area. Thus, at the higher end, one might expect a reversal in the relationship between population density and level of entrepreneurship. Taken together, these arguments imply a U-shaped curve, initially negative and then turning positive, between population density and level of entrepreneurship.

## Cultural Determinants of Level of Entrepreneurship

Though the economic factors influencing level of entrepreneurship are clearly important, there remains a high level of unexplained variation across countries when only economic variables are taken into account. Thus, more recently, researchers have also looked towards cultural factors to explain this variation. This section reviews the basic terminology used with respect to culture, how it has been applied to entrepreneurship research and, finally, how certain culture variables, including competitiveness, bureaucratic orientation and the Hofstede indices may be thought to influence entrepreneurial activity.

### Definition of culture

Kroeber and Parsons (1958, p. 583) define culture as 'patterns of values, ideas and other symbolic-meaningful systems as factors in the shaping of human behaviour'. Barnouw (1979, p. 5) defines culture as configurations of 'stereotyped patterns of learned behaviour which are handed down from one generation to the next'. Hofstede (1980, p. 25) refers to culture as 'the collective programming of the mind which distinguishes the members of one human group from another and includes systems and values'. Since values are typically determined early in life (Barnouw, 1979; Hofstede, 1980) they tend to be 'programmed' into individuals resulting in behaviour patterns consistent with the cultural context and enduring over time (Hofstede, 1980; Mueller and Thomas, 2000).

Culture can be defined for a variety of levels or systems in society with potential interactions between levels. Ulijn and Weggeman (2001) identify four different cultures: occupational or professional culture (PC), organizational or corporate culture, branch or industry culture (BC) and national culture (NC). Then there are those that argue that, due to shifting national borders, at least as important if not more important is the concept of culture as defined by a civilization. Huntington (1996) identifies five or six contemporary civilizations: Sinic, Japanese, Hindu, Islamic, Orthodox, Western and African (possibly), with Western further subdivided into three components: Europe, North America and Latin America. At each level of culture, one can identify distinct values, norms, language and symbols. Though all these layers are important, differences in cultures may be explained in turn by variations in influences from ancient and modern civilizations from which these national cultures derive (Huntington, 1996).

Since extensive research at the psychological level shows a link between values, beliefs and behaviour, it is plausible that differences in national culture, in which these values and beliefs are embedded, may influence a wide range of behaviours including the decision to become self-employed rather than to work for others (Mueller and Thomas, 2000). Using this logic, several past studies explore the relationship between various aspects of culture and entrepreneurial behaviour across cultures (Busenitz, Gómez and Spencer, 2000; Davidsson, 1995; Huisman, 1985; Lee and Petersen, 2000; McGrath and MacMillan, 1992; Mueller and Thomas, 2000; Tiessen, 1997; Uhlaner, Thurik and Hutjes, 2002; Wennekers et al., 2001).

### Views regarding the relationships between cultural values and entrepreneurial behaviour

Davidsson (1995) identifies two overall views regarding the relationship between cultural values and entrepreneurial behaviour. The first, the *aggregate psychological trait* explanation for entrepreneurship, is based on the idea that if a society contains more people with entrepreneurial values, more people will be entrepreneurs. Davidsson notes that this is essentially the perspective taken by McClelland (1961) and other proponents of the individualistic view of culture. Davidsson also identifies a second view, first set forth by Etzioni (1987), referred to as *social legitimation.* This latter view assumes that variation in entrepreneurship is based upon differences in values and beliefs between the population as a whole and potential entrepreneurs. It is precisely the clash of values between the groups that drives potential entrepreneurs away from the average organization and into self-employment (Wennekers et al., 2001).

### Competitiveness

Research by Lynn (1991) compares the four psychological theories of economic growth described previously (Weber's work ethic, Schumpeter's competitiveness, McClelland's achievement motivation and Wiener's status of the landowner). In a study of 43 countries, they present empirical evidence to support the conclusion that competitiveness is the only attitude that explains variation across populations, best supporting Schumpeter's theory.

### Bureaucracy and corruption

Mauro (1995) analyses subjective indices of corruption, bureaucracy, and the efficiency of the judicial system (combined with a bureaucratic efficiency index) and finds that corruption lowers private investment and thereby reduces economic growth. This might imply that corruption also hampers entrepreneurship.

## Linking Hofstede's cultural indices to innovation and entrepreneurship

Many articles and books discussing the relationship between culture and economy refer to the four cultural indices of Hofstede (1980), power distance (PDI), uncertainty avoidance (UAI), masculinity (MAS) and individualism (IDV). However, the existing hypotheses with respect to the influence of the indices on entrepreneurship, or the hypotheses that can be inferred from indirectly related phenomena, are often contradictory.

For example, Shane (1992) investigates the relationship between culture and *inventions*, and finds that countries with small power distance (PDI−) and high individualism (IDV+) are more inventive than others. Shane (1993) examines the influence of culture on rates of *innovation* (per capita number of trademarks), and finds that weak uncertainty avoidance (UAI−) has the strongest influence, even stronger than per capita income. PDI− and IDV+ are related to innovation as well, though to a lesser extent. Since innovation is more directly related to entrepreneurship than inventiveness, the latter article shows more evidence for the influence of culture on entrepreneurship than Shane (1992). Although the relationships with culture are indirect, the results of the two references suggest that countries with PDI−, UAI− and IDV+ are more entrepreneurial and hence may have more entrepreneurs than others.

Using Hofstede's indices, McGrath, MacMillan and Scheinberg (1992) compare entrepreneurs and non-entrepreneurs within eight countries, although they do not make cross-country comparisons. Using discriminant analysis, they differentiate entrepreneurs v. non-entrepreneurs as follows: entrepreneurs tend to score high on power distance (PDI+), individualism (IDV+), and masculinity (MAS+) while scoring low on uncertainty avoidance (UAI−). Note that although the results for power distance seem to contradict Shane's findings (1992; 1993), the analyses were different, one comparing countries, and the other comparing entrepreneurs with non-entrepreneurs across countries and identifying certain entrepreneurial values, independent of culture.

Baum et al. (1993) hypothesize a reverse role of individualism (at the level of countries). The authors argue that not high but low individualism may stimulate entrepreneurship (self-employment): an individualistic society is more adapted to deal with people who want to do it their own way; both entrepreneurs and non-entrepreneurs might be able to satisfy their motivational needs in a common organizational environment. In a less individualistic society, organizations and institutions do not yield these opportunities and, as a result, people with entrepreneurial needs are more inclined to start for themselves, as they cannot satisfy their needs within the existing structures.

In another study using Hofstede's indices for culture and self-employment, Acs, Audretsch and Evans, (1994) empirically examine culture and self-employment at the level of nations. They focus primarily on economic explanations and consider culture just marginally. Nevertheless, the authors find that UAI+ and IDV− are related to higher levels of self-employment.

Other research proposes that more than one satisfactory blend of cultural attributes leads to innovation (and thus perhaps to entrepreneurship). Ulijn and Weggeman (2001) propose a fit between certain corporate and national cultures such that depending upon the national culture, different types of corporate cultures that may still obtain equally good results. They identify four types of corporate cultures that may be influenced by national culture including the clan (low in UAI and PDI), the guided missile or well-oiled machine (high UAI and low PID), the family, closed system (low UAI but high PDI) and the Eiffel tower or pyramid of people (high UAI and PDI). Within the proper national context, all types may still lead to appropriate innovation. Thus, these interactions may help to explain some of the contradictions in the literature.

More recent work also attempts to apply Hofstede's indices to the prediction of new product development, which might be viewed as a corollary of entrepreneurship (Nakata and Sivakumar, 1996). Based on a literature review, Nakata and Sivakumar outline some possible new directions to explore linking national culture and firm performance.

Altogether, there are several contradicting hypotheses with respect to the influence of Hofstede's indices of culture on entrepreneurship and/or self-employment. Consistent with the 'aggregate psychological traits' perspective, one might surmise that PDI−, UAI−, MAS+ and IDV+ stimulate entrepreneurship (Shane, 1992; 1993). This is based on the assumption that countries with this cultural profile have relatively more individuals with entrepreneurial values. However, according to the social legitimation perspective, regarding the level of entrepreneurship, the opposite could also be true. Thus, applying the reasoning of Baum et al. (1993) to all four indices, one could argue that 'entrepreneurial' individuals in countries with PDI+, UAI+, MAS−, and IDV− have more difficulties in 'doing things their own way', since organizations and existing structures are less suited to them. Dissatisfied as they are in their situation, they may choose self-employment, to be as independent as possible. The findings of Acs, Audretsch and Evans (1994) empirically confirm this reverse role, at least for the indices UAI+ and IDV−. We refer to this latter interpretation as the 'dissatisfaction hypothesis' in subsequent discussion in this chapter. That is, would-be entrepreneurs are 'pushed' toward self-employment because they are unhappy working in mainstream companies.

## Further Links among Culture, Dissatisfaction and Entrepreneurship

As suggested earlier in the chapter, previous research on dissatisfaction and entrepreneurship suggests that it may well serve as a push factor. Dissatisfaction as a motive at the micro-level has often been confirmed in survey studies with respect to both job mobility and business start-ups (Wennekers et al., 2001). Brockhaus (1982) finds the self-employed to be relatively strongly dissatisfied with several dimensions of job satisfaction, including the work itself, with supervision and with opportunities for promotion (but more satisfied with actual pay). More generally, the state of being out of place or between things (Shapero and Sokol, 1982, p. 81) often precedes the formation of a company. So at the level of the individual, a strong dissatisfaction with life in general is probably associated with a stronger propensity to become self-employed. What exists at the micro-level appears also to exist at the macro-level. We will explore this further with our own data set.

In addition to the direct effects of (dis)satisfaction on entrepreneurship, there may also be indirect effects. Following the logic of the 'dissatisfaction hypothesis', at the macro-level, one might surmise that in cultures where the mainstream corporate cultures (as a reflection of the national culture) are unappealing to potential entrepreneurs, they are then 'pushed' to start their own firms to provide some distance from a culture they find undesirable.

## A Summary of Research Hypotheses to be Tested

In summary of the research to be presented in this chapter, we propose a number of hypotheses as follows at the country level of analysis

### Propositions linking economic variables and level of entrepreneurship
With respect to economic variables, we propose the following:

*Proposition 1.1*　A U-shaped curve is predicted between a nation's economic prosperity and level of entrepreneurship.

*Proposition 1.2*　An inverse relationship is predicted between female labour share and level of entrepreneurship.

*Proposition 1.3*　An inverse relationship is predicted between labour income quota and overall level of entrepreneurship.

*Proposition 1.4*　In principle, a positive relationship is predicted between unemployment and level of entrepreneurship, though for extremely high levels of unemployment, the relationship is expected to reverse itself (inverse U-shaped relationship).

*Proposition 1.5*  Population density is expected to have a U-shaped relationship with level of entrepreneurship.

## Propositions linking culture variables and level of entrepreneurship

With respect to cultural variables, as measured by the Hofstede indices, we state the following propositions. The rationale, in all four of these propositions, consistent with the social legitimation perspective, is that the corporate cultures of the mainstream companies run counter to the entrepreneurial personality, thus 'pushing' these individuals to start their own companies since they cannot satisfy their needs in the existing structures:

*Proposition 2.1*  Countries with higher power distance (PDI+) in the general population will have a higher level of entrepreneurship.

*Proposition 2.2*  Countries with higher uncertainty avoidance (UAI+) in the general population will have a higher level of entrepreneurship.

*Proposition 2.3*  Countries with lower masculinity (MAS−) in the general population will have a higher level of entrepreneurship.

*Proposition 2.4*  Countries with lower individualism (IDV−) in the general population will have a higher level of entrepreneurship.

In addition, we suggest, consistent with Schumpeter's theory and Lynn's work, the following proposition:

*Proposition 2.5*  The greater the competitiveness within the culture, the higher the level of entrepreneurship.

And consistent with Mauro's work:

*Proposition 2.6*  The greater the perceived corruption in mainstream companies, the lower the level of entrepreneurship.

## Propositions linking dissatisfaction and level of entrepreneurship

Finally, with respect to satisfaction with life and with society, and consistent with the overall 'dissatisfaction hypothesis', we propose the following:

*Proposition 3.1*  The lower the satisfaction with life and with society, the higher the level of entrepreneurship.

## 3.   RESEARCH METHOD

### The Variables and the Sample

In order to test our central hypotheses about the influences of economic, cultural and psychological attitude variables on entrepreneurship, data are used from different compiled sources collected by EIM Business and Policy Research and the Institute for Research on Intercultural Cooperation (IRIC). We provide more details regarding the source of data and construction of the variables in the Appendix to this chapter.

### Level of entrepreneurship
As used in this study, level of entrepreneurship is measured on the basis of the number of self-employed per labour force. For the period under study, 1974–94, the data are available for 23 countries (see Table 8.1). Self-employment is measured for 11 periods of time between 1974 and 1994, for each of the even years.

*Table 8.1    The 23 countries studied in the research (in alphabetical order) with their abbreviations*

| | | | | | | | |
|---|---|---|---|---|---|---|---|
| Australia | AUL | France | FRA | Italy | ITA | Portugal | POR |
| Austria | AUT | Germany (W) | GER | Japan | JPN | Spain | SPA |
| Belgium | BEL | Great Britain | GBR | Luxembourg | LUX | Sweden | SWE |
| Canada | CAN | Greece | GRE | Netherlands | NET | Switzerland | SWI |
| Denmark | DEN | Iceland | ICE | New Zealand | NZL | USA | USA |
| Finland | FIN | Ireland | IRE | Norway | NOR | | |

### Economic variables
The economic variables used to predict level of entrepreneurship in this study include the following:

- labour income quota
- population density per square kilometre
- female labour force as a percentage of the total labour force
- per capita income (GDP per capita)
- unemployment as a percentage of the total labour force.

These variables are also available for the 23 countries listed in Table 8.1, and for the even years of the period 1974–94. The main sources are: OECD, Main Economic Indicators; OECD, Labour force statistics 1974–94; and OECD, National Accounts 1960–94, Detailed Tables. For the missing measurement period, data was provided from the Eurostat Labour Force Survey.

### Cultural variables

Measures for the various cultural variables are also derived from a variety of sources, the most important being from Hofstede (1980) and the European Values Studies project (Ester, Halman and De Moor, 1993; Halman, 1990; Harding and Phillips, 1986; Stoetzel, 1983). Different variables are measured during different time periods as described below. Data are missing for a number of countries, depending upon the index. Thus, it was not possible to analyse the culture-related propositions for the full sample of 23 countries.

*Corruption: Mauro's bureaucratic efficiency index*   Mauro's bureaucratic efficiency index is intended as an inverse indicator of the level of corruption in a particular society. That is, the higher the score on bureaucratic efficiency, the lower the corruption level is estimated to be. Mauro's bureaucratic efficiency index was measured between 1980 and 1983 (Mauro, 1995).

*Lynn's competitiveness measure*   Lynn's competitiveness measure is available between 1986 and 1989 (see Lynn, 1991). Data are available for 17 countries. Referring to Table 8.1, these include all but Austria, Denmark, Finland, Italy, Luxembourg and the Netherlands.

*Hofstede's cultural indices*   Hofstede's indices were collected by two different groups of researchers. The original data was collected from 1976 and 1973 and was available for 22 of the 23 countries (excludes Iceland) (Hofstede, 1980).[2] Hoppe also collected cultural data using a version of Hofstede's indices in 1984 (Hoppe, 1990). Hoppe's study overlaps 17 countries from our data set. We use both datasets in order to provide more complete coverage of countries and time periods.

### Dissatisfaction variables

Overall life satisfaction was measured in 1990, 1993 and 1995. Satisfaction with democracy was measured in 1977 and 1993. Satisfaction with society was measured in 1977. The measure for dissatisfaction with life was measured based on the percentage of respondents answering they are 'not at all satisfied with life'. Dissatisfaction with democracy was measured based on the percentage 'not at all satisfied with the way democracy works'. These variables are collected from the Eurobarometer Trends (1994) and are available for 12 European countries (Belgium, Denmark, France, Great Britain, Germany, Greece, Ireland, Italy, Luxembourg, the Netherlands, Portugal and Spain).

**Data Analysis**

The data analysis has three parts. First we present descriptive statistics for self-employment levels by country, including the average level and dispersion during the 1974–94 time period. Second, we present results of the tests of the propositions for bivariate relationships between the various economic, cultural and dissatisfaction indicators and level of entrepreneurship. Third, we examine the effects of satisfaction on level of entrepreneurship while controlling for economic factors. Results for these first three parts of the data analysis are presented in Section 4. Finally, we examine the interaction effects of culture with economic and dissatisfaction variables. Because the Hofstede data is not available during the period for which other time-series data is available, it is used instead as the basis for forming cultural country clusters. The regression results using this clustering technique are presented in Section 5.

## 4. INITIAL RESULTS

### Descriptive Statistics for Level of Entrepreneurship

To get some idea of the differences between countries with respect to their entrepreneurial activity, we calculated for each country the average level of self-employment in the period 1974–94 (see Table 8.2). The countries are grouped partly by language and partly by geography. Where multiple languages are dominant in a culture (for example Switzerland, Belgium and Luxembourg), a country was grouped based on similarities in cultural values, which in turn were based on preliminary analyses using the Hofstede indices. Thus, Switzerland is grouped with Germany and Austria, even though in addition to German, three Romance languages (French, Italian and Romansch) are spoken. Belgium and Luxembourg are grouped with France for the same reason, even though at least one other official language is Germanic (Flemish in the case of Belgium; Letzeburgish in the case of Luxembourg). Bilingual Canada (English–French) rates Anglo-Saxon.

As can be seen from this list, several of the Southern European countries score quite high on self-employment. A less clear pattern emerges for the Anglo-Saxon countries. They are relatively wide apart, with Australia and New Zealand scoring comparatively high, Canada and Great Britain relatively low, and Ireland and the USA in between. Japan, Belgium and France are about average. The Nordic countries, Germanic countries and Luxembourg, score somewhat below the average.

The dispersion shown in Table 8.2 indicates for each country the absolute

Table 8.2   *Average level (and dispersion) of self-employment levels between 1974 and 1994, per country*

| Country | Average disp. | Country | Average disp. | Country | Average disp. |
|---|---|---|---|---|---|
| *Nordic:* | | *Anglo-Saxon:* | | *(Greco-) Latin North* | |
| Denmark | 7.6 (2.8) | (Europe) | | Belgium* | 10.5 (1.7) |
| Finland | 5.7 (3.7) | Great Britain | 8.6 (5.3) | France | 9.5 (2.6) |
| Netherlands | 8.7 (2.0) | Ireland | 10.2 (3.4) | Luxembourg* | 7.8 (4.3) |
| Norway | 8.8 (1.6) | (outside of Europe) | | *(Greco-) Latin South* | |
| Iceland | 8.4 (5.7) | Australia | 13.8 (3.5) | Greece | 18.6 (2.8) |
| Sweden | 6.7 | Canada* | 8.6 (3.7) | Italy | 16.1 (4.0) |
| *Germanic* | | New Zealand | 13.3 (6.7) | Portugal | 11.9 (9.5) |
| Austria | 5.9 (1.3) | USA | 9.9 (1.5) | Spain | 15.5 (2.9) |
| W. Germany | 6.8 (1.5) | | | *Asia:* | |
| Switzerland* | 9.8 (0.9) | | | Japan | 11.2 (2.8) |

*Notes:*
Dispersion refers to the absolute difference between the minimum and the maximum level of self-employment in the period 1974–94.
* Has multiple official languages but grouped based on results of cluster analysis on Hofstede's cultural indices.

difference between the minimum and the maximum level of self-employment in the period 1974–94. In many countries the number of self-employed (per labour force) increased during the 1974–94 period. For example, Portugal's self-employment increased monotonically from 7.9 per cent in 1974 to 17.4 per cent in 1994, that is, 9.5 percentage points, moving from sixteenth to third place. Other countries declined in self-employment. On the other hand, Luxembourg's number of self-employed per labour force decreased monotonically from 9.8 per cent, dropping from tenth to last place. Several countries also have U-shaped functions, including Austria, the Netherlands and New Zealand, dropping during the middle of the period, and then recovering most of or all of the losses in self-employment experienced during the middle of the 20-year period.

To determine how much a country's level of self-employment fluctuates compared to other countries, we calculated the correlations between the self-employment levels in the various years. Although all correlations are significant ($p < .001$), there is a clear progression with weaker correlations between more distant years (for instance with a correlation of .67 between 1974 and 1994). This suggests that a country's entrepreneurial activity compared to other countries is changing, however slowly. In a more recent study by Uhlaner, Thurik and Hutjes (2002), an analysis of variance of 14 OECD countries and 12 observations over the same 20-year period shows that the majority of variation can be explained by country variation ($eta^2 = .88$) rather than time period ($eta^2 = .024$). Taken together, these findings suggest that country provides an important source of explanation for variation in entrepreneurial activity. Its relative stability suggests that certain institutional and/or cultural factors may plan a role in this stability, consistent with conclusions drawn from past research by Hofstede (1980; 2001) and others.

## Economic Variables and Level of Entrepreneurship

### Bivariate relationships between economic variables and level of entrepreneurship

In a first set of analyses, the five economic variables are correlated with level of entrepreneurship for each of the 11 time periods. Of these five, only two – GDP per capita and female labour share – correlate significantly with level of entrepreneurship. In these initial analyses, the other three variables (labour income quota, population density and unemployment) are not significant for the years under study.

The results for GDP per capita clearly show a time-lagged pattern. Whereas the relationship is negative for all periods, it gets stronger for periods closer to and following the 1984 measurement period for GDP.

Thus, the results imply a clear direction of causality: GDP influencing self-employment ($r = -.66$, $p < .001$ for self-employment and prosperity in 1994) rather than the converse ($r = -.37$, non-significant, in 1974).

The direction of the relationship between female labour share and self-employment is less clear. The relationship is indeed negative, as predicted, although in this case, the correlation becomes slightly weaker after the measurement of female labour share in 1984, rather than the reverse ($r = -.62$, $p < .01$ in 1974; $r = -.50$, $p < .05$) raising doubts about the direction of causality for this variable.

*Regression of all five economic variables and level of entrepreneurship*
Table 8.3 shows the results of a regression of the five economic variables on self-employment for the full set of 23 countries. In the first column, the time series of variables are 'pooled' over time, so that we obtain 253 cases (23 countries × 11 years). In this analysis, three of the five economic variables turn out to be significant: female labour share and GDP per capita, both negatively associated with level of entrepreneurship and unemployment, for which the relationship is positive.

**Preliminary discussion of results for propositions 1.1 to 1.5**
Reviewing the results from this section, and based on the use of the data set of 23 countries with time-series data between 1974 and 1994, we can conclude the following. First, there appears to be support for a negative relationship, rather than a U-shaped curve, between a nation's economic prosperity and level of entrepreneurship, at least for the period under study and the countries examined. Thus, proposition 1.1. is not supported, at least for this initial series of analyses.

Second, there does appear to be an inverse relationship between female labour share and level of entrepreneurship, supporting proposition 1.2. However, time-series data casts doubt on the hypothesized direction of causality in the relationship. Third, there is no support for proposition 1.3. In particular, the regression analyses do not support the hypothesis that labour income quota and overall level of entrepreneurship are inversely related. Nor is there support for a linear relationship between population density and level of entrepreneurship, though a multiple regression does not test for curvilinear relationships (proposition 1.5). Finally, there does appear to be support for a positive relationship between unemployment and level of entrepreneurship, supporting the view that unemployment may indeed be a 'push factor' leading people to set up their own firms (proposition 1.4).

Table 8.3   *Regressions on self-employment across 23 countries*

| Variable | Standard Beta | T-Value | Standard Beta | T-value | Standard Beta | T-value |
|---|---|---|---|---|---|---|
| Labour income quota | −0.025 | −0.424 | −0.035 | −0.388 | −0.055 | −0.832 |
| Population density | −0.069 | −1.210 | −0.157 | −1.779 | −0.034 | −0.498 |
| Female labour share | −0.265 | −4.148* | −0.028 | −0.328 | −0.029 | −0.455 |
| GDP per capita | −0.228 | −3.487* | −0.438 | −4.724* | −0.139 | −1.740 |
| Unemployment | 0.226 | 3.919* | 0.126 | 1.455 | 0.121 | 1.776 |
| Dissatisfaction (life) | | | | | 0.483 | 5.228* |
| Dissatisfaction (democracy) | | | | | 0.265 | 3.384* |
| R2 | 0.24 | | 0.32 | | 0.64 | |
| N (countries × time ) | 253 | | 119 | | 119 | |
| N (countries) | 23 | | 12 | | 12 | |

*Note:*   * p<.001.

**Culture Variables and Level of Entrepreneurship**

This section presents results of bivariate analyses between selected culture variables and level of entrepreneurship. In Section 2 we mentioned some cultural determinants that might play a role in determining level of entre- preneurship. These are (among others) Schumpeter's competitiveness (see Lynn, 1991), the bureaucratic efficiency index of Mauro (1995), and Hofstede's indices of power distance, uncertainty avoidance, masculinity and individualism (Hofstede, 1980). We also include measurement of these same four 'Hofstede' indices by Hoppe (1990), to obtain a data point at a different period of time, and during the 20-year interval under study. Note that although each of the culture variables are measured at one point in time only, we correlate them with the level of entrepreneurship for each year (the even years between 1974 and 1994) to check for possible lagged effects. Table 8.4 presents results of these analyses.

In reviewing the results from Table 8.4, the only cultural index among the Hofstede cultural variables that consistently predicts level of entrepreneur- ship is power distance. The other results are equivocal. Thus, whereas uncertainty avoidance is positively associated with level of entrepreneur- ship in the Hofstede study, Hoppe's findings are not significant. Neither study finds support for the link between masculinity and level of entrepren- eurship. Finally, whereas Hoppe's results suggest a positive association between individualism and level of entrepreneurship, Hofstede's index leads to the conclusion that the two variables are not associated with one another.

Competitiveness does appear, on the other hand, to predict level of entre- preneurship with the time-series data suggesting the causal direction to be in the predicted direction. Finally, the bureaucratic efficiency index is neg- atively associated with level of entrepreneurship, implying a positive corre- lation between corruption and level of entrepreneurship.

In spite of the lacklustre results, the stability of the correlations between the various Hofstede and Hoppe measures of culture with level of entre- preneurship are themselves worthy of note. This is consistent with other literature that suggests that culture is a stable part of a country's character- istics (Hofstede, 2001).

**Preliminary discussion of results for propositions 2.1 to 2.6**
Reviewing first the results for Hofstede's culture indices and level of entre- preneurship, we find mixed support for the predictions made in propositions 2.1 to 2.6. The positive relationship found between power distance and level of entrepreneurship is consistent with proposition 2.1. Second, the direction of proposition 2.2 is also supported, however it is only significant in

Table 8.4 *Correlations between level of entrepreneurship and culture variables*

| | Level of entrepreneurship (the number of self-employed per labour force) in the year | | | | | | | | | | |
|---|---|---|---|---|---|---|---|---|---|---|---|
| Variable | 1974 | 1976 | 1978 | 1980 | 1982 | 1984 | 1986 | 1988 | 1990 | 1992 | 1994 |
| Power distance-HF | .47[a] | .47[a] | .49[a] | .55[b] | .54[a] | .55[a] | .52[a] | .52[a] | .49[a] | .49[a] | .46[a] |
| Power distance-HP | .67[b] | .68[b] | .70[b] | .71[b] | .71[b] | .71[b] | .73[c] | .73[c] | .72[b] | .70[b] | .67[b] |
| Uncertainty Avoidance-HF | .52[a] | .52[a] | .54[a] | .57[b] | .56[b] | .56[b] | .55[b] | .54[a] | .51[a] | .52[a] | .49[a] |
| Uncertainty Avoidance-HP | .30 | .31 | .32 | .30 | .33 | .35 | .39 | .42 | .38 | .35 | .32 |
| Masculinity-HF | .23 | .24 | .26 | .24 | .26 | .28 | .30 | .32 | .29 | .23 | .20 |
| Masculinity-HP | .07 | .09 | .13 | .16 | .21 | .24 | .24 | .26 | .28 | .26 | .27 |
| Individualism-HF | -.09 | -.11 | -.13 | -.16 | -.15 | -.13 | -.12 | -.13 | -.15 | -.18 | -.17 |
| Individualism-HP | -.44 | -.49 | -.51[a] | -.53 | -.50[a] | -.48 | -.49 | -.47 | -.49 | -.52[a] | -.52[a] |
| Competitiveness-LY | .34 | .38 | .44 | .43 | .43 | .46 | .50[a] | .55[a] | .54[a] | .54[a] | .55[a] |
| Bureaucratic Efficiency-MA | -.48[a] | -.47[a] | -.49[a] | -.55[b] | -.54[a] | -.58[b] | -.56[b] | -.59[b] | -.63[b] | -.66[c] | -.64[b] |

*Notes:*
Significance levels: a$p < 0.05$, b$p < 0.01$, c$p < 0.001$.
HF = Hofstede index; HP = Hoppe index; LY = Lynn, MA = Mauro.
Year of variable's measurement is underlined (Lynn's competitiveness was measured between 1986 and 1989, Mauro's bureaucratic efficiency index between 1980 and 1983, and Hofstede's indices between 1967 and 1973).

Hofstede's research, not based on the data from Hoppe's smaller group of countries. Further, proposition 2.3, predicting a negative relationship between masculinity and level of entrepreneurship, is definitely not supported. In fact, the correlation coefficients are not only nonsignificant, but (though weakly) in the opposite direction to that predicted. Finally, there is some weak support for proposition 2.4. Based on Hoppe's study, the correlation between individualism and level of entrepreneurship is indeed negative, as predicted, for several of the years. However, this finding does not hold for Hofstede's dataset.

Results linking competitiveness and level of entrepreneurship are more encouraging with significant results during and after the period when competitiveness is first measured (proposition 2.5). However, the range in coefficients for competitiveness also suggests less stability for this trait, possibly in a particular society. Finally, the relationship between corruption and level of entrepreneurship is significant, but in the opposite direction to that proposed in proposition 2.6 but perhaps more in line with the dissatisfaction hypothesis mentioned previously in the chapter.

## Dissatisfaction Variables and Level of Entrepreneurship

We now consider the bivariate relationships between dissatisfaction and level of entrepreneurship. As shown in Table 8.5, overall life satisfaction is consistently, strongly and negatively associated with level of entrepreneurship as measured by self-employment, across the 20-year period. Similar results are found for satisfaction with democracy and societal satisfaction. Moreover, although correlations are significant for each of the 11 time periods, typically the correlations are greater on or after the time in which satisfaction is measured, suggesting a possible lagged effect, that is, that satisfaction appears to influence level of entrepreneurship, rather than the other way around. Take for instance the measure of overall life satisfaction from 1985. Although significant for all 11 periods, the relationship between life satisfaction and level of entrepreneurship is strongest within a few years following measurement, and weakest prior to measurement ($r = -.64$, $p < .05$ in 1974; $r = -.77$, $p < .01$ in 1986; $r = -.73$, $p < .01$ in 1994) (see Table 8.5). These findings support the predictions in proposition 3.1.

One might argue that dissatisfaction is a surrogate for economic variables. Perhaps dissatisfaction is greater in countries that are less prosperous. Table 8.3 presents a multiple regression, which includes both economic, and dissatisfaction variables in the same multiple regression analysis. Controlling for the two dissatisfaction variables, we first observe that some economic variables that were not significant, now are.

Table 8.5  *Most significant correlations between level of entrepreneurship and dissatisfaction*

| Variable | Level of entrepreneurship (the number of self-employed per labour force) in the year | | | | | | | | | | |
|---|---|---|---|---|---|---|---|---|---|---|---|
| | 1974 | 1976 | 1978 | 1980 | 1982 | 1984 | 1986 | 1988 | 1990 | 1992 | 1994 |
| Satisfied with democracy (1977) | −.66 | −.67$^a$ | −.68$^a$ | −.73$^a$ | −.81$^b$ | −.87$^b$ | −.87$^b$ | −.87$^b$ | −.86$^b$ | −.83$^b$ | −.80$^b$ |
| Satisfied with democracy (1993) | −.56 | −.56 | −.57 | −.60$^a$ | −.68$^a$ | −.76$^b$ | −.78$^b$ | −.79$^b$ | −.77$^b$ | −.76$^b$ | −.77$^b$ |
| Satisfied with society (1977) | −.68$^a$ | −.68$^a$ | −.68$^a$ | −.72$^a$ | −.78$^a$ | −.80$^b$ | −.80$^b$ | −.76$^a$ | −.73$^a$ | −.71$^a$ | −.69$^a$ |
| Overall life satisfaction (1985) | −.64$^a$ | −.65$^a$ | −.66$^a$ | −.68$^a$ | −.73$^a$ | −.75$^b$ | −.77$^b$ | −.78$^b$ | −.74$^b$ | −.75$^b$ | −.73$^b$ |
| Satisfied with life (1990, male) | −.58$^a$ | −.60$^a$ | −.63$^a$ | −.71$^b$ | −.74$^b$ | −.81$^c$ | −.82$^c$ | −.83$^c$ | −.81$^c$ | −.82$^c$ | −.79$^c$ |
| Satisfied with life (1990, female) | −.61$^a$ | −.63$^a$ | −.66$^b$ | −.74$^b$ | −.77$^c$ | −.85$^c$ | −.86$^c$ | −.86$^c$ | −.85$^c$ | −.86$^c$ | −.83$^c$ |
| Overall life satisfaction (1993) | −.71$^a$ | −.72$^a$ | −.73$^a$ | −.73$^a$ | −.77$^b$ | −.79$^b$ | −.81$^b$ | −.82$^b$ | −.78$^b$ | −.78$^b$ | −.74$^b$ |

*Notes:*
Significance levels: $^a$p < 0.05, $^b$p < 0.01, $^c$p < 0.001.
Year of measuring variable is underlined (two underlined years: measurement was in the odd year in between).

The explained variance ($R^2$) increases significantly when the dissatisfaction variables are included in the regression. Results do suggest on the one hand that there is some overlap in variation explained. The standardized regression coefficient for GDP per capital decreases considerably when dissatisfaction variables are added to the model. On the other hand, dissatisfaction with life and dissatisfaction with democracy both contribute substantially to overall variation explained (a change in $R^2$ of .32) suggesting that dissatisfaction is an important factor in explaining level of entrepreneurship over and above economic factors.

**Summary of Key Bivariate Findings between Economic, Cultural and Psychological Attitude Variables and Level of Entrepreneurship**

In this section, we summarize the analyses presented to this point. Across countries, the following cultural and non-cultural phenomena are related to self-employment.

- *Wealth.* There is a higher level of entrepreneurship in countries that are relatively poor.
- *Kind of society.* In countries with higher levels of entrepreneurship, the power distance is larger and there is more competitiveness and more corruption. There is also a lower female labour participation.
- *Dissatisfaction with society.* In countries with a higher level of entrepreneurship, people are less satisfied with the kind of society in which they live. They like less the way democracy is functioning and they have less confidence in the legal system.
- *Life satisfaction.* In countries with more self-employment, the overall life satisfaction is lower. Besides, there are larger differences in happiness between the happy and less happy people than in other countries.

## 5.  RESULTS CONTROLLING FOR DIFFERENCES IN CULTURE

In this section we examine the interrelationships among the cultural, economic and psychological attitude variables that predict level of entrepreneurship. We use the Hofstede ratings to cluster countries as an alternative to using the indices in regression analyses. This is done because comparable time-series data is not available. We justify the use of the Hofstede ratings, however, because these ratings are quite stable within cultures (see Hofstede, 1980; 2001). The technique we use enables us to examine whether in different clusters the five economic and the two dissatisfaction variables influence level of entrepreneurship in different ways. Data is available on 22 of the 23 countries (excludes Iceland).

## Clustering of Countries

Each Hofstede index was first used individually to divide the countries into two clusters (PDI+ versus PDI−; UAI+ versus UAI−, MAS+ versus MAS−, and IDV+ versus IDV−). In addition to these four classifications, countries were also divided into two groups based on a cluster technique, using all four of the Hofstede indices based on a technique that uses the K-means algorithm.[3] The results of this latter clustering are referred to in Tables 8.6 and 8.7 as All_4. All_4=1 includes the Nordic (Denmark, Finland, the Netherlands, Norway and Sweden), Anglo-Saxon (Australia, New Zealand, Ireland, the USA, Canada and Great Britain) country clusters. All_4=2 includes the Germanic (Austria, West Germany and Switzerland), both Northern and Southern 'Greco-Latin' countries (Belgium, France, Luxembourg in the North and Greece, Italy, Portugal and Spain in the South) and Japan. Note that the clustering according to the K-means algorithm is fairly similar to the divisions for high and low PDI and UAI, with the exception of the Germanic countries (which in spite of their low PDI and low UAI, were clustered with high PDI and high UAI countries as a result of the K-means algorithm technique).

## Multiple Regressions Controlling for Culture

We now consider regressions for the various country clusters based on the indices of Hofstede, first for the economic variables alone, then together with the dissatisfaction variables. Note that due to limited data availability for the dissatisfaction variables, the latter analyses were done for only 12 of the 23 countries studied in this chapter, so they are not entirely comparable.

### Multiple regressions of economic variables on level of entrepreneurship, controlling for culture

Table 8.6 summarizes the results of multiple regressions based on various clusters. Note that the number of cases used for each analysis equals the product of the number of countries times and number of years in the time series. Thus, for All_4=1, analyses are based on 121 cases (11 countries × 11 years).

Considering Table 8.6, we make the following observations:

- The variable labour income quota (a proxy for earning differentials and assumed to be inversely related) is itself negatively associated

*Table 8.6   Regressions on self-employment in country clusters, excluding dissatisfaction*

| Name of Cluster[a] | Countries included in cluster (number of countries in cluster) | N | $R^2$ | Labour income quota | Population density | Female labour share | GDP per capita | Unemployment |
|---|---|---|---|---|---|---|---|---|
| All_4=1 | Nordic, Anglo-Saxon (11) | 121 | .36 | **−0.29**[c] (−3.45) | **−0.33**[c] (−4.21) | **−0.53**[c] (−4.92) | **0.27**[a] (2.43) | **0.18**[a] (2.35) |
| All_4=2 | Germanic, (Greco-)Latin North and South, JPN (11) | 121 | .48 | **0.19**[a] (2.57) | 0.01 (0.18) | **−0.22**[b] (−2.93) | **0.40**[c] (−5.22) | **0.33**[c] (4.60) |
| PDI− | Nordic, Germanic, Anglo-Saxon (14) | 154 | .34 | **−0.21**[b] (−2.95) | **−0.40**[c] (−5.57) | **−0.53**[c] (−6.18) | **0.322**[c] (3.70) | **0.24**[c] (3.52) |
| PDI+ | (Greco-)Latin North and South, JPN (8) | 88 | .45 | 0.18 (1.94) | −0.04 (−0.43) | −0.13 (−0.46) | **−0.47**[c] (5.14) | **0.31**[c] (3.47) |
| UAI− | Nordic, GER, SWI, Anglo-Saxon (13) | 143 | .38 | **−0.27**[c] (−3.66) | **−0.42**[c] (−5.80) | **−0.54**[c] (−6.24) | **0.30**[c] (3.35) | **0.20**[b] (2.85) |
| UAI+ | (Greco-)Latin North and South, AUT, JPN (9) | 99 | .50 | **0.20**[a] (2.44) | 0.10 (1.31) | **−0.21**[b] (−2.62) | **−0.46**[c] (−5.66) | **0.37**[c] (4.72) |
| MAS− | Nordic, FRA, POR, SPA (8) | 88 | .68 | **−0.39**[c] (−5.93) | **−0.32**[c] (−4.06) | **−0.55**[c] (−6.21) | **−0.17**[a] (−2.19) | **0.30**[c] (4.51) |
| MAS+ | Germanic, Anglo-Saxon, BEL, LUX, GRE, ITA, JPN (14) | 154 | .24 | **0.19**[a] (2.35) | **−0.16**[a] (−2.19) | 0.10 (1.07) | **−0.37**[c] (−3.74) | 0.09 (1.11) |
| IDV− | AUT, GRE, POR, JPN (4) | 44 | .57 | **0.31**[a] (2.05) | 0.25 (1.64) | −0.07 (−0.35) | **−0.63**[c] (−3.89) | 0.09 (0.52) |
| IDV+ | Nordic, Anglo-Saxon, GER, SWI, (Greco-)Latin North, ITA, SPA (18) | 198 | .39 | **−0.28**[c] (−4.84) | **−0.20**[c] (−3.43) | **−0.46**[c] (−6.75) | 0.06 (0.83) | **0.35**[c] (5.78) |

*Notes:*

Significance levels: [a] $p < 0.05$, [b] $p < 0.01$, [c] $p < 0.001$. Tabulated are the standardized regression coefficients (T-values between brackets); coefficients with |T| > 2 are written in bold. Abbreviations used for individual countries are listed in Table 8.1.

Nordic = {DEN, FIN, NET, NOR, SWE}; Germanic = {AUT, GER, SWI}; Anglo-Saxon = {AUL, CAN, GBR, IRE, NZL, USA}; (Greco-) Latin North = {BEL, FRA, LUX}; (Greco-)Latin South = {GRE, ITA, POR, SPA}.

a: 'All_4 = 1' and 'All_4 = 2' are clusters formed by using a K-means algorithm for data on all four Hofstede indices. Other clusters are formed by values on Hofstede indices as shown (low is negative; high is positive).

with level of entrepreneurship for the clusters All_4 = 1, PDI−, UAI−, MAS− and IDV+. For the other clusters the influence is positive (though less significant). This reversal is puzzling and counter to the predictions made in proposition 1.3. Population density always appears with a negative sign when it is significant in the regression equation. The standardized regression coefficient is significant for the following clusters: All_4 = 1, PDI−, UAI−, MAS− and MAS+, and IDV+. These findings are not consistent with the U-shaped relationship posited in proposition 1.5.

- In accordance with proposition 1.2, female labour share always has the (expected) negative relationship with level of entrepreneurship, with the exception of the MAS+ cluster, suggesting that the influence of this variable is independent of culture.
- The sign for GDP per capita varies depending upon the cluster. Thus, it is inversely related with level of entrepreneurship for the clusters PDI+, UAI+, MAS+, MAS− and IDV−. It has a positive influence for most of the other clusters with the exception of IDV+.
- Unemployment always has a positive influence, irrespective of culture, consistent with proposition 1.4. However, the influence is stronger for certain clusters.

### Regressions in Country Clusters, including Dissatisfaction Variables

Now we will consider the 12 countries for which the dissatisfaction variables are given. For each clustering we have first carried out a regression without the dissatisfaction variables, to see whether for the 12 countries the influence of the five economic variables is different than for the 22 countries studied in the previous subsection. Subsequently, we add the two dissatisfaction variables to discern their extra explaining power. Table 8.7 summarizes the results. The clusters according to PDI and UAI involve the same countries and are thus equivalent. The clustering according to IDV is omitted, since IDV− contained only two countries.

Comparing first the regressions for the 'economic variables only' models presented in Table 8.6 (based on 23 countries) and Table 8.7 (based on 12 countries), we see some similarities and differences:

- Labour income quota is only significant in MAS− (negatively) though the signs are still negative for the other subgroups.
- Population density is always negative, but only significant for 'All_4 = 2' and MAS−. Again, however, the signs remain negative, though nonsignificant for the other clusters.

*Table 8.7  Regressions on self-employment in country clusters, including dissatisfaction*

| Country cluster[a] | Countries included in cluster (no. of countries in cluster; total n) | $R^2$ | Dissatisfaction with life | Dissatisfaction with society | Labour income quota | Population density | Female labour share | GDP per capita | Unemployment |
|---|---|---|---|---|---|---|---|---|---|
| All_4=1 | DEN, GBR, IRE, NET (4; 44) | .30 | | | −0.09 (−0.36) | −0.40 (−1.41) | **−0.75[a]** (−2.25) | 0.58 (1.46) | 0.24 (1.17) |
| | | .47 | 0.07 (0.38) | **0.53[b]** (2.74) | −0.06 (−0.28) | **−0.55[a]** (−2.17) | **−1.05[c]** (−3.42) | **1.27[b]** (3.13) | 0.20 (1.04) |
| All_4=2 | GER, (Greco-)Latin North and South (8; 75) | .61 | | | 0.10 (1.09) | **−0.20[a]** (−2.46) | −0.11 (−1.33) | **−0.52[c]** (−6.22) | **0.31[c]** (3.73) |
| | | .76 | −0.04 (−0.27) | **0.44[c]** (4.85) | 0.04 (0.56) | **−0.23[b]** (−2.94) | −0.04 (−0.57) | **−0.47[c]** (−4.98) | **0.16[a]** (2.14) |
| PDI− or UAI− | DEN, GER, GBR, IRE, NET (5; 55) | .35 | | | −0.01 (−0.02) | −0.11 (−0.50) | −0.41 (−1.68) | 0.19 (0.61) | **0.45[b]** (2.71) |
| | | .50 | −0.05 (−0.32) | **0.55[c]** (3.56) | −0.04 (−0.23) | −0.22 (−1.12) | **−0.57[a]** (−2.58) | **0.65[a]** (2.15) | **0.38[a]** (2.51) |
| PDI+ or UAI+ | (Greco-)Latin North and South (7; 64) | .58 | | | 0.14 (1.17) | −0.19 (−1.33) | −0.08 (−0.89) | **−0.59[c]** (−6.32) | **0.28[b]** (3.04) |
| | | .72 | −0.13 (−0.89) | **0.46[c]** (4.47) | 0.07 (0.82) | **−0.22[a]** (−2.52) | −0.02 (−0.28) | **−0.60[c]** (−5.35) | 0.14 (1.62) |
| MAS− | DEN, FRA, POR, SPA, NET (5; 45) | .84 | | | **−0.49[c]** (−5.85) | **−0.53[c]** (−4.86) | **−0.34[c]** (−3.33) | **−0.31[b]** (−3.24) | 0.12 (1.50) |
| | | .87 | **−0.40[b]** (−3.25) | 0.17 (1.91) | **−0.69[c]** (−6.97) | **−0.79[c]** (−5.58) | **−0.38[c]** (−3.65) | **−0.34[c]** (−3.80) | 0.04 (0.56) |
| MAS+ | GER, GBR, IRE, BEL, LUX, GRE, ITA, (7; 74) | .29 | | | 0.20 (1.12) | −0.22 (1.124) | 0.19 (1.12) | −0.29 (−1.68) | 0.13 (0.91) |
| | | .78 | **0.54[c]** (5.20) | **0.39[c]** (4.36) | 0.11 (1.08) | −0.17 (−1.53) | 0.17 (1.65) | 0.07 (0.63) | 0.05 (0.55) |

*Notes:*
Significance levels: [a]p<0.05, [b]p<0.01, [c]p<0.001, two-tailed. Tabulated are the standardized regression coefficients (T-values in parentheses); coefficients with |T|≥2 are written in bold. Abbreviations used for individual countries are listed in Table 8.1. Nordic={DEN, FIN, NOR, SWE}; Germanic={AUT, GER, SWI}; Anglo-Saxon={AUL, CAN, GBR, IRE, NZL, USA}; (Greco-)Latin North={BEL, FRA, LUX}; (Greco-)Latin South={GRE, ITA, POR, SPA}.
a: 'All_4=1' and 'All_4=2' are clusters formed by using a K-means algorithm for data on all four Hofstede indices. Other clusters are formed by values on Hofstede indices as shown (low is negative; high is positive).

- Female labour share is only significant in 'All_4 = 1' and MAS− (negatively). Again, however, signs for other clusters remain in the same directions, including a positive direction for the MAS+ cluster.
- GDP per capita is (again) the most significant variable for the clusters 'All_4 = 2', and PDI+/UAI+. However, the relationship between GDP per capita and level of entrepreneurship is negative for the smaller group of eight countries, opposite to that reported in Table 8.6.
- Female labour share is only significant in 'All_4 = 1' and MAS− (negatively). Again, however, signs for other clusters remain in the same directions, including a positive direction for the MAS+ cluster.
- GDP per capita is (again) the most significant variable for the clusters 'All_4 = 2', and PDI+/UAI+. However, the relationship between GDP per capita and level of entrepreneurship is negative for the smaller group of eight countries, opposite to that reported in Table 8.6.
- Unemployment is always positive, but only significant in 'All_4 = 2', PDI−/UAI−, and PDI+/UAI+. In PDI−/UAI− it is the only significant variable.

Controlling for the two dissatisfaction variables, we first observe that some economic variables that were not significant, now are. For example: in 'All_4 = 1' three of the five economic variables are now significant, whereas only one of them was significant with the dissatisfaction variables excluded. Furthermore, we observe the following:

- The explained variance ($R^2$) increases substantially when the dissatisfaction variables are included in the regression, in all but the MAS− cluster.
- Dissatisfaction with life seems less important as a predictor of level of entrepreneurship than does dissatisfaction with democracy, except when controlled for by masculinity. It appears that in the high masculinity countries (which emphasize material goals), dissatisfaction with life serves as a push factor into entrepreneurship whereas in the low masculinity countries, it leads to the opposite result. Perhaps in the low masculinity countries, dissatisfaction with life has less to do with material wealth (and thus less likely solved via self-employment).
- Dissatisfaction with democracy now plays a very important role (positively). Only in MAS− it is not significant. It is the most significant variable in PDI−/UAI−, and the second most significant variable in PDI+/UAI+ (after GDP per capita).

## Summary of Analyses Testing the Moderating Effects of Culture

Table 8.8 provides a summary of the regression analyses presented in this chapter, including results presented already in Tables 8.3, 8.6 and 8.7. Considering first the economic variables, we see that across all countries that only the economic variables, female labour share (−), unemployment (+), and GDP per capita (−) predict level of entrepreneurship when the full set of 23 countries is included in the analysis. Within country clusters, which control for cultural differences, other economic factors also emerge as important predictors, but in some cases (GDP per capita and labour income quota, most notably) in opposite directions.

*Table 8.8　Significant variables in the regressions on level of entrepreneurship*

**Only economic variables:**
*Across all (23) countries:*
1. Female labour share (−)
2. Unemployment (+)
3. GDP per capita (−)

| *In countries with PDI− or UAI−:* | *In countries with PDI+ or UAI+:* |
|---|---|
| 1. Female labour share (−) | 1. GDP per capita (−) |
| 2. Population density (−) | 2. Unemployment (+) |
| 3. GDP per capita (+) | 3. Female labour share (−) |
| 4. Unemployment (+) | 4. Labour income quota (+) (3 and 4 |
| 5. Labour income quota (−) | only for UAI+) |

**Economic and Dissatisfaction Variables:**
*Across all (12) countries:*
1. Dissatisfaction with life (+)
2. Dissatisfaction with democracy (+)

| *In countries with PDI− or UAI−* | *In countries with PDI+ or UAI+* |
|---|---|
| 1. Dissatisfaction with democracy (+) | 1. GDP per capita (−) |
| 2. Female labour share (−) | 2. Dissatisfaction with democracy (+) |
| 3. Unemployment (+) | 3. Population density (−) |
| 4. GDP per capita (+) | |

When all seven independent variables are included, we see that across all 12 countries in the initial analysis, dissatisfaction with life (+) and with democracy (+) are the most (and the only) significant variables (see Table 8.3). In the country cluster PDI−/UAI−, dissatisfaction with democracy (+), female labour share (−), unemployment (+) and GDP per capita (+) all predict level of entrepreneurship (see Table 8.7). For PDI+/UAI+ the significant variables are GDP per capita (−), dissatisfaction with democracy (+) and population density (−).

Considering this summary, we conclude that the influence of PDI and UAI on the role of the economic variables in explaining self-employment levels is especially clear for GDP per capita and labour income quota. For the PDI−/UAI− cluster, GDP per capita has a positive influence, and for PDI+/UAI+ it is negative. Labour income quota (inversely related to earning differential) is negatively associated with level of entrepreneurship for PDI−/UAI− and positive for PDI+/UAI+ (but for PDI+ not significantly). Across the 12 countries, the positive influence of labour income quota in PDI+/UAI+ is not significant. For the other variables, the signs do not change. The only difference is that some variables lose their significance in the other cluster, or change their order.

## 6. DISCUSSION

### Cultural Variables, Dissatisfaction and Level of Entrepreneurship

The results reported on in Section 4 and Section 5 provide a relatively coherent picture. Countries in which people are less satisfied with life as a whole have a higher level of entrepreneurship. These are societies with larger power distance, stronger uncertainty avoidance, more bureaucracy, more corruption and which are relatively poor. People in these countries are less satisfied with the way their democracy is functioning and with their society in general. Perhaps people in such countries are more easily forced into self-employment because they do not feel comfortable in existing structures and organizations. In other countries, people possibly have more opportunities to find an appropriate job within existing structures and, as a result, are less inclined towards starting for themselves.

The dissatisfaction hypothesis is further confirmed by the results of the regressions in Section 5. Dissatisfaction with life and dissatisfaction with democracy are even stronger determinants of level of entrepreneurship, as measured by self-employment than are the economic variables. The moderating effects of masculinity are interesting. They suggest that perhaps in future research, it may be helpful to distinguish between the effects of dissatisfaction in more or less post-materialistic societies. This is consistent with research findings by Uhlaner, Thurik and Hutjes (2002) who find a negative relationship between post-materialism and level of entrepreneurship. Taken together with the findings from our own studies, these results suggest that dissatisfaction with life may be a stronger push factor toward entrepreneurship in positive masculinity (that is, materialistic) cultures because material wealth and satisfaction with life are themselves more closely linked in such cultures. Future research should explore these connections in more detail.

## Economic and Demographic Variables and Level of Entrepreneurship

Reviewing the results for economic variables and level of entrepreneurship, other trends also emerge. First, we find a positive relationship between unemployment and level of entrepreneurship. Unemployment can be seen as a push factor in all countries. Since a negative relation was never found, we conclude that in the countries considered the unemployment rate generally remained below the level where it discourages people to start a business.

With respect to prosperity, a negative correlation with self-employment dominates. However, when cultural clusters are distinguished, sometimes (for example, in PDI− or UAI− clusters) a positive relation is found. Since the countries in for instance the PDI− cluster are relatively affluent and those in PDI+ are less prosperous, these findings are in conformity with the U-shaped relationship between self-employment and prosperity, as hypothesized in Section 2. In countries that have a relatively low level of GDP per capita, there is a negative relation due to the yet unexploited possibilities for economies of scale. In countries with a high level of GDP per capita, there is a positive relationship because a change toward greater differentiation of markets, dis-economies of scale and movement toward a service economy (also known as 'tertiarization') has set in.

Since prosperity is negatively correlated with power distance, as well as with uncertainty avoidance (albeit weakly), and positively with individualism (see Hofstede, 1991), it is likely that it is the level of prosperity that provides an indirect link between these cultural dimensions and self-employment. The triangular relationship between cultural dimensions, prosperity and self-employment obviously deserves further research.

Concerning labour income quota, only in some cases do we find significant evidence for the expected negative relation with self-employment (implying that a higher level of profitability is a stimulus towards self-employment). When (cultural) clusters are distinguished, a positive relationship is sometimes found (for instance in UAI+ and IDV−), which is not confirmed by theory. This may, however, be due to a reversed causality when a high level of self-employment causes a low level of profitability. In a country with little social security and a low supply of jobs, this situation may perpetuate itself. At the same time, the compensation of entrepreneurial labour is also counted within the labour income quota, which may cause a statistical artefact.

Population density appears to be negatively related to level of entrepreneurship, which implies that the minimum level of provisions (shops, crafts) needed in thinly populated areas and the effect of economies of scales in densely populated areas overrule the effect of the attractiveness of networks.

Finally, as predicted, the overall proportion of women in the labour force is negatively associated with the level of entrepreneurship. This is not to say, however, that the overall proportion of women in the labour force has a negative impact on the growth of female entrepreneurship, as pointed out by Verheul et al. (2002).

## 7.   CONCLUSIONS

The determinants of level of entrepreneurship are complex (Audretsch et al., 2002). But as far as national differences are concerned, one clear determinant appears: dissatisfaction with society and with life in general. Across nations, dissatisfaction with society in particular seems to be a distinguishing factor even controlling for different cultural characteristics.

Two caveats are appropriate here. First, the relationship between dissatisfaction and self-employment holds across nations, and may not be true for individuals within countries. It might be that dissatisfaction also plays a role within countries as is often stated in the literature, but this cannot be concluded from this cross-national study. Secondly, one must be prudent in extrapolating the conclusions found in this study to worldwide relationships. This study is based on Western countries (with the exception of Japan). Further research is needed to test our conclusions for different country samples. In particular, this study is based primarily on more affluent cultures based on Western traditions. But this limitation does not disqualify important findings from this study, which shows that even within Western countries, national culture may have powerful moderating effects on the relationship between economic and attitude variables on the level of entrepreneurship.

In sum, we draw the following inferences from our research. The cultures of relatively poor countries can often be characterized by large power distance and low individualism, and often also by strong uncertainty avoidance (at least in the Western countries). At the same time, their population is often relatively dissatisfied with society and life in general. All these circumstances give rise to a high incidence of (small-scale) self-employment. When these countries develop further economically, they start reaping hitherto unexploited economies of scale, prosperity rises and dissatisfaction seems to diminish. The result is a definite decline of level of entrepreneurship. Finally, when countries are fully industrialized and a service economy sets in, several countervailing forces seem to dominate the scene. First, information technology and differentiation of markets create dis-economies of scale and invite new, innovative entrepreneurship. Simultaneously, a high level of satisfaction with life in these societies may, however, slow down the drive towards entrepreneurship. But when unemployment increases for a longer period, due to the transition to the knowledge-based economy, this may again elicit new (and perhaps marginal) business start-ups. As far as cultural characteristics are concerned, individualism has been documented to rise with increasing wealth (Hofstede, 2001). There are no clear indications of the influence of economic development on other cultural characteristics.

## APPENDIX: ECONOMIC DATA – DEFINITIONS AND SOURCES

The following countries are in the estimation sample (1974–94):

| | | | |
|---|---|---|---|
| Austria | Greece | Spain | USA |
| Belgium | Ireland | Sweden | Japan |
| Denmark | Italy | UK | Canada |
| Finland | Luxembourg | Iceland | Australia |
| France | Netherlands | Norway | New Zealand |
| Germany (W.) | Portugal | Switzerland | |

The main definitions and sources are listed below.

### 1.  Self-employment

There are several definitional aspects to the concept of self-employment or business ownership, which have to be taken into account when measuring the number of self-employed. First one must distinguish between four different categories of self-employment. These are the owners of enterprises that are not legally incorporated, the owner/managers of incorporated businesses, so-called unpaid family workers and wage-and-salary workers operating a side-business as a secondary work activity.[4]

Self-employment as defined in the present report includes the owners of both incorporated and unincorporated businesses, but excludes the other categories. Data on the number of self-employed used in this report are taken from the OECD Labour Force Statistics 1974–94. However, in the OECD statistics the definitions of self-employed were not fully compatible between countries. In some countries self-employed are strictly defined as individuals owning a business that is not legally incorporated. In other countries, owner/managers of an incorporated business who gain profits as well as a salary, are also considered self-employed. Australia, Canada, Denmark, France, Ireland, the Netherlands, New Zealand, Norway, Portugal, Spain and the USA use the narrow definition, while the other countries apply the broader characterization. For the countries not following the broader definition, EIM made an estimation of the number of owner/managers by using information derived from statistical bureaus in these countries. Another difference in definition is that in some countries unpaid family workers are included in the data of self-employed as well. The unpaid family workers were eliminated from the data by using ratios derived from other variables, recent years or other domestic sources. This work has resulted in a unified data set of self-employed persons, which includes the owners of both the incorporated and unincorporated businesses but excludes the unpaid family workers. As far as we know the data set also exclude side-businesses. In this data set possible discontinuities in time series have not been corrected for.

Finally, the number of self-employed, as defined above, was expressed as a percentage of the labour force. Data on the labour force were also taken from the OECD Labour Force Statistics 1974–94. Again, some missing data have been filled up from other sources.

## 2. Gross Domestic Product per Capita

The underlying variables gross domestic product and total population are from OECD, National Accounts 1960–94, Detailed Tables, and from the OECD Labour Force Statistics 1974–94, respectively. Gross domestic product is measured in constant prices of 1990. Furthermore, purchasing power parities per US$ in 1990 are used to make the monetary units comparable between countries.

## 3. Unemployment Rate

This variable measures the number of unemployed as a fraction of the total labour force. Employees, self-employed persons, unpaid family workers, people who work in the army and unemployed persons form the labour force. The main source for this variable is OECD Main Economic Indicators. Some missing data on the number of unemployed have been filled up with help of data from the OECD Labour Force Statistics and the Yearbook of Labour Statistics from the International Labour Office.

### 4. Labour Income Quota

The following definition is used. Total compensation of employees is multiplied by the proportion total employment/number of employees to correct for the imputed wage income for the self-employed persons. Next, the number obtained is divided by total income (compensation of employees plus other income). The data on the separate variables are from the OECD, National Accounts 1960–94, Detailed Tables. Some missing data have been filled up with help of data from the OECD Labour Force Statistics.

## NOTES

1. Cultural traits are not directly included in the regressions, since they are not available in time series.
2. For Luxembourg, estimates were provided by the Institute for Training in Intercultural Management (ITIM) and are based on extensive data from training sessions.
3. Given a Hofstede index, the two corresponding clusters are determined using the K-means algorithm. In this algorithm the countries are assigned in turn to the nearest of the two cluster centres (which are initialized as the lowest and the highest score among the 22 countries). When all cases have been added, each cluster centre is updated as the average score of the countries it contains. This process iterates until the solution converges.
4. For more information on the various measures of self-employment, see *The State of Small Business; A Report of the President 1986*, Washington: US Government Printing Office, ch. 4.

## REFERENCES

Acs. Z.J. (1992), 'Small business economics; a global perspective', *Challenge*, **35**, 38–44.
Acs, Z.J., D.B. Audretsch and D.S. Evans (1994), 'The determinants of variations in self-employment rates across countries and over time'. Mimeo.
Audretsch, D.B. and A.R. Thurik (2000), 'Capitalism and democracy in the 21st century: from the managed to the entrepreneurial economy', *Journal of Evolutionary Economics*, **10** (1), 17–34.
Audretsch, D.B. and A.R. Thurik (2001), 'What is new about the new economy: sources of growth in the managed and entrepreneurial economies', *Industrial and Corporate Change*, **10** (1), 267–315.
Audretsch, D.B., M.A. Carree and A.R. Thurik (2001), 'Does entrepreneurship reduce unemployment?', *Tinbergen Institute Discussion Paper TI01-074/3*, Erasmus University, Rotterdam.
Audretsch, D.B., A.R. Thurik, I. Verheul and A.R.M. Wennekers (eds) (2002), *Entrepreneurship: Determinants and Policy in a European–US Comparison*, Boston and Dordrecht: Kluwer Academic.
Bais, J., W.H.M. van der Hoeven and W.H.J. Verhoeven (1995), *Determinanten van Zelfstandig Ondernemerschap*, Den Haag: OSA (in Dutch).
Barnouw, V. (1979), *Culture and Personality*, Homewood, IL: Dorsey Press.
Baum, J.R., J.D. Olian, M. Erez, E.R. Schnell, K.G. Smith, H.P. Sims, J.S. Scully

and K.A. Smith (1993), 'Nationality and work role interactions: a cultural contrast of Israeli and U.S. entrepreneurs' versus managers' needs', *Journal of Business Venturing*, **8**, 499–512.

Blau, D. (1987), 'A time series analysis of self-employment', *Journal of Political Economy*, **95**, 445–67.

Brock, W.A. and D.S. Evans (1989), 'Small business economics', *Small Business Economics*, **1**, 7–20.

Brockhaus, R. (1982), 'The psychology of the entrepreneur', in C. Kent, D. Sexton and K. Vesper (eds), *Encyclopedia of Entrepreneurship*, Englewood Cliffs, NJ: Prentice-Hall.

Busenitz, L.W., C. Gómez, and J.W. Spencer (2000), 'Country institutional profiles: unlocking entrepreneurial phenomena', *Academy of Management Journal*, **43** (5), 994–1003.

Carree, M.A. and A.R. Thurik (2003), 'The impact of entrepreneurship on economic growth', in D.B. Audretsch and Z.J. Acs (eds), *Handbook of Entrepreneurship Research*, Boston and Dordrecht: Kluwer Academic Publishers, 437–71.

Carree, M.A., A.J. van Stel, A.R. Thurik and A.R.M. Wennekers (2002), 'Economic development and business ownership: an analysis using data of 23 OECD countries in the period 1976–1996', *Small Business Economics*, **19** (3), 271–90.

Davidsson, P. (1995), 'Culture, structure and regional levels of entrepreneurship', *Entrepreneurship and Regional Development*, **7**, 41–62.

Ester, P., L. Halman and R. de Moor (eds) (1993), *The Individualizing Society: Value Change in Europe and North America*, Tilburg: Tilburg University Press.

Etzioni, A. (1987), 'Entrepreneurship, adaptation and legitimation: a macro-behavioural perspective', *Journal of Economic Behaviour and Organization*, **8**, 175–89.

Eurobarometer Trends 1974–93 (1994), Brussels: European Commission.

European Commission (1999), *Action Plan to Promote Entrepreneurship and Competitiveness*, Brussels: Directorate-General for Enterprise.

Evans, D.S. and L.S. Leighton (1989), 'The determinants of changes in US self-employment, 1968–1987', *Small Business Economics*, **1**, 111–19.

Evans, D.S. and L.S. Leighton (1990), 'Small business formation by unemployed workers', *Small Business Economics*, **2**, 319–30.

EZ (1999), *The Entrepreneurial Society. More Opportunities and Fewer Obstacles for Entrepreneurship*, Den Haag: Ministry of Economic Affairs.

Foti, A. and M. Vivarelli (1994), 'An econometric test of the self-employment model: the case of Italy', *Small Business Economics*, **6**, 81–93.

Halman, L. (1990), *Waarden in de Westerse Wereld: Een Internationale Exploratie van de Waarden in de Westerse Samenleving*, Tilburg: Tilburg University Press (in Dutch).

Hamilton, R.T. (1989), 'Unemployment and business formation rates: reconciling time series and cross-sections', *Environment and Planning A*, **11**, 249–55.

Harding, S. and D. Phillips, with M. Fogarty (1986), *Constrasting Values in Western Europe*, London: Macmillan.

Hofstede, G. (1980), *Culture's Consequences: International Differences in Work-Related Values*, Beverly Hills, CA: Sage.

Hofstede, G. (1991), *Cultures and Organizations: Software of the Mind*, London: McGraw-Hill.

Hofstede, G. (2001), *Culture's Consequences; Comparing Values, Behaviours, Institutions and Organizations Across Nations*, 2nd edition, Thousand Oaks, CA: Sage.

Hoppe, M.H. (1990), 'A comparative study of country elites: international differences in work-related values and learning and their implications for international management training and development', PhD thesis, University of North Carolina at Chapel Hill.

Huisman, D. (1985), 'Entrepreneurship: economic and cultural influences on the entrepreneurial climate', *European Research*, **13** (4), 10–17.

Huisman, D. and W.J. de Ridder (1984), *Vernieuwend Ondernemen*, Utrecht: SMO (in Dutch).

Huntington, S.P (1996), *The Clash of Civilizations and the Remaking of World Order*, London: Simon and Schuster.

Klundert, T. van de (1997), *Groei en instituties; Over de oorzaken van economische ontwikkeling*, Tilburg: Tilburg University Press (in Dutch).

Kroeber, A.L. and T. Parsons (1958), 'The concepts of culture and of social system', *American Sociological Review*, **23**, 582–3.

Lee, S.M. and S.J. Peterson (2000), 'Culture, entrepreneurial orientation, and global competitiveness', *Journal of World Business*, **35** (4), 401–16.

Lucas, R.E. Jr (1978), 'On the size distribution of business firms', *Bell Journal of Economics*, **9**, 508–23.

Lynn, R. (1991) *The Secret of the Miracle Economy: Different National Attitudes to Competitiveness and Money*, London: The Social Affairs Unit.

Mauro, P. (1995), 'Corruption and growth', *Quarterly Journal of Economics*, **110** (3), 681–712.

McClelland, D.C. (1961), *The Achieving Society*. Princeton, NJ: Van Nostrand.

McClelland, D.C. (1976), *The Achieving Society*, Princeton, NJ: Van Nostrand.

McGrath, R.G. and I.C. MacMillan (1992), 'More like each other than anyone else? Cross-cultural study of entrepreneurial perceptions', *Journal of Business Venturing*, **7** (5), 419–29.

McGrath, R.G., I.C. MacMillan and S. Scheinberg (1992), 'Elitists, risk-takers, and rugged individualists? An exploratory analysis of cultural differences between entrepreneurs and non-entrepreneurs', *Journal of Business Venturing*, **7**, 115–35.

Meager, N. (1992), 'Does unemployment lead to self-employment?', *Small Business Economics*, **4**, 87–103.

Mueller, S.L. and A.S. Thomas (2000), 'Culture and entrepreneurial potential: a nine country study of locus of control and innovativeness', *Journal of Business Venturing*, **16**, 51–75.

Nakata, C. and K. Sivakumar (1996), 'National culture and new product development: an integrative review', *Journal of Marketing*, **60** (1), 61–72.

North, D.C. and R.P. Thomas (1973), *The Rise of the Western World: A New Economic History*, Cambridge: Cambridge University Press.

OECD (1998a), *Fostering Entrepreneurship: The OECD Jobs Strategy*, Paris: OECD.

OECD (1998b), *Women Entrepreneurs in Small and Medium Enterprises*, OECD Conference, Paris, 1997, Paris: OECD.

OECD (2000), *OECD Employment Outlook*, Paris: OECD.

Olson, M. (1982), *The Rise and Decline of Nations; Economic Growth, Stagflation and Social Rigidities*, New Haven, CT, and London: Yale University Press.

Reynolds, P.D., D.J. Storey and W. Westhead (1994), 'Cross national comparisons of the variation of new firm formation rates', *Regional Studies*, **28** (4), 443.

Reynolds, P.D., M. Hay, W.D. Bygrave, S.M. Camp and E. Autio (2000), *Global Entrepreneurship Monitor: 2000 Executive Report*, Kauffman Center for

Entrepreneurial Leadership, London: Apex Partners Co Ltd and London Business School.

Santarelli, E. and A. Sterlacchini (1994), 'New firm formation in Italian industry', *Small Business Economics*, **6**, 95–106.

Schumpeter, J.A. (1934), *The Theory of Economic Development*, Cambridge, MA: Harvard University Press.

Shane, S.A. (1992), 'Why do some societies invent more than others?', *Journal of Business Venturing*, **7**, 29–46.

Shane, S.A. (1993), 'Cultural influences on national rates of innovation', *Journal of Business Venturing*, **8**, 59–73.

Shapero, A. and L. Sokol (1982), 'The social dimensions of entrepreneurship', in C. Kent, D. Sexton and K. Vesper (eds), *Encyclopedia of Entrepreneurship*, Englewood Cliffs, NJ: Prentice-Hall.

Stanworth, M.J.K. and J. Curran (1973), *Management Motivation in the Smaller Business*, London: Gower Press.

Stoetzel, J. (1983), *Les Valeurs du Temps Present*, Paris: Presses Universitaires de France (in French).

Teece, D.J. (1993), 'The dynamics of industrial capitalism: perspectives on Alfred Chandler's scale and scope', *Journal of Economic Literature*, **31**, 199–225.

Thurik, A.R. (1996), 'Small firms, entrepreneurship and economic growth', in P.H. Admiraal (ed.), *Small Business in the Modern Economy*, Oxford: Basil Blackwell, pp. 126–52.

Tiessen, J.H. (1997), 'Individualism, collectivism, and entrepreneurship: a framework for international comparative research', *Journal of Business Venturing*, **12**, 367–84.

Uhlaner, L., R. Thurik and J. Hutjes (2002), 'Post-materialism and entrepreneurial activity: a macro perspective', *Proceedings, the 2002 Small Business and Entrepreneurship Development Conference*, 15–16 April, University of Nottingham.

Ulijn, J. and M. Weggeman (2001), 'Towards an innovation culture: what are its national, corporate, marketing, and engineering aspects, some experimental evidence', in C. Cooper, S. Cartwright and C. Early (eds), *Handbook of Organizational Culture and Climate*, London: Wiley, pp. 487–517.

Uxem. F.W. van and J. Bais (1996), *Het Starten van een Bedrijf; Ervaringen van 2000 Starters*, EIM: Zoetermeer (in Dutch).

Verheul, I., S. Wennekers, D. Audretsch and A.R. Thurik (2002), 'An eclectic theory of entrepreneurship', in D.B. Audretsch, A.R. Thurik, I. Verheul and A.R.M. Wennekers (eds), *Entrepreneurship: Determinants and Policy in a European–US Comparison*, Boston and Dordrecht: Kluwer Academic.

Weber, M. (1904), *The Protestant Ethic and the Spirit of Capitalism*, translated by T. Parsons, New York: Scribner, 1929.

Wennekers, A.R.M. and A.R. Thurik (1999), 'Linking entrepreneurship and economic growth', *Small Business Economics*, **13**, 27–55.

Wennekers, A.R.M., L.M. Uhlaner and A.R. Thurik (2002), 'Entrepreneurship and its conditions: a macro perspective, *International Journal of Entrepreneurship Education*, **1** (1), 25–64.

Wennekers, A.R.M., N.G. Noorderhaven, G. Hofstede and A.R. Thurik (2001), 'Cultural and economic determinants of business ownership across countries', in W.D. Bygrave et al. (eds), *Frontiers of Entrepreneurship Research 2001*, Wellesley, MA: Babson College, 179–90.

Wiener, M.J. (1981), *English Culture and the Decline of the Industrial Spirit 1850–1980*, Cambridge: Cambridge University Press.

# 9. Towards cooperation between European start-ups: the position of the French, Dutch and German entrepreneurial and innovative engineer

**Jan Ulijn and Alain Fayolle**

## 1. INTRODUCTION

People who want to start their own business often try to survive or die again on their own. The very fact is that 'others', apart from family, friends and fools who invest in their venture, are quickly seen as probable competitors, who want to steal the idea, prevent start-ups from cooperation with partners. Setting up a personal network might even cause more risk, since one has to share ideas for technological development of the idea or look for a market for it. The consequence is that within five years most new start-ups are already out of business (OECD, 1998). The key would be cooperation with others, but with whom and to what extent? Since most of the engineers know that to develop an innovation, they might need anything up to a whole R&D laboratory to help, they might be less reluctant to cooperate than others. On the other hand, they might forget to look for a market or cooperate with a potential customer to design the product, for instance in the ICT-sector (see van Luxemburg, Ulijn and Amare, 2002), because of a technology push syndrome.

Authors, such as Birley (1985) and Aldrich and Zimmer (1986) have not failed during the last 10 years to develop the idea of, and study the effect of, networking and strategic alliancing between start-ups, entrepreneurship as teamwork and at least a shared concept for starters who have the same objective in mind. University incubators, such as the one at Imperial College in London are very successful in promoting this concept (see Theunissen, 2002), but is this the case only in the UK or the USA, where the culture of free enterprise is more strongly developed? What about countries, such as France, the Netherlands and Germany? What is the position, for instance, of the entrepreneurial and innovative engineer who wants to start his/her own business? May a lack of cooperation or a fear of cooperating with others be a result of how engineers traditionally are educated in those countries? In 1998 Albert Rubinstein identified technical entrepreneurship in the firm as the focus of the future of our intellectual discourse on technology and innovation management. How entrepreneurial are French, German and Dutch engineers, and what is their innovation culture and that of the firms in which they work? Are those who are leaving those firms to start their own businesses, willing to cooperate with others, and do they not fade away in splendid isolation?

To tackle these questions a few definitions are needed with some international scope. In their strategic definition Hitt and Reed (2000, p. 24) link entrepreneurship to innovation right away:

> Entrepreneurship is a way of thinking and doing things that transforms innovation into market opportunities or competitive advantage.

Who is an entrepreneur? Kao (1997) defines as follows:

> An entrepreneur is a person who undertakes a wealth-creating and value adding process, through incubating ideas, assembling resources and making things happen.

Several authors since Schumpeter (1934), have underlined a definition of innovation should always imply an entrepreneurial mindset: an innovation has to be implemented to lead to a marketable product, an entrepreneur is a person of ideas and actions who looks constantly for new product and market opportunities (see Drucker, 1985; Mueller and Thomas, 2000; the authors they cite; and Ulijn and Weggeman, 2001, the latter more for the relation between innovation and culture as a mindset). We might summarize the definitions of innovation mentioned in those sources as follows:

> Innovating is a group process that is characterized by its multidisciplinary character and its (limited) controllability, and this process leads to an innovation, which is a new product, process or service or a part of those.

This definition indicates well the cooperation element of this process, which is also evident in the concept of *international* entrepreneurship, although this is still seen too much as doing things abroad in marketing terms (see the literature cited by Kandasaami and Wood, 1996), than thinking and innovating through networking or strategic alliancing. The impressive comparison of 18 multinational corporation (MNC) cases of global innovation (six in each of the following sectors: pharmaceutical, chemical and food, the electronics and software industry, and the electrical and machinery industry), with DuPont, Canon and ABB as best in class in each sector by Boutellier, Gassmann and von Zedwitz (1999), might lead to recommendations to intrapreneurship within those firms, but is not linked to spinned out start-ups as a result of that innovation management process. We all are aware, of course, that MNCs in crisis often lead to the birth of numerous start-ups, as the Eindhoven area in the Netherlands in the 1990s has shown. The ASML company, as a spin-out of the Philips R&D laboratories with its chip-making equipment is just one of them. Although some small firms might be dependent only on an international market, the very start of small business development might be too often a strict national, regional or, even, individual affair. (International) cooperation seems not to be on the agenda of the would-be entrepreneur. A missed opportunity? What is his or her position, for instance, on the European scene?

## 2.   A MODEL OF THE ENTREPRENEURIAL AND INNOVATIVE EUROPEAN ENGINEER AND HIS/HER INTERACTION WITH THE ENVIRONMENT: NETWORKS AND COOPERATION

Entrepreneurship theory, as summarized by Kandasaami and Wood (1996) encompasses a broad range of perspectives: sociocultural, population ecological, economic, psychological and, last but not least, as discussed above, international. Those perspectives all affect the personal environment of the technology entrepreneur in his/her start-up. He/she, therefore, needs to have a global vision, a pioneering-innovative motive, networking skills, trustworthiness, tolerance for cultural differences, tolerance for ambiguity and locus of control. To cooperate entrepreneurs need to access all those characteristics, because who can master all this on his/her own? On the other hand, as the study by Paffen (1998) on career paths by Dutch engineers towards general management shows, these can be signposted by experiential, evolutionary, transdisciplinary and for cooperation, above all, interactive aspects. In the career from technical professional, via line manager and division director to top manager, management, entrepreneurship and leadership (in this time line) are important steps in personal development (ibid., p. 317). One of the recommendations is *Think as an entrepreneur* (or intrapreneur within a firm). Interaction is key also in entrepreneurship, as the French study by Fayolle and Livian (1995) and Fayolle (1996) pinpoints. How can cooperation create value for the technology entrepreneur to support his/her personal, economic and social environment? This chapter cannot answer all the above questions with respect to entrepreneurship and cooperation, but it can try to develop a model of the entrepreneurial and innovative European engineer and his/her interaction with the environment (see next section) through networks and cooperation illustrated with examples from countries, such as France, the Netherlands and Germany.

**Presentation of our Model**

Figure 9.1 shows an interactive model of the entrepreneurial and innovative engineer in his/her personal (and also professional) environment.

In Figure 9.1, which comes from a previous study (Fayolle, 2002), two logics meet within a process where interaction is a key element. The first logic (logic of the subject) concerns the individual, in our perspective the engineer. The engineer, any engineer, is, in a certain way an entrepreneur who is not necessarily aware of it, and whose personal and professional life is made up of a variety of different stages. The first stage, at which the engineer can remain all his life, is characterized by an indifference towards (or unawareness of) entrepreneurship. Any engineer can, according to influences through interactions, develop a taste for entrepreneurship, which we define as an inclination, a desire to begin an entrepreneurial process. An engineer who shows entrepreneurial inclination is someone who is aware of, or sensitive to, entrepreneurship as we can observe in a study on the entrepreneurial behaviours of the French engineers (Fayolle, 1996). This propensity can develop towards an entrepreneurial intention. For many years, the theory of planned behaviour, initially proposed by Ajzen (1991), has been used to model entrepreneurial intention (Autio et al., 1997; Kolvereid, 1996; Krueger and Carsrud, 1993; Tkachev and Kolvereid, 1999). This, and other theories, comes from the fields of sociology and psychology. The intention often, but not always, precedes entrepreneurial behaviour, which suggests both a decision to act and an involvement in entrepreneurial action. The final stage is the appraisal (advantages and benefits at an individual level) of the results of the entrepreneurial action.

In this progression, each engineer can acquire and develop entrepreneurial potential, defined as a collection of personal resources (knowledge, experience, skills, relations, networks, ... ), which are useful for entrepreneurial action. The path, which leads an engineer to setting up a business, is strongly influenced by his initial training, by the social status of the school from which he/she graduated, by the professional experience, which he/she has acquired, by the technical skills, which he/she has developed, and by some personal factors. This path leads to very contrasting entrepreneurial profiles, as we have seen in a previous work (Fayolle, Ulijn and Nagel, 2002).

The second logic (logic of the object), we are showing in our model, concerns the creation of value, or rather the intangible and/or tangible support

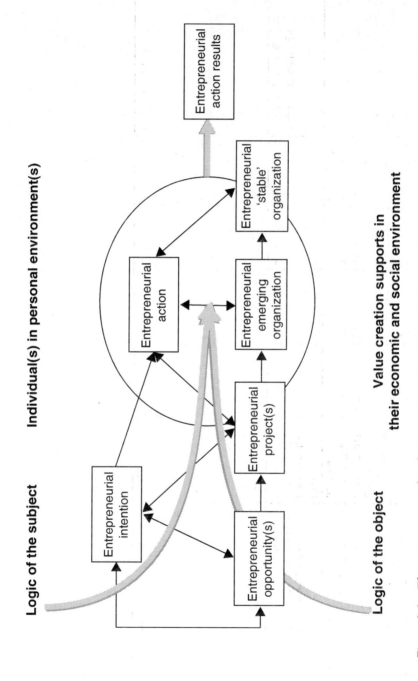

**Logic of the subject**

**Individual(s) in personal environment(s)**

Entrepreneurial
intention

Entrepreneurial
action

Entrepreneurial
action results

Entrepreneurial
'stable'
organization

Entrepreneurial
emerging
organization

Entrepreneurial
project(s)

Entrepreneurial
opportunity(s)

**Value creation supports in
their economic and social environment**

**Logic of the object**

*Figure 9.1    The entrepreneurial and innovative engineer in his/her personal environment*

for the creation of value and the notions, which are used to describe it. This support has varying value-creating potential, which can be freed and expressed under certain conditions. If we look at this second logic, the first step is probably the entrepreneurial first idea (not mentioned in Figure 9.1), which an engineer can have and which can turn out to be an entrepreneurial opportunity following a study of the environment in question and an initial assessment of possibilities. Following the opportunity, the entrepreneurial project begins to take shape, get a structure and possibly become the object of material formalization. The fact of using concepts of opportunity and project means that there will be interaction, transactions and co-operations with the environments and professional and/or personal milieu. The importance of these relations is probably in relation with the intensity and the level of technological innovation in the entrepreneurial project (Mustar, 1997). The next stage corresponds to the emergence of the entrepreneurial organization. Imagined, visualized, formalized and proportioned in the project stage, it will come in existence at the launching time. The final stage is the creation of a 'stable' entrepreneurial organization or a new firm, which can be assessed using business performance and results indicators.

In this second logic, each stage contains a varying potential for the creation of value which depends on the quality of the observations, the entrepreneurial orientation, the marketing orientation, the processing of information, the quality of environment interactions and, finally, the aptness of the choices made by the engineer within his/her process. However, the 'real' creation of value only happens at the end of the process and this raises the question of the best transformation of a given potential of value creation through an organizational set-up, a level of resources and strategic moves and decisions.

The main interest of our model is to suggest that even if it is necessary to take into consideration each of these two logics, the one of the entrepreneurial and innovative engineer and the one of the value creation material, the best way to develop a comprehensive view of this phenomenon is to analyse the engineer-value creation material couple in a more systemic approach. On the one hand, the entrepreneur engineer profile influences the entrepreneurial action results and, on the other hand, the nature of the entrepreneurial opportunity or the characteristics of the entrepreneurial project influences and probably changes the initial orientation of the entrepreneurial engineer. One of the stronger consequences of this could be seen by discovering the entrepreneurial behaviour differences of two contrasted profiles of entrepreneur engineers, those who are technology orientated and those who are management and/or market orientated (Fayolle, 2001). To give, here, a few insights: the former is launching industrial activities, developing new technologies, innovating in technologies, using technological networks, choosing partners and associates among engineers and scientists; the latter is launching a wider range of activities, innovating in product and service areas, choosing managers and not engineers as partners or associates, financing his/her enterprise through external sources, and developing the firm using a strong growth orientation.

Needless to say that this model of technology entrepreneurship which reflects the evolution of the engineer combined with a cubical action model with, on one face, opportunity identification and implementation, and a second face with profit-seeking, organizing, creating and innovating with skills required, such as motivation and finance, on a third face is affected by the personal characteristics, such as country, age, gender (see authors such as Shane and Stevens quoted by Ulijn and Brown, Chapter 1 in this book; Mueller and Thomas, 2000) and education (Reynolds et al., 2000).

### Comparison Elements between French, Dutch and German Entrepreneurship

Figure 9.1 has linked the environment of the person of the entrepreneurial and innovative engineer with her/his enterprise, be it high, low or any tech. We deal with technology entrepreneurship at all levels. Table 9.1 presents some answers to eight research questions related to data about the general economic environment the entrepreneur works in, the rate and difficulty of self-employment, such as the costs, satisfaction levels, and the possible effect of national culture on willingness to start and the profile traits of the successful innovator and entrepreneur from different empirical sources for France, the Netherlands and Germany.

The answers to the following research questions (RQs) will now be dealt with, concluding with a comparison between the three countries in general.

1. How productive are French, Dutch and Germans?
2. What is the relation between Employment (E) and Labour productivity (LP)?
3. How many people are self-employed (percentage of total workforce)
4. How difficult is it to start a business?
5. What are the approximate average initial costs to set up a private limited company?
6. How satisfied are those self-employed v. those employed?
7. What is the possible relation between national culture and entrepreneurship?
8. What is the ideal profile of the innovative entrepreneur?

One question is lacking: is there a strong relation between innovation and employment as well, as Schumpeter already suggested. Jaffe (1989) demonstrated for 29 American states over eight years a link of both with investment in R&D and patents, although in the EU member states employment was negatively correlated with patent activity (Laafia, 2001). We do not have the United States of Europe yet; in the EU other factors might affect that link, such as a different role of the national governments in this process. The Dutch government does not mingle too much with the national economy affairs, spends less on R&D and education, whereas the French and the German governments do a lot more and protect their much bigger domestic markets.

Compared to the USA (100), the Dutch are per capita (77) more productive than the EU average (65) and that of Japan (71), and this leads to an employment rate above average. Germany (and Japan) on the other side has an employment below average. France and the USA are close to average in this respect, but in the USA this might be explained partly by a higher labour productivity (we are dealing with correlation coefficients which do not predict causal relationships). Although the periods compared do not match (1995–2001 v. 1974–94), it seems that the Eurobarometer 2000 index finding that in the USA 69 per cent of the population would prefer to be self-employed v. 51 per cent in the EU, might partly account for the 9.9 per cent self-employed of the total workforce in the reality of the previous period of 1974–94 (Japan: 11.2 per cent). Notwithstanding (or because of, to oppose it, in France?) the bureaucratic culture of both France and Japan (see RQ 7), those countries have a higher self-employment rate (9.5 per cent and 11.2 per cent) than the Netherlands (8.7 per cent) and Germany (6.8 per cent).

We come now to a number of RQs related to the personal situation and satisfaction of the self-employed and to a possible national culture effect on entrepreneurship and entrepreneur. In all countries compared, starting your own business is perceived as rather difficult, but in the Netherlands less so than in the EU in general (35 out of 100 v. 29/100). Even Americans do not find it so easy to start their own business (26)! The low cost of setting up a business in France (€200) might explain partly the higher percentage of self-employed, but for Dutch and German entrepreneurs it would not do so (€800 and €700, but a higher self-employment rate in the Netherlands). The same holds true for Austria and Denmark, which are the extremes in cost (€2200 v. zero), but a representative sample from the population in both countries prefer the employment and not the self-employed status (57 and 55 per cent, Eurobarometer, 2000). Denmark seems to have a unique position where with low cost to start a business people still prefer to have a boss! More than 80 per cent of the 8000 people questioned in the USA and

*Table 9.1   Comparative table of research outcomes about French, Dutch and German entrepreneurs and entrepreneurship in general*

| Research question (RQ) | Source | | French | Dutch | German | Remarks |
|---|---|---|---|---|---|---|
| 1. How productive are French, Dutch and Germans (GDP per capita)? | OECD (2000) | | 64 | 77 | 68 | USA = 100, Jap = 71, EU = 65 |
| 2. What is the relationship between employment (E) and Labour productivity (LP) (1995–2001)? | OECD (2000) | LP | All close to average | | | USA: LP > average |
| | | E | Close to average, as US | > Average | < Average, as Japan | |
| 3. How many people are self-employed (% of total work-force) (1974–94)? | Hofstede et al., Chapter 8 | | 9.5 | 8.7 | 6.8 | Only West Germany |
| 4. How difficult is it to start a business (% of respondents)? | Eurobarometer Survey (2000) | | 26 | 35 | 29 | EU: 29 / USA: 26 |
| | | | Max: 100 = very easy | | | |
| 5. What are the approximate average initial costs to set up a private limited company? | European Commission Enterprise DG (2002) | | €200 | €800 | €700 | Highest: Austria, €2,200 / Lowest: Denmark, €0 |
| 6. How satisfied are those self-employed (% of respondents)? | Blanchflower, Oswald and Stutzer (2001); Eurobarometer (1995 and 2000) | Fairly | 61 | 47 | West 52 | East 57 |
| | | Very | 20 | 44 | 32 | 33 |
| What about the employed? | | Fairly | 53 | 39 | 40 | 50 |
| | | Very | 28 | 59 | 49 | 41 |

| 7. What is the possible relationship between national culture and entrepreneurship? (Maximum score of Hofstede: 100) | Hofstede et al., Chapter 8; Hofstede (2001) | | 68 | 35 | 38 | Ideal: Low | Nakata and Sivakumar (1996); Uljin and Weggeman (2001) |
|---|---|---|---|---|---|---|---|
| | | Power Distance | | | | | |
| | | Individualism | 71 | 67 | 80 | High | |
| | | Masculinity | 43 | 66 | 14 | Low | |
| | | Uncertainty Avoidance | 86 | 65 | 53 | Low | |
| | Barnes (2000); Harris and Moran (1996) | | Bureaucratic, as Japan | Managerial as USA | Technical | | |
| 8. What is the ideal profile of the innovative entrepreneur? | Trompenaars and Hampden-Turner (1999) | | I | R | L | H | Ideal order suggested by the top management team of Shell: |
| | | | A | A | A | A | |
| | | | L | H | R | I | |
| | | | H | L | I | R | |
| | | | R | I | H | L | |

Key: decreasing order of priority of Analysis (A), Helicopter view (H), Imagination and Creativity (I), Leadership (L), Reality (R) (given in alphabetical order)

*Note:* Italicized numbers are percentages.

213

the EU (Eurobarometer, 2000) believe that inadequate financial support makes it difficult to start a business. Another striking finding from this last survey, is that the Dutch would prefer to be employed (58 per cent), whereas French prefer the opposite (55 per cent), which is in line with a higher self-employment. In Germany the preference is slightly in favour of self-employment (East and West together, 48 v. 46 per cent). With a preference of 51 per cent to be self-employed the whole of the EU scores clearly lower than the Americans (69 per cent). How satisfied are those self-employed v. those employed (RQ 6)? The Dutch are the happiest people here both as self-employed and employed, but yet more so as the latter (44 and 59 per cent high satisfaction). Then comes Germany (West: 49 and 32 per cent), whereas the French and the Eastern Germans were the unhappiest in 1995 on this point. Combined with RQ 3 one may conclude, as Hofstede et al., Chapter 8 in this book indicates in much more detail, that dissatisfaction might also explain partly a higher preference to be self-employed (Eurobarometer, 2000) and a higher self-employment rate (RQ 3).

What is the possible relation between National Culture (NC) and innovation/entrepreneurship (RQ 7)? We have to refer here again to Hofstede et al., Chapter 8 in this book, but can look in more detail at the countries of comparison selected. Nakata and Sivakumar (1996) and Ulijn and Weggeman (2001) could evidence on the basis of their empirical studies that, ideally, innovation in its initiation stage would require low power distance, masculinity and uncertainty avoidance, and a high individualism in companies for entrepreneurship to emerge (intrapreneurship inside). The Dutch NC would then be ideal, with the Germans next and the French in the last position, but for the implementation of the innovation a high power distance, masculinity and uncertainty avoidance, and a low individualism would work better. On those scores the ideal order would be the opposite: France, Germany, the Netherlands. If we make a plea in this chapter for more cooperation and teamwork, which is particularly required to make the start-up a success in the long run, the three countries combined would warrant an ideal European start-up! It is not sure if the characterization by Harris and Moran (1996) of the working cultures in some countries would work in a comparable way to the (dis)advantage of entrepreneurship development. In Japan and France bureaucratic culture might lead to high employment rates, as said above, but the Dutch managerial culture seems to lead to a lot less willingness to start your own business (41 per cent) than the USA one (69 per cent, Eurobarometer, 2000). Finally, regarding the ideal profile of the innovative entrepreneur (RQ 8) the three countries might cooperate again in a complementary way. All agree on analysis as a sound base of technology entrepreneurship in the second place, but the French give priority to imagination and creativity, the Dutch are realistic and the Germans need some leadership in an entrepreneurial team. This finding by Trompenaars and Hampden-Turner (1999) for Shell has been confirmed by later findings for students, business executives and experts (Klafft and Daum, 2001; Ulijn and Fayolle, in preparation and below). In sum, the three countries are not too far apart when it comes to the position of being an entrepreneur. Some differences might be mutually supportive, when it comes to cooperation between start-ups. Across the EU it is striking, however, that most countries in Northern Europe (including the Benelux countries) prefer the employed status, with the exception of Ireland, which together with the Southern/Latin countries prefer to be self-employed. This finding and that of France contradicts the recent survey by Reynolds et al. (2000), where Ireland and France present only 2 to 3 per cent of new jobs in new firms (cf. 12 to 16 per cent in Brazil, Korea, the USA and Australia). One-third of the world's new jobs are created in new firms, but there is no equal distribution across country borders. The UK and Germany are divided on this issue, the UK perhaps because of lower welfare arrangements as in the other North-Western European countries. Germany, certainly, because of an East–West divide, as discussed above. Some available details for each of the three countries are added below.

**The French**

As Neft (1995) mentioned about Rhone-Poulenc, this chemical giant makes the change of culture part of its formal personnel planning and succession processes. In their preference for innovation and creativity, the French engineers appear to be more interested in pure science than in solving difficult technical problems with less concern about immediate marketability, on what the US and UK engineers would have working primarily in this global enterprise. This seems in line with Fayolle's view (2000 and the sources he mentions) that French students would be a lot less interested in self-employment. Entrepreneurs would have a rather negative image in France. This seems in strong relation to the specificities of the French educational system, which is very hierarchical and is based on the reputation of the schools. A particularity of the French system is that the 'Grandes Ecoles' fulfil a social function. The 'Grandes Ecoles' allow the ruling class to reproduce itself, first, by allowing the transmission of privileges and, secondly, by organizing a whole series of barriers into the social group. The dominating class, the 'Noblesse d'Etat', as the French sociologist Bourdieu (1989) refers to it, legitimizes its reproduction through an academic meritocracy. Under these conditions, the most important thing, in France, social recognition and position, does not come from entrepreneurship and from successes in business, but it is mainly related to the graduation from a prestigious French 'Grande Ecole'. This gives a cultural explanation to the very low entrepreneurial propensity of the French engineers (Ribeil, 1984). The cultural dimension is useful and relevant to have a comprehensive view of behavioural differences among managers and engineers in a country. Important research works from d'Iribarne (1993) have put into evidence three key behavioural logics among people working in the same international company in three different countries: France, the USA and the Netherlands. These logics could explain a wide diversity of entrepreneurial attitudes and behaviours in these countries. France certainly has the weakest entrepreneurial orientation and the Netherlands seems to have a stronger entrepreneurial culture.

**The Dutch**

In the Netherlands, there is a consistent pattern of business-related practices built around a 'consensus' principle (see d'Iribarne, 1993). It is important that decisions are made after everyone has been listened to and, if there are disagreements, then there will be a search for a better solution that is agreed on by everyone. In connection with this, a Dutch manager also wants freedom to adopt his/her own approach to the job and for creating personal ideas. A Dutch manager takes his/her tasks seriously. 'Business is business' and 'Business for pleasure' are two Dutch expressions. The orientation of a Dutch manager is short-term planning. He/she wants to see results quickly. On the other hand, when the results do not come fast, he/she has perseverance, you almost call it stubbornness. The Dutch engineer is less specialized in a technical area than his/her German counterpart. To obtain technical knowledge the Dutch engineer thinks it necessary to buy or develop it him/herself rather than obtain it from internal education programmes. Still, a Dutch manager's authority is also based on knowledge. The Dutch are more impressed by actions than by words. Another point mentioned by Kympers (1992) is their efficient and economic way of managing. The negative side of this way of managing is an urge towards perfection, which leads to rigidness. But again, as with the French, the Dutch engineers might be less willing to take the risk of trying to be self-employed. A recent internal survey among about 4000 alumni of two management-orientated engineering programmes shows that only 3 to 5 per cent work in small companies of up to nine employees and 7 per cent of all Dutch students wish to be entrepreneurs (Verhoef, in Ulijn and Fayolle, in preparation). It seems as though lower education levels lead more easily to a start-up: the Turkish minority in the Netherlands have more start-ups than the average of the majority Dutch population. Here, and in other countries, low education and less access to high levels of education might just be one reason to start your own business. Less access to mainstream managerial positions and high levels of society might be other reasons. Entrepreneurs seem to be ill prepared and run unnecessary risks, which might explain 75 per cent of the bankruptcy of Dutch firms in 2001 (Blom, in Ulijn and Fayolle, in preparation). Are the German engineers with less market orientation than the Dutch (see Ulijn, Nagel and Tan, 2001) more successful in entrepreneurial ventures? An engineer might have to 'unlearn' things as well. Reynolds et al. (2000) found that the influence of education level on entrepreneurship should not be exaggerated, as the above example shows.

**The Germans**

In Germany, there is a consistent pattern of business-related practices around 'competence first'. The professional culture of the German engineer is strongly based on this principle. The German apprentice system leads to an exceptionally well-trained workforce. About two-thirds of German supervisors hold a Master certificate. German managers are chosen for their positions on the basis of their expert knowledge and they consider this knowledge to be the most important basis of their authority. The German engineer finds it self-evident that he/she teaches his/her subordinates his/her knowledge and experience. If personnel are highly qualified and they respect their supervisors, there will be little guidance needed. Therefore in Germany the average percentage of staff personnel is less than 30 per cent and this leads to a flat organization. A flat organization has the advantage that new technologies can be introduced more easily (also because personnel have a high level of education). Considering innovation, the German engineers are technology orientated. Marketing is seen as a distraction from the primary goal. To maintain knowledge for innovation German managers think there has to be investment in R&D instead of buying knowledge through acquisitions, joint ventures and so on. German managers consider unions and work councils to be stabilizing factors. This leads to less time spent on labour disputes. A German manager thinks and acts in a businesslike manner. He/she tries to reduce uncertainties.

To illustrate the differences between the French, the Germans and the Dutch, we give below some results of quick tests we did to assess the profiles of the ideal innovator and the ideal entrepreneur using samples of Germans and French.

Klafft and Daum (2001) were able to compare 10 regular industrial engineering, 9 start-ups and 48 personnel recruiters (at the annual Konactiva job fair to attract new personnel right on the campus of Darmstadt University of Technology), all in Darmstadt. They did this on the basis of two lists. One profiles the ideal entrepreneur, which has the innovator as one of its 10 basic elements (in alphabetical order): creative (C), hard worker (H), independent thinker (IT), innovator (IN), leader (L), optimist (OPT), recognizes/takes advantage of opportunities (OPP), resourceful (RES), risk-taker (RIS) and visionary (VIS). The Ernst & Young survey with Rope Starch Worldwide from 1995 gives the following ideal order: OP, RES, C, IT, H, OPT, IN, RIS, V and L. For Germany the top three would be Visionary, Creative and Independent thinker (for 48 personnel recruiters), for the nine start-ups it would be Innovator, Creative/Leader, and for the students Opportunities user, Visionary and Risk-taker. The two orders we could gather for French students (15 industrial engineering and 23 telecommunication) were again different (Ulijn and Fayolle, in preparation), but mostly the above top elements were included: OPP, VIS, Creative, Leader (probably meant market or technology leader).

The second list uses the HAIRL model explained in Table 9.1, assessing the profile of the ideal innovator which the Shell top management team considered to be: Helicopter view (H), Analysis (A), Imagination and Creativity (I), Reality (R) and Leadership (L) (Trompenaars and Hampden-Turner, 1999). Surprisingly the LARIH model for the ideal German innovator by Shell (see Table 9.1) is only partly confirmed by the personnel recruiters, since they also mentioned other elements related more to the entrepreneurial success of the innovation: top 3 – Human resources, Innovation and Leadership. Start-ups would give A/I, H and L/R, and students IHARL. Another German set of 31 students (Da Campo, Gruescu and Nehrbass, 2000) including an association of students willing to start up a venture (JADE) gave AHILR. So leadership seems to be a controversial issue, when it comes to innovation in Germany, perhaps because of the confusion about the term: leader of a team or leader in the competitive marketing sense. Nineteen Dutch civil engineering students gave the following order, IARHL, which differs from the Shell sample, RAHLI. The above two samples of French students gave almost the same profiles, IHARL and IAHRL, with imagination and creativity at the top. Comparing all ideal innovator profile sets, however, it seems as if the French favour more imagination and creativity in an innovation, that the Germans prefer the analysis and that the Dutch prefer to be realistic on an innovation; again the three NCs are complementary.

To conclude this section, we would say an entrepreneurial and innovative engineer as outlined in Figure 9.1 needs a strong interaction with his/her environment, be it within the firms he/she wishes to depart from, or once started in the search of partners and a market for his/her innovative idea. We have demonstrated how complicated this picture of networking and cooperating may become once a European dimension is envisaged. On the other hand, the natural and cultural diversity brought in by French, Dutch and German managers and engineers in start-up cooperation, may help to overcome potential hurdles. If it is easier and less expensive to start in France, why not do so? If Dutch personnel would be more productive, why not use this, for instance, for marketing purposes? If a better design and more R&D are needed, why not commit a French engineer to the venture? If the production could be 'sourced out' to a group of German engineers, who are good in manufacturing, why not do so? This way the best of all worlds can be achieved in one entrepreneurial team on the European scene.

## 3. THE EUROPEAN ENTERPRISE AND ITS CULTURE: AN INTERACTION OF NATIONAL, PROFESSIONAL AND CORPORATE CULTURES (NC, PC AND CC) WITHIN THE MINDS OF FRENCH, DUTCH AND GERMAN ENGINEERS

So far we have seen that a European engineer who wants to start his/her own business faces the effect of his/her NC on his/her perceptions of the ideal entrepreneurial behaviour. Da Campo, Gruescu and Nehrbass (2000) could not confirm the following hypothesis in their pilot study with Dutch, German, Russian and Rumanian students:

> The cultural differences regarding entrepreneurship are very low. Under similar conditions, individuals belonging to different cultures seem to have a similar perception of entrepreneurial behaviour.

The rankings of Trompenaars HAIRL model for Shell varied significantly across those NCs, although this needs further verification in well controlled studies, including the other NCs and population samples, such as start-up engineers and business executives (see Ulijn and Fayolle, in preparation). This study and others referred to above by Reynolds et al. (2000), Blanchflower, Oswald and Stutzer (2001) and Hofstede et al. (Chapter 8 in this book), indicate that there is a lot of latent entrepreneurship across nations, which cannot only be explained by NC effects. Mueller and Thomas's (2000) study could relate NC in nine countries, ranging from the USA, via Slovenia and Croatia to China and Singapore, including Germany to personality traits associated with an entrepreneurial potential. What Ulijn and Weggeman (2001) summarized as the ideal innovation culture, a mix of high individualism and low uncertainty avoidance, leads to innovativeness and internal locus of control, but those are two entrepreneurial behaviour traits. Others might relate to other dimensions of Hofstede, as Nakata and Sivakumar (1996) evidence for innovative behaviour. What should be the ideal incubator then for the emerging technology entrepreneur, as outlined by Paffen (see above)? The MNCs and SMEs and even universities or 'Grandes Ecoles' which display a CC including low power distance and low uncertainty avoidance, as Ulijn and Weggeman could illustrate, might not only lead to effective innovation inside with the effective intrapreneurship, but also a nice offspring of technical start-ups outwards.

Taking Hofstede's (2001) cultural development model, we might see a European innovative and entrepreneurial engineer who may grow up in a family business (where a CC comes on the top of his/her NC development at an early age), and then assimilates through his/her education a certain professional culture (PC). What is this PC, which might help or discourage him/her to be an entrepreneur? Both van der Hart (2001) and Gaillard (2002) suggest that a lot more marketing culture is needed in general industrial and even R&D contexts, the lack of which might hamper cooperation in technical start-ups. *The idea is good, but there is no market for it.* We will now compare for the three countries selected how NC, PC and CC may interact in the minds of engineers. The findings of the studies are not comparable on a one-to-one basis. The French part still has to be replicated for samples of Dutch and German enterprises, because their CCs of MNCs and SMEs (<500 employees) are not comparable to start-ups and small-business settings. The Dutch and the German part have to be redone within the educational and historical setting of the original French study on a large sample of French engineers originating from the Grandes Ecoles d'Ingénieurs which prevent alumni perhaps more than in other countries from becoming entrepreneurial (innovative should be OK!). The managerial culture of the Dutch might provide a better setting for market aspects, whereas the technical culture of Germany would be a better safeguard for quality. So we have to be partly speculative here! What is needed first is an entrepreneurial culture from which a particular CC of start-up may develop, once it is in operation.

Cooperation between start-ups in Europe is certainly not a question only of national culture; a merger or a clash between professional and corporate cultures might foster or hamper as well. Entrepreneurial and innovative engineers build up their experiences of this through a lifetime based on the logics outlined in Figure 9.1. Our chapter is based upon data from three different European countries, which includes a survey among French engineers and a case comparison of 12 innovative German and Dutch firms. How does this transition take place in different parts of Europe? How many engineers become successful entrepreneurs through a happy reconciliation of technological and marketing orientations within a given historical context?

In trying to bring some elements to answer the above questions our data reveal interesting things. Obviously, in relation to invention, innovation and entrepreneurship behaviours, we can observe the discriminating character of the technological dimension for the engineers. Technological dimension is a key one which strongly shapes the career of engineers in France, in Germany and in the Netherlands. But we also know the importance of the market orientation in the innovation process and the influence of cultural variables in the transition from the technological orientation to the market orientation. The transition processes are not similar for German, Dutch and French engineers. One of our previous studies, for example, is highlighting one difference between Dutch and German engineers. The Dutch engineer appears to be more market orientated than the German one and his/her transition from a technological orientation to a market perspective takes place earlier. This study suggests the importance of cultural explanations at the corporate and the professional levels.

In France, the social and educational context is still playing a great role in shaping the French engineer attitudes and behaviours. Our survey among French engineers highlights two different profiles of entrepreneurs and two different ways to reach innovation. The 'technician' entrepreneur engineer profile is very close to the one of inventor. This type of entrepreneur engineer invents new technologies, new products or new manufacturing processes. He very often needs other competencies (related mainly to marketing, finances and human resource management) to carry out these inventions and to bring them to the markets. One way could be in acquiring these competencies; the other could be to build up an entrepreneurial team. The latter is generally the one chosen, for a lot of reasons, such as time constraint and efficiency or requirements from the financial environment. The second profile, that of 'manager' entrepreneur engineer, is very close to the profile of innovator. This type of entrepreneur engineer innovates more or less in the service activities, business to business or business to consumer. He/she has a good ability to manage all the aspects of the innovation process and he/she is particularly interested in and orientated to the market orientation. The 'manager' entrepreneur engineer is, therefore, an engineer who succeeds earlier than the 'technician' entrepreneur engineer in the transition from the technological orientation to the market orientation. In some cases the transition will not be easy or possible for the latter.

Hence, the results of our study show that both 'technician' and 'manager' entrepreneur engineers are involved in the innovation phenomena. The nature and the processes of innovation are not similar in the two cases, but both types of innovation are useful for our economies. Under these conditions one main question could be related to the improvement of our understanding about the different forms of using the scientific, technological and managerial knowledge of European engineers in our European societies.

As we have shown, technical culture is a key variable influencing the behaviours of engineers towards innovation and entrepreneurship in Germany, in France and in the Netherlands.

Technical culture (see Harris and Moran, 1996), as it exists in a long tradition of technical expertise (Germany) and the one rooted in a pure science of mathematics and physics tradition (France), might not always be beneficial to an entrepreneurial culture. Meyer and Heppard (2000) argue that elements, such as organizational learning, innovation as creating new knowledge, implementing strategic decisions quickly and increasing speed to the marketplace, and having teams are keys to this. So far as the organizational level is concerned, start-ups rather need an 'enterprising' culture related to the person of technology entrepreneur. Kao (1993) defines this as follows:

> Enterprising culture is a commitment of the individual to the continuing pursuit of opportunities and developing an entrepreneurial endeavor to its growth potentials for the purpose of creating wealth for the individual and adding value to society.

It is obvious that such an entrepreneurial endeavour needs cooperation between the start-up and the actors of its environment.

## 4. HOW TO FOSTER COOPERATION BETWEEN EUROPEAN START-UPS FOR A BETTER ENTERPRISING AND INNOVATIVE CULTURE

Finally, this chapter addresses the question of how to foster cooperation between European start-ups for a better enterprising and innovative culture. Research projects aimed at this issue, might start by comparing national entrepreneurship phenomena, such as suggested partly by Lichtenberger and Naulleau (1993) and Trompenaars and Hampden-Turner (1999), followed by studying cooperation, networks and alliances (Aliouat, 2000) including globalization (Birley and Stockley, 1998) and the heterogeneity of teams, for instance by mixing marketers and engineers (Bantel and Jackson, 1989, Geletkanycz and Hambrick, 1997; Shaw and Shaw, 1998). Cooperation requires more mobility. Within the European Union, the individual member states face an influx of economic refugees (who might create excellent start-ups, by the way) rather than welcoming an invasion of entrepreneurial and innovative engineers from each other. There is a lot of exchange of students, but very much less so of professors. The flexibility of the job market across member state borders is poor. Which French engineer would like to start a business with a German colleague who could implement his idea perfectly? Which German engineer seeks a market-orientated partner in Britain or the Netherlands (NL) to fulfil his dream of a successful start-up? Which Dutch engineer looks for technology entrepreneurship in France and vice versa? It seems as though new virtual borders also prevent start-ups from cooperating. That is why this chapter presents a summarizing model of a new cultural identity of Europe based upon entrepreneurship, innovation and mobility using the onion culture metaphor by Hofstede (1991) and Schein (1991) to increase the mobility of the European engineer (Ulijn and Gould, 2002). A new culture is needed to foster the cooperation between high, low and other tech start-ups to facilitate a genuine European technology entrepreneurship.

The above outline of an enterprising and innovative culture pinpoints apart from a low power distance (PD) and uncertainty avoidance (UA) for the initiation of the innovation (Nakata and Sivakumar, 1996), a low uncertainty avoidance (Mueller and Thomas, 2000) for entrepreneurship. This does not mean that countries with high PD and UA do not create self-employment. As Hofstede et al. (Chapter 8 in this book) show, dissatisfaction with bureaucracy, poverty and corruption might be a strong incentive for entrepreneurship. Most of those countries (in East Asia, South America and Africa) are very collectivistic and have tight cultures (Triandis, 1995) with high context/implicit communication (Hall, 1996 and 1998). A lot of knowledge and experience are constantly shared and do *not* have to be specifically stated and spelled out over and over in a very explicit way (see Ulijn and Kumar, 2000). It seems as though cooperation in such settings, with natural teaming up and group solidarity, could be very beneficial to entrepreneurship. On the other hand, high PD and UA and a high collectivism foster the implementation of the innovation. Since neither France, nor NL or Germany has a high collectivism, cooperation might not be a given fact. On the one hand, high individualism might lead to entrepreneurship in the countries compared by Muller and Thomas; on the other hand, cooperation would have to be learned in those situations. This might be easier in the technical culture of the well-oiled machine in Germany than in a bureaucratic French culture, with the Dutch managerial culture in the middle. What ways of cooperating between start-ups may be suggested?

International comparisons of entrepreneurship, such as the ones on the basis of HAIRL (Trompenaars and Hampden-Turner, 1999) and for the South Pacific and South-East Asia (Dana, 1999; 2002) might break away potential hurdles for international cooperation, in particular if a start-up has the market in the other country as a focus or opportunity. Although the concept of global entrepreneurship (Birley and MacMillan, 1997) does not imply yet such true international comparison, the surveys of studies by Birley and others (for instance, Birley and Stockley, 1998; Ulijn and Weggeman, 2001) suggest a lot of ideas for an ideal composition of entrepreneurial and innovative teams. Important factors here are heterogeneity

v. homogeneity (Bantel and Jackson, 1989; Geletkanycz and Hambrick, 1997), team size, the cooperative setting of an incubator or clan (Ouchi, 1980), of loose v. tight groups (Triandis, 1995), and the need for conflict resolution (using the work by Jehn, 1995 and 1997). Job satisfaction fuels those team processes at project level (Nerkar, McGrath and MacMillan, 1997).

Interculturally countries could learn from each other. If high PD and UA work better for efficient implementation of an innovation, why not have French work with Germans to combine the best of some worlds. If the low masculinity score of the Dutch is beneficial to creativity, why not have them together with a French colleague to design an innovation in one entrepreneurial team? But NC is not the only cultural factor in international teams, also in national teams a possible clash and conflict between engineers and marketers (Shaw and Shaw, 1998; Ulijn, Nagel and Tan, 2001) might be transformed into an asset for effective cooperation in design and innovation with the client, as van Luxemburg, Ulijn and Amare (2002) show in five Dutch cases. They suggest that engineering culture, for instance, might be high context, implicit and tight (*we, as inside experts, know what we are talking about*), where marketing culture would be much more open (low context) and tend to exchange explicit messages with customers. The right mix of professional cultures might be essential for effective cooperation between start-ups. Of course, cooperation can take on some standardized and structural forms, such as the different ways of strategic alliancing, joint ventures, mergers or acquisitions, once a start-up has come to some maturity. In a study of 60 technological alliances between French firms, it appeared that entrepreneurs might start with simply saving transactions costs, but end up with sharing a lot of crucial knowledge sources essential for new start-ups (Aliouat, 2000). Of course, such collaboration, as for instance in French–German joint ventures, create conflicts, but also synergy, once the right mutual perception leads to effective problem-solving (Lichtenberger and Naulleau, 1993). National cultures might also network differently. A study by Burt, Hogarth and Michaud (2000) indicates that the social capital of French managers differs from that of American ones. The French are anchored in long-standing personal relationships to which they add recent acquaintances from work. The American do the opposite adding personal to work. This has implications for cooperation between French and American/Dutch/German start-ups, the American behaviour being similar to that of the Dutch and Germans. As Brown (Chapter 6 in this book) and Gwynne (1997) indicate, a special culture of skunks is needed to look for start-up opportunities, which requires the mobility of that animal.

Van Gorp et al. (2002) report on several sources that show that the mobility of scientists and engineers is greatest in the USA, where they change jobs every four years (OECD, 2000). In Japan only 20 per cent do so over their lifetime. The EU is short of internal mobility and risks a brain drain towards the USA, which is a constant threat to its internal economy, as has been already mentioned in an early NATO study (1982). Lack of transferability of pensions between public and private sectors and between member states might cause such lack of mobility and job change. On the basis of an inquiry among 40 European advanced students of engineering and five Members of the European Parliament (MEPs, members of the Commission on External Trade, Industry, Research and Energy) on the causes of this issue and how to take measures to make the EU more competitive for entrepreneurship and innovation, Ulijn and Gould (2002) propose a new cultural identity for Europe, that of entrepreneurship, innovation and mobility (see Figure 9.2).

The onion metaphor of the different layers of artefacts and products (explicit) towards the implicit inner core of the basic assumptions is used to show that once engineers were to feel more as European innovative entrepreneurs, they would develop norms and values towards that mobility, having the right perceptions of the complementarities of their partners from other EU member states. Cooperation between start-ups across the state borders might then be as easy as in the USA. *A conditio sine qua non* for this would be, however, that both the European Commission and the European Parliament adopt the appropriate regulations in the outer layer of the onion to protect and foster the inner layers of this mobility culture. Both students (future entrepreneurial and innovative engineers?) and MEPs agreed upon the need for such regulations and culture.

To be more specific, we would like to develop, as an example, a proposed CLUSTER programme initiated by Eindhoven University of Technology (ECIS: Eindhoven Centre of Innovation Studies) and INP Grenoble (EPI: Entrepreneurship and Process of Innovation). In order to promote and stimulate a better enterprising and innovative culture in Europe, this cooperation programme is developing some initial and key measures.

One of the academic measures to take will be a joint CLUSTER PhD training programme for Entrepreneurship and Innovation (Taskforce VI), an initiative of ECIS and EPI. The hope is then that some cooperation between start-ups among the best universities of technology in Europe would naturally occur.

A second academic measure is to organize, each year as part of the above, a European conference on entrepreneurship and innovation research. The first conference, 'Entrepreneurship research in Europe: specificities and perspectives', was held in September 2002 at Valence (France). The second conference could be organized in the Netherlands at Eindhoven. The aim

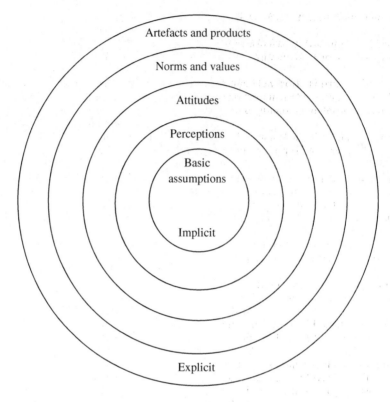

*Source:* The onion model (based on Hofstede, 1991, and Schein, 1991) from Ulijn and Gould (2002).

*Figure 9.2*    *A new cultural identity of Europe: entrepreneurship, innovation and mobility ( EIM )*

of such conferences is to highlight the European particularities in the field of research in entrepreneurship and innovation. For instance, concerning entrepreneurship, we are dealing with these topics:

- Teaching entrepreneurship: theories, practices and main effects.
- The study of entrepreneurial processes: why, what and how?
- Theories in the field of entrepreneurship.
- Innovative methodologies in the study of entrepreneurship phenomenon.
- High-technology, innovation and entrepreneurship.
- Frontiers of entrepreneurship and relationship with other scientific fields.

The first two measures try to set up structures and framework for training, exchanging ideas and research materials around entrepreneurship and innovation at the academic level.

A lot of more classical measures will take place in the cooperation programme such as the PhD's joint supervision, the exchange of people (teachers, researchers, students, and so on). Within the European network, the design of joint research projects and also the development of a strong relationship with the professional world of innovation and entrepreneurship in each country of the CLUSTER group.

## 5. CONCLUSIONS AND IMPLICATIONS FOR BUSINESS

Across the EU it is striking, however, that most countries in Northern Europe (including the Benelux countries) prefer the employed status, with the exception of Ireland, which together with the Southern/Latin countries, prefers to be self-employed. This finding and that of France contradicts the recent survey by Reynolds et al. (2000), where those two countries present only 2 to 3 per cent of new jobs in new firms (12 to 16 per cent in Brazil, Korea, the USA and Australia). The UK and Germany are divided on this issue, the UK because of lower welfare arrangements as in the other North-Western European countries; Germany, certainly, because of an East–West divide, as discussed in this chapter. A lot of things need to be done to explain these differences between countries and also to identify the main factors which are playing a role. Our research is certainly bringing some answers to the key questions we asked in the introductory part.

If we look at the national culture level in the development of a strong entrepreneurial orientation, the Dutch culture would be ideal, with the Germans next and the French in the last position, but for the implementation of the innovation a high power distance, masculinity and uncertainty avoidance, and a low individualism would work better. On those scores the ideal order would be the opposite: France, Germany, the Netherlands. If we make a plea in this chapter for more cooperation and teamwork, which is particularly required to make the start-up really a success in the long run, the three countries combined would warrant an ideal European start-up! *( Let the French design, the Germans implement and the Dutch sell? )*

Regarding the ideal profile of the innovative entrepreneur (RQ 8) the three countries might cooperate again in a complementary way: all agree on analysis as a sound basis of technology entrepreneurship in the second place, but the French give priority to imagination and creativity, the Dutch are realistic and the Germans need some leadership in an entrepreneurial team. Comparing all ideal innovator profile sets, however, it seems the French favour more imagination and creativity in an innovation, that the Germans prefer the analysis and that the Dutch prefer to be realistic about an innovation, again the three national cultures are complementary.

We were able to interpret our data according to new 'cultural' lines based upon Nakata and Sivakumar (1996), Hofstede (2001) and Ulijn and Weggeman (2001). Cooperation between start-ups in Europe is certainly not a question only of national culture. A perfect innovation culture seems to merge not only at the national level, but should match perfectly the professional culture of the European engineers and the corporate culture of their firms (start-up, SME or MNC) researched.

An entrepreneurial and innovative engineer as outlined in this chapter needs a strong interaction with his/her environment, be it within the firms he/she wishes to leave or, once started, in the search of partners and a market for his/her innovative idea. We have demonstrated how complicated this picture of networking and cooperating may become once a European dimension is envisaged. On the other hand, the natural and cultural diversity brought in by French, Dutch and German managers and engineers in start-up cooperation, may help to overcome potential hurdles. If it is easier and less expensive to start in France, why not do so? If Dutch personnel would be more productive, why not use this, for instance, for marketing purposes? If a better design and more R&D is needed, why not commit a French engineer to the venture? If the production could be 'sourced out' to a group of German engineers, who are good at manufacturing, why not do so? This way the best of all worlds can be achieved in one entrepreneurial team on the European scene.

Should French engineers design the technical innovation, their German colleagues implement it into a well-controlled manufacturing process and the Dutch, for instance, sell to the market, as they are often positively stereotyped? Our research suggests that diversity might already be built in systematically in a cross-border innovation team as a competitive asset and not as something which happens to us as a handicap on the European and global scene. Cooperation between start-ups within and across countries may serve as a key example of this. Our earlier plea for a European development of technology management beneficial to both high-tech enterprises and engineering education has obvious implications for the position of French, Dutch and German entrepreneurial and innovative engineers in such cooperation of start-ups (Fayolle, Ulijn and Nagel 2002).

We are conscious, at the end of our exploratory work, that few things have been done concerning the key topic – the cooperation between European technological start-ups. More research is needed with adequate sampling in each of our three countries. Research projects could have a focus on the cultural aspects and have as a main objective the test of hypotheses we have elaborated. Other projects could use a longitudinal approach to study the questions related to the foundation and the development of technological start-ups in France, Germany and the Netherlands. At a theoretical level, depending on the type of research project, the network theory and the resource-based theory could be of interest to develop scientific knowledge about the potential of cooperation between technological start-ups in Europe.

# REFERENCES

Ajzen, I. (1991), 'The theory of planned behavior', *Organizational Behavior and Human Decisions Processes*, **50**, 1–63.

Aldrich, H.E. and C. Zimmer (1986), 'Entrepreneurship through social networks', in D.L. Sexton and R.W. Smilor (eds), *The Art and Science of Entrepreneurship*, Cambridge, MA: Ballinger, pp. 3–24.

Aliouat, B. (2000), 'Entrepreneurship culture and technological strategic alliances between competitors: from saving transaction costs to common knowledge dynamics', *Journal of Enterprising Culture*, **8** (3), 271–90.

Autio, E., R. Keeley, M. Klofsten and T. Ulfstedt (1997), 'Entrepreneurial intent among students: testing an intent model in Asia, Scandinavia and USA', *Frontiers of Entrepreneurship Research*, Babson College, Wellesley, pp. 133–47.

Bantel, K. and S. Jackson (1989), 'Top management and innovations in banking: does the composition of the top team make a difference?', *Strategic Management Journal*, **19**, 107–24.

Barnes, P.E. (2000), 'A comparative analysis of multinational facilities in the European Union and the United States: how environmental regulations and culture affect the implementation of an international environmental standard', PhD thesis, Erasmus University of Rotterdam.

Birley, S. (1985), 'The role of networks in the entrepreneurial process', *Journal of Business Venturing*, **1** (1), 107–18.

Birley, S. and I. MacMillan (1997), *Entrepreneurship in Global Context*, London: Routledge.

Birley, S. and S. Stockley (eds) (1998), 'Entrepreneurial teams and venture Growth', unpublished paper, Imperial College Entrepreneurship Centre.

Blanchflower, D.G., A. Oswald and A. Stutzer (2001), 'Latent entrepreneurship across nations', *European Economic Review*, **41**, 680–91.

Bourdieu, P. (1989), *La noblesse d'Etat. Grandes Ecoles et esprit de corps*, Paris: Les Editions de Minuit.

Boutellier, R., O. Gassmann and M. von Zedtwitz (1999). *Managing Global Innovation: Uncovering the Secrets of Future Competitiveness*, Berlin: Springer.

Burt, R.S., R.M. Hogarth and C. Michaud (2000), 'The social capital of French and American managers', *Organisation Science*, **11** (2), 123–47.

Da Campo, S., R. Gruescu and E. Nehrbass (2000), 'Entrepreneurship and innovation: what is the ideal profile of an entrepreneur, how should an entrepreneur prioritise the assessment of an innovation and negotiate it in an international context', small thesis, TU Darmstadt (Germany).

Dana, L.P. (1999), *Entrepreneurship in Pacific Asia: Past, Present, and Future*, London: World Scientific.

Dana, L.P. (2002). *When Economies Change Paths: Models of Transition in China, the Central Asian Republics, Myanmar and the Nations of Former Indochine Française*, London: World Scientific.

Drucker, P. (1985), *Innovation and Entrepreneurship*, New York: Harper & Row.

Eurobarometer Survey (1995 and 2000), *Flash Eurobarometer 83: Entrepreneurship*, Brussels: European Commission http://europa.eu.int/comm/enterprise_policy/survey/eurobarometer83.htm.

European Commission Enterprise DG (2002), *Benchmarking the administration of business start-ups*, http://europa.eu.int/comm/enterprise/entrepreneurship/support_measures/start-ups/benchmarking.htm.

Fayolle, A. (1996), 'Contibution à l'étude des comportements entrepreneuriaux des ingénieurs français', thèse de doctorat en sciences de gestion, Université de Lyon.

Fayolle, A. (2000), 'Exploratory study to assess the effects of entrepreneurship programs on French student entrepreneurial behaviors', *Journal of Enterprising Culture*, **8** (2), 169–84.

Fayolle, A. (2001), D'une approche typologique de l'entrepreneuriat chez les ingénieurs à la reconstruction d'itinéraires d'ingénieurs entrepreneurs, *Revue d'Entrepreneuriat*, **1** (1), 77–97.

Fayolle, A. (2002), 'Research and researchers at the heart of entrepreneurial situations', in C. Stayeart and al. (eds), *Movements in Entrepreneurship*, Cheltenham, UK and Northampton, MA, USA: Edward Elgar.

Fayolle, A. and Y.F. Livian (1995), 'Entrepreneurial behavior of French engineers. An exploratory study', in S. Birley and I. MacMillan (eds), *International Entrepreneurship*, London: Routledge, pp. 202–228.

Fayolle, A., J. Ulijn and A. Nagel (2002), 'The entrepreneurial orientation towards technology management: the example of French, German and Dutch engineers', in D. Probert, T. Durand, O. Granstrand and H. Tschirky (eds), *Bringing Technology into the Boardroom*, Basingstoke: Palgrave.

Gaillard, J.M. (2002), *Marketing et Gestion dans la Recherche et Développement*, 2nd edition, Paris: Economica.

Geletkanycz, M.A. and D.C. Hambrick (1997), 'The external ties of top executives: Implications for strategic choice and performance', *Administrative Quarterly*, **42**, 654–81.

Gorp, K. van, B. Piscaer, V. Prins and R. de Vaan (2002), 'The road to innovative success', small thesis, TU Eindhoven Jean Monnet chair.

Gwyne, P. (1997), 'Skunks work: 1990s style', *Research Technology Management*, **40** (4), 18–23.

Hall, E.T. (1976), *Beyond Culture*, New York: Doubleday.

Hall, E.T. (1998), 'Three domains of culture and the triune brain', in S. Neimeier, C.P. Campbell and R. Dirven (eds), *The Cultural Context in Business Communication*, Amsterdam: John Benjamins, pp. 11–30.

Harris, P.R. and R.T. Moran (1996), *Managing Cultural Differences*, London: Gulf.

Hart, H. van der (2001), 'Techniek en marketing: Van polarisatie naar integratie (Technology and marketing: from polarization to integration)', farewell address, Eindhoven University of Technology.

Hitt, M.A. and T.S. Reed (2000), 'Entrepreneurship in the new competitive landscape', in G.D. Meyer and K.A. Heppard (eds), *Entrepreneurship as Strategy: Competing on the Entrepreneurial Edge*, pp. 23–48, Thousand Oaks, CA: Sage.

Hofstede, G. (1991), *Culture and Organizations: Software of the Mind*, London: McGraw Hill.

Hofstede, G. (2001), *Culture's Consequences: Comparing Values, Behaviours, Institutions, and Organizations across Nations*, 2nd edition, London: Sage.

d'Iribarne, P. (1993), *La logique de l'honneur: Gestion des entreprises et traditions nationales*, Paris: Editions du Seuil.

Jaffe, A. (1989), 'Real effects of academic research', *American Economic Review*, **79** (5), 957–70.

Jehn, K.A. (1995), 'A multimethod examination of the benefits and detriments of intragroup conflict', *Administrative Science Quarterly*, **40**, 256–82.

Jehn, K.A. (1997), 'A qualitative analysis of conflict types and dimensions in organizational groups', *Administrative Science Quarterly*, **42**, 530–57.

Kandasaami, S. and J. Wood (1996), 'International entrepreneurship in born global firms', in ENDEC (ed.), *Globalisation and Entrepreneurship*, Supplement to proceedings, pp. 158–73, Singapore: NTU.

Kao, R. (1993), 'Defining entrepreneurship: past, present and future', *Creativity and Innovation Management*, **2** (1), 22–35.

Klafft, M. and M. Daum (2001), 'Innovation, entrepreneurship and culture as factors of entrepreneurial success', small thesis, TU Darmstadt (Germany).

Kolvereid, L. (1996), 'Organizational employment versus self-employment: reasons for career choice intentions', *Entrepreneurship Theory and Practice*, Spring, 23–31.

Krueger, N.F. and A.L. Carsrud, (1993), 'Entrepreneurial intentions: applying the theory of planned behavior', *Entrepreneurship and Regional Development*, **5**, 315–330.

Kympers, L. (1992), 'Een Belgisch-Vlaamse kijk op Nederlands zakendoen', *Holland Management Review*, **33**, 59–69.

Laafia, I. (2001), *Statistics in Focus: How Much Do Governments Budget for R&D Activities?* EU, www.europe.eu.int.

Lichtenberger, B. and G. Naulleau (1993), 'French–German joint-ventures: cultural conflicts and synergies', *International Business Review*, **2** (3), 297–307.

Luxemburg, A.P.D. van, J. Ulijn and N. Amare (2002), 'Interactive design process including the customer in 6 Dutch SME cases: traditional and ICT-media compared', contribution to a special issue of the *IEEE Journal of Professional Communication* on *The future of ICT-studies and their implications for human interaction and culture in the innovation management process* (eds J. Ulijn, T. Bemelmans and D. Vogel).

Meyer, G.D. and K.A. Heppard (eds) (2000), *Entrepreneurship as Strategy: Competing on the Entrepreneurial Edge*, pp. 23–48, Thousand Oaks, CA: Sage.

Mueller, S.L. and A.S. Thomas (2000), 'Culture and entrepreneurial potential: A nine country study of locus of control and innovations', *Journal of Business Venturing*, **16**, 51–75.

Mustar, P. (1997), 'How French academics create hi-tech companies: the conditions for success or failure', *Science and Public Policy*, **24** (1), 37–43.

Nakata, Ch. and K. Sivakumar (1996), 'National culture and new product development: an integrative review', *Journal of Marketing*, **60** (1), 61–72.

NATO (1982), *International Mobility of Scientists and Engineers*, Lisbon: Science commission.

Neft, P. (1995), 'Cross-cultural research teams in a global enterprise', *Industrial Research Institute*, May–June, 15–19.

Nerkar, A., R.G. McGrath and I. MacMillan (1997), 'Team processes in innovation: the role of job satisfaction at project level', in S. Birley and I. MacMillan (eds), *Entrepreneurship in Global Context*, pp. 103–38, London: Routledge.

OECD (1998), *Fostering Entrepreneurship*, Paris: OECD.

OECD (2000), *Science, Technology and Industry Outlook*, Paris: OECD.

Ouchie, W.G. (1980), 'Markets, bureaucracies and clans', *Administrative Science Quarterly*, **25**, 129–41.

Paffen, P. (1998), 'Careers of engineers in general management', PhD thesis, Twente University (NL).

Reynolds, P., M. Hay, W.D. Bygrave, S.M. Camp and E. Auto (2000), *Global Entrepreneurship Monitor: 2000 Executive Report*, Babson College, Ernest & Young, Kauffman Centre, London Business School.

Ribeil, G. (1984), 'Entreprendre hier et aujourd'hui: la contribution des ingénieurs', *Culture Technique*, **12**, 77–92.

Schein, E.R. (1991), 'What is culture?', in P.J. Frost, L.F. Moore, M.R. Louis, C.C. Lundberg and J. Martin (eds), *Reframing Organizational Culture*, London: Sage, pp. 243–53.

Schumpeter, J.A. (1934), *The Theory of Economic Development*, Cambridge, MA: Harvard University Press.

Shaw, V. and C.T. Shaw (1998), 'Conflict between engineers and marketers', *Industrial Marketing Management*, **27**, 279–91.

Theunissen, C. (2002), *Supporting Student Start-ups at Imperial College*, internship report of Imperial College, London.

Tkachev, A. and L. Kolvereid (1999), 'Self-employment intentions among Russian students', *Entrepreneurship and Regional Development*, **11** (3), 269–80.

Triandis, H.C. (1995), *Culture and Social Behaviour*, New York: McGraw-Hill.

Trompenaars, F. and C. Hampden-Turner (1999), *Riding the Waves of Culture: Understanding Cultural Diversity in Business*, London: Nicolas Brealey.

Ulijn, J. and A. Fayolle (in preparation), *The Ideal Entrepreneurship and Innovation Profile Preferences of French, Dutch and German Engineers.*

Ulijn, J. and R. Gould (2002), 'Towards a new European cultural identity of entrepreneurship, innovation and mobility through technology (by increasing the mobility of entrepreneurial and innovative engineers): an issue and discourse analysis of the views of 41 students and 5 MEPs', contribution to the Jean Monnet conference on Intercultural Dialogue, Brussels, 20 and 21 March.

Ulijn, J. and R. Kumar (2000), 'Technical communication in a multi-cultural world: How to make it an asset in managing international businesses, lessons from Europe and Asia for the 21st century', in P.J. Hager and H.J. Scherber. *Managing Global Discourse: Essays on International Scientific and Technical Communication*, New York: Wiley, pp. 319–48.

Ulijn, J. and M. Weggeman (2001), 'Towards an Innovation Culture: what are its national, corporate, marketing and engineering aspects, some experimental evidence', in C. Cooper, S. Cartwright and C. Early (eds), *Handbook of Organisational Culture and Climate*, London: Wiley, pp. 487–517.

Ulijn, J.M., A.P. Nagel and W.-L. Tan (2001), 'The impact of national, corporate and professional cultures on innovation: German and Dutch firms compared', contribution to a special issue of the *Journal of Enterprising Culture*, **9** (1), 21–52 on *Innovation in an International Context* (eds A. Nagel, J. Ulijn and W.-L. Tan).

# 10. Multi-path system emergence: an evolutionary framework to analyse process innovation

## Takahiro Fujimoto

## 1. INTRODUCTION: PROCESS INNOVATION AND EVOLUTION

The main purpose of this short chapter is to propose an additional concept to analyse an evolutionary type of innovation – *multi-path system emergence*. It focuses on a long-term *process innovation* that creates a new and competitive manufacturing system, such as the Ford production system and the Toyota-style production system. Such a manufacturing system is often described and analysed as a coherent set of organizational routines (Nelson and Winter, 1982).

Thus, one of the central questions to the issue of process innovations (that is, creation of new manufacturing systems) is whether a set of manufacturing routines are developed all at once by a deliberate plan of the innovating individual or organization. However, the history of manufacturing systems, and that in fabrication-assembly industries in particular, seems to indicate that such innovations tended to be a result of trial and error (Hounshell, 1984), or a complex interplay of plans and chances, visions and imperatives, creations and imitations (Fujimoto, 1999). Also, the creation of a coherent manufacturing system is often described as a long-term cumulative process rather than a one-time 'big bang' (Hounshell, 1984). If this is the nature of the process innovations in question, what kind of conceptual framework should we adopt for better understanding of such phenomena?

Generally speaking, an artificial system, which looks as if it were deliberately designed as a rational one in terms of competitiveness or survival, may have been formed through a complex dynamic process which itself cannot be reduced to an *ex ante* rational planning alone. When we observe an *ex post* rational object which may not have been formed in an *ex ante* rational way, a certain *evolutionary framework* can often be applied effectively to such a case. By evolutionary framework I mean a dynamic perspective that separately explains an observed system's survival (that is, the functional logic) and its formation (that is, the genetic logic). For example, a prevalent neo-Darwinian (or synthetic) theory of biological evolution assumes natural selection for explaining a living system's survival, and random variation for its origin. Indeed, a number of past researchers applied some sort of evolutionary approaches to dynamic analyses of biological, social or economic systems of this kind.

The present chapter aims to propose a kind of evolutionary framework that may be applicable to an artificial system that I believe is *ex post* rational: for example, the manufacturing system of Toyota Motor. Although my analysis here is by no means a direct application of neo-Darwinism or biological models in general, it is still evolutionary in that I separate the functional logic and the genetic logic on the manufacturing system at Toyota.

In this chapter, there are two main concepts that I try to add to the existing evolutionary framework to innovations – *multi-path system emergence* and *evolutionary learning capability*. I try to describe historical formation of a highly coherent and competitive set of production-development-purchasing routines (for example, Toyota-style manufacturing system) as 'multi-path system emergence', or a complex and irregular combination of both intended and unintended system changes. In other words, the author proposes an evolutionary view that incorporates the concept of system emergence, as opposed to pure randomness (that is, neo-Darwinism) or foresight (that is, teleology), as the genetic logic for system variations.

I also propose the concept of 'evolutionary learning capability' as a firm's distinctive ability to create a set of effective (that is, *ex post* rational) routines faster and earlier than its competitors despite the complex and chaotic process of multi-path system emergence. It is a kind of organization's learning capability, but it incorporates not only intentional (*ex ante*) but also opportunistic (*ex post*) learning processes. In this way, I aim to combine the concept of organizational learning (that is, creation of new organizational routines; Leavitt and March, 1988), emergent strategy (Mintzberg and Waters, 1985) and evolutionary theory of the firm (Nelson and Winter, 1982).

## 2. AN EVOLUTIONARY FRAMEWORK FOR MANUFACTURING SYSTEMS

Let us first clarify the concept of the evolutionary framework itself. Since the modern evolutionary theory originated from Darwin's work on living systems, such a framework has also been applied to the cases of social, economic and managerial systems. The notion of evolution, however, has been quite equivocal, which often created misunderstanding among researchers. For example, an 'evolutionary model' may imply different things to different people: random system variations, domination of environmental forces as a selection mechanism, regular succession of stages or progression to a supreme goal, and so on. This chapter adopts none of these specific interpretations, however. Thus, I need to clarify what I mean by an 'evolutionary framework' as broadly defined.

In this regard, it is important to distinguish two levels of an evolutionary framework: a general scheme and a specific scheme. The present evolutionary approach shares its basic logical structure with many other evolutionary theories of biological and social systems at the first level, while it is more or less specific to the present analytical purpose: the empirical research of manufacturing systems and process innovations at the second level.

### General Scheme of Evolutionary Framework

By evolutionary framework at this level, I do not mean any specific theories of biological or social evolution, but a general logical scheme that such theories may share. It shows what I think is a common denominator for any models or theories to be called 'evolutionary'. At this level, the present framework shares basic logical patterns with contemporary synthetic (neo-Darwinian) theory of biological evolution, as well as evolutionary theory of the firm, technologies, organizations and strategies. Here is my checklist for a general evolutionary scheme.

1.  *Variety and stability*: the framework's main purpose is to explain why we observe a certain variety or difference of stable patterns (for example, species) in the objects concerned (for example, living systems).
2.  Ex-post *rationality*: the objects observed behave so functionally that they *look as if* someone had purposefully designed them for survival, regardless of whether such purposive motivation actually existed beforehand.
3.  *History*: the present pattern of the objects is conjectured to have been formed historically through a certain path over a long period.
4.  *Genetic and functional logic*: the framework prepares three complementary explanations for a given dynamic phenomenon: the logic for system *variation* (generation of a variety of patterns), *selection* (elimination of low-performing patterns) and *retention* (preservation of the remaining patterns). In other words, the evolutionary perspective provides *genetic* and *functional* explanations separately to the same object. The former shows how it evolved into what we see now, whereas the latter demonstrates how it behaves effectively for higher performance or survival rate.
5.  *Anti-teleology*: because of the above logical separation, this framework

does not have to depend on *ex ante* rational foresight of omnipotent decision-makers for explaining the formation of the *ex post* rational system. In other words, the evolutionary logic denies depending totally upon teleology.

The evolutionary framework of this chapter shares the above logical scheme with many other evolutionary theories for biological and social systems.

Note, again, that the generic evolutionary framework separates genetic analysis (that is, how the system was created and has changed to yield its present form) and functional analysis (that is, how a system's structure has contributed to its survival and growth), which is the heart of evolutionary thinking.

### Specific Scheme of Evolutionary Framework to Process Innovations

At the second level, the evolutionary framework is applied specifically to the present theme, the evolution of a certain manufacturing system, or cumulative process innovations. At this level, the evolutionary framework is more or less 'customized' to the task of this chapter – empirical-historical analyses of innovations in manufacturing systems – although it partially adopts various elements of other evolutionary models.

It should be noted here that, considering the nature of this chapter's theme (that is, long-term changes in manufacturing routines within a single surviving company), I assume that individual firms (for example, Toyota) can adapt their internal system to the environments and thereby survive at the firm level. As Barnett and Burgelman (1996) point out, one may also conceive of another type of evolutionary model, in which individual firms are unable to adapt its internal structures to the selection environment, and that those firms with ineffective routines are simply weeded out; it is the population of firms as a whole that adapt (for example, Hannan and Freeman, 1989). This chapter does not adopt such neo-Darwinian (or population ecology) versions of evolutionary models, though. It instead assumes that individual firms may internally select their manufacturing routines through what Burgelman would call an 'intraorganizational ecological process' (Burgelman, 1994 p. 24), before being selected by external ecological process.

The specific scheme for cumulative process innovations that this chapter proposes can be summarized as follows (its application to the world automobile industry is assumed as an example):

1.  *Retention:* based on the author's view that production is transmission of product design information from the process to the product (Fujimoto,

1999), the present framework assumes that what is retained in a manufacturing system is a stable pattern of *information assets and flows* that collectively influence manufacturing performance. This informational pattern, or 'gene' of the manufacturing system, may also be called *routines, productive resources* or routinized capabilities. In other words, the present study reinterprets manufacturing routines as a detailed pattern of stocks and flows of value-carrying design information.

2. *Variation*: the present framework treats changes in manufacturing routines as a *multi-path system emergence*, a complex and irregular combination of rational plans, entrepreneurial visions, historical imperatives, pure chance, and so on. In this sense, the present evolutionary model is *not* neo-Darwinian – the latter only assumes pure randomness as an ultimate source of genetic variation, denying the possibility of feedback from the environment to the genes (routines). The present model is rather Lamarckian in that it recognizes individual firm's efforts to adapt its routines to the environment, although imperfectly.

    The multi-path system emergence also differs from intentional 'search' activities that some theories of evolutionary economics assume in that the former may include unintended trials. The system emergence is obviously akin to the concept of 'emergent strategy' (Mintzberg and Waters, 1985), but the former assumes a situation in which managers do not even know if a deliberate strategy works or emergent strategy is the case for the next system change.

3. *Selection*: the present framework assumes a *lenient selection mechanism*. As mentioned earlier, selection of routines may occur when firms with low-performing routines are immediately eliminated through market competition – a situation that so-called organizational ecology may assume (Hannan and Freeman, 1989). This kind of 'harsh' selection seldom happens in today's automobile industry though.[1] For the present empirical analysis, a more realistic assumption is that firms with lower performance can still survive for some time, but that competitive pressures from 'best practice' rivals tend to force such firms to select and change routines in the long run. In other words, the selection environment in this case is generous enough to allow automobile firms of different performance levels to survive. This study does not deal with direct selection of individual firms by the market environment, but analyses selection of routines within a surviving firm (that is, Toyota).

    The market does function as a routine selection mechanism, but its impact is at most indirect in most cases of today's automobile firms (that is, existing firms may switch routines in response to signals from the market). For long-term survival, what matters as a market signal is relative performance. The survivor's routines do not have to be optimal, but they need only to be better than competitors in the long run. To sum up, the selection process of the present framework is milder than the neo-Darwinian models of biology, population ecology of organizations or equilibrium models of microeconomics assume. Accordingly, the present framework regards relative manufacturing performance as a surrogate indicator of individual firms' 'probability of future survival'.

4.  *Compared with biological neo-Darwinian models*: overall, the evolutionary framework of the present chapter is by no means new, but it is clearly different from some other interpretations of evolutionary models. For instance, whereas the present framework shares a general logical scheme with today's synthetic theory of biological evolution, it is not a direct application of the biological model at the specific level (Table 10.1).

    The prevalent paradigm in biology theorizes that variation (mutation as random changes of genetic information or DNA), selection (natural selection caused mostly by different propagation rates) and retention (reproduction of genetic DNA information in and across individuals) jointly create changes and diversification of genetic information, which then materialize in living systems through adaptation to changing environments.

    For the purposes of microscopic empirical analyses of social/technical systems, however, I do not follow the biological model at the level of specific scheme.

In the context of a social system, *variation* is explained not by the purely random process that neo-Darwinism[2] may define in a biological system, but by a complex interaction of forces ranging from purely random to purely purposeful changes – a multi-path system emergence.

As for *selection*, as mentioned earlier, the present framework assumes a rather lenient selection environment, in that relatively weak organizations, with lower competitive performance, can still survive at least for a certain period. That way, it is possible to observe significant cross-organizational differences in performance for survival at a certain point in time (Clark and Fujimoto, 1991; Womack, Jones and Roos, 1990). Also, the framework may include certain internal selection mechanisms inside the organization that pre-screen the routines that have higher probabilities of survival in the external selection environment.

Finally, I only assume an incomplete mechanism for *retention* and duplication of organizational knowledge or information in a social system, unlike a relatively strict mechanism of gene or DNA duplication in the case of living systems. As anyone who has worked in a company knows,

*Table 10.1   Comparison of evolutionary frameworks*

|  | Framework in this book | Neo-Darwinian (synthetic) theory in biology |
|---|---|---|
| Object | Manufacturing systems | Living systems |
| Criteria of *ex post* rationality | Relative manufacturing performance | Survival/reproduction |
| Logic of retention | Object to be retained = manufacturing routines as informational patterns | Object to be retained = genes as information |
|  | Routines are stored in the firm; it may be diffused across firms | Genetic information is stored in the organism; it may be reproduced across generations |
| Logic of variation | Emergent process changes routines | Random chance changes genetic information |
|  | Feedback from the environment may trigger routine changes (Lamarckian) | No feedback from the environment to gene |
| Logic of selection | Long-term elimination of low-performing routines by either market or organization | Long-term elimination of low-performing genotypes by the environment |
|  | Rather 'generous' selection environment is assumed | Rather harsh selection environment is assumed |
|  | Individual firms may select high-performing routines | Individual organism cannot select high-performing genes |
| Separation of functional and genetic explanations | Genetic explanations = emergent processes result in changes in manufacturing routines | Genetic explanations = random variations of DNA result in variations of phenotypes |
|  | Functional explanations = certain routines result in relatively high performance (static and improvement capability) | Functional explanations = certain phenotypes result in higher performance for survival in the environment (natural selection) |
| Anti-teleology | Reject the idea that omnipotent decision-makers create the entire system through perfect foresight | Reject the idea that the omnipotent creator made all of the living system through predetermined plans |

organizational routines and memories erode quickly. Also, they are often difficult to imitate by other organizations.

To sum up, the specific framework of this chapter is indeed evolutionary, but it is not neo-Darwinian – the latter assumes random variation and harsh selection, while the former features emergent variation and lenient selection.

## 3. EVOLUTIONARY CAPABILITY AND SYSTEM EMERGENCE

### Multi-path System Emergence

Let us define the concept of multi-path system emergence in a more systematic manner. Generally speaking, a new manufacturing routine gradually emerges as a result of complex interactions of firms and environments, in which firm-specific capability may play only a partial role. In other words, system emergence can occur through a number of different paths, and a combination of them may be required to explain a particular system change. In my evolutionary framework for analysing a manufacturing firm, I include the following paths (see Figure 10.1):

- *Random trials*: those who take this path believe that an organization's trials are a matter of pure chance. A lucky one gets a better system, while an unlucky one gets a poor one – so in that case, you might as well try everything.
- *Rational calculation*: here decision-makers deliberately choose a new course of action that satisfies or maximizes an organization's objective function; they examine feasible alternatives based on their understanding of environmental constraints and capability limits.[3] This is the *ex ante* rational problem-solving many managers believe is the only way to create successful change.
- *Environmental constraints*: decision-makers detect certain constraints imposed by objective or perceived environments, and voluntarily prohibit a certain set of actions. The constraints may be objective (for example, laws and regulations), or they may be 'self-restraints' based on managerial perception of the environment (for example, perceiving that the market is rapidly diversifying, planning an ambitious product proliferation to match this perception and facing the constraint of a current shortage of engineers).
- *Entrepreneurial vision*: a desirable set of activities is directly chosen by entrepreneurs, based on their visions, philosophies or intuitions without much analysis of organizational capabilities and constraints.

**Rational calculation**

activity 2

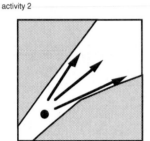

**Random trials**

activity 2

activity 1

**Environmental constraints**

activity 2

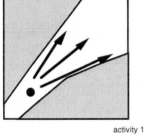

activity 1

**Entrepreneurial vision**

activity 2

vision

activity 1

**Knowledge transfer**

activity 2

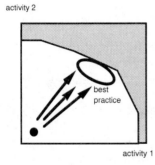

best practice

activity 1

Key:

☐ = constrained area

● = current position

➤ = direction of system change

For visual simplicity, a space of two system activities (properties) is assumed for each case.

*Source:* Modified and adopted from Fujimoto (1995).

*Figure 10.1    Multi-path system emergence*

- *Knowledge transfer*: a certain pattern is transferred from another organization to the one in question. The transfer may happen within the industry (competitor, supplier, customer) or across industries. Also, the transfer may be a 'pull' type, in which the adopter-imitator of the system takes initiative, or it may be a 'push' type, in which the source organization is the driving force behind the transfer.

Although pure chance and historical imperatives often play important roles in the system emergence and capability-building process, a company may still be able to build certain manufacturing capabilities faster and more effectively than competitors through a strong evolutionary learning capability. For example, historical imperatives may explain why the Japanese auto-makers in general acquired certain region-specific capabilities; but it does not explain why certain Japanese companies like Toyota have had better capabilities than others.

### Evolutionary Learning Capability

In applying the concept of organizational capability to the case of manufacturing systems (for example, at Toyota), researchers need to distinguish three different layers of capabilities: *routinized manufacturing, routinized learning, and evolutionary learning capabilities*. The first two are organizational routines that have been analysed by much of the past literature; but the last category is a new and non-routine concept (Table 10.2):

1. *Routinized manufacturing capability*: a set of organizational routines that affects the level of competitive performance in a steady state.
2. *Routinized learning capability*: a set of organizational routines that affects the pace of continuous performance improvements (as well as recoveries from frequent system disruptions or deterioration).
3. *Evolutionary learning capability*: a non-routine ability that affects creation of the above capabilities themselves.[4]

More specifically, given the present evolutionary framework, in which variation of manufacturing capabilities occurs through the process of multi-path system emergence, evolutionary learning capability can be redefined as a firm's *ability to manage the multi-path system emergence processes of routine-capability building better than its competitors*. As such, it is a non-routine dynamic capability embedded in the organization.

Note here that the evolutionary learning capability plays only a partial role in the overall evolutionary process of manufacturing systems. Indeed, when a company changes its organizational routines over the long run, the

*Table 10.2   Three levels of manufacturing capability*

|  | Basic nature | Influence on: | Interpretation |
|---|---|---|---|
| Routinized manufacturing capability | Static and routine | Level of competitive performance (in stable environments) | Firm-specific pattern of the steady-state information system in terms of efficiency and accuracy of repetitive information transmission |
| Routinized learning capability | Dynamic and routine | Changes or recoveries of competitive performance | Firm-specific ability of handling repetitive problem-solving cycles or a routinized pattern of system changes |
| Evolutionary learning capability | Dynamic and non-routine | Changes in patterns of routine-capability | Firm-specific ability of handling the system emergence or the non-routine pattern of system changes in building the above routine capabilities |

firm-specific dynamic capability may facilitate this system emergence process, but other factors such as environmental imperatives and pure luck may also have significant influence. For a manufacturing firm, its capability-building process is neither fully controllable nor totally uncontrollable. This is why an evolutionary framework for social systems can be effectively applied to the case of long-term process innovation.

**Operational Definition**

Now that the main concepts and logic of the evolutionary framework for analysing cumulative process innovations are illustrated, we can now apply this scheme to the actual case of manufacturing systems' evolution.

For historical and empirical analysis, the multi-path system emergence and the evolutionary learning capability may be operationally redefined as follows: (1) when a wide variety of system change patterns (rational calculation, environmental constraints, entrepreneurial vision, knowledge transfer, random trials) are observed historically; (2) and when no correlation is observed between the patterns of the system change paths and the changing systems themselves, we see that the system in question is an outcome of a multi-path system emergence. In addition, when we also observe that the resulting system (that is, a set of routines) demonstrate stable and firm-specific competitive performance, we infer from these facts that the firm had a certain evolutionary learning capability.

### Result of Historical Analysis

Based on the above operational definition of system emergence and evolutionary learning capability, the author explored the evolution of various core elements of the Toyota-style system (Fujimoto, 1999). Just-in-time, mechanisms for productivity improvement, multi-tasking, flexible production, total quality control, suppliers' design capability and the heavyweight product manager system were examined as main components of the system.

Although the details of the historical analysis are omitted in this chapter (see Fujimoto, 1999, for details), the result may be summarized as in Table 10.3, in which Toyota's capability-building cases were classified according to types of routines and types of paths.

It is now clear from this analysis that: (1) there were a variety of system change paths for each main component of the Toyota-style manufacturing system (see the variety of explanations at each column of Table 10.3); and (2) there was no clear correlation between the nature of the routines and the types of the paths (compare the patterns of explanations across the columns of Table 10.3).

Therefore, by applying the operational definition specified earlier, I argue that Toyota's routine capability building can be characterized as a *multi-path system emergence* and that Toyota, creating distinctively competitive routines through the emergent process, possessed an *evolutionary learning capability*.

## 4. CONCLUSION

This chapter presented an evolutionary framework for analysing certain types of long-term process innovations. By introducing such concepts as multi-path system emergence and evolutionary learning capability, the chapter argued that the cumulative process innovation of a manufacturing system may be explained more persuasively by applying this present framework of multi-path system emergence and evolutionary learning capability. A case of Toyota-style manufacturing system was briefly illustrated as an example.

Based on empirical and historical researches of the world automobile industry to date, we know that a wide variety of system performances and practices exist at different firms, and that these systems have changed in

*Table 10.3  Summary of evolution of selected production-development capabilities*

| | Just-in-time | Multi tasking with product-focus layout | Jidoka and flexible equipment | Kaizen and TQC | Black box parts | Heavyweight product manager |
|---|---|---|---|---|---|---|
| Competitive effect (rationality) | Creating pressure for productivity improvement Throughout time Inventory cost | Productivity improvement | Pressures for quality improvement Flexibility | Quality improvement Productivity improvement | Cost reduction by manufacturability Development lead time and productivity | High product integrity Development lead time and productivity |
| Entrepreneurial vision | Kiichiro Toyoda, 1930s ('just in time' slogan) Taiichi Ohno, 1940s–1950s (system building) | Kiichiro Toyoda, 1945 (a vision of rapid productivity catch-up without economy of scale) | Kiichiro Toyoda, 1931 (a vision of high productivity with small volume production) | | | |
| Transfer from other industry | Textile (benchmarking of Nichibo) Pre-war aircraft production | Textile: multi-machine operation in spinning (Through Ohno) | Textile: Sakichi Toyoda's automatic loom | TQC was established in other industries (e.g. process industry) | Pre-war locomotive or aircraft parts supplier | Pre-war aircraft industry (chief designer system) Forced transfer (collapse of aircraft industry) |
| Transfer from Ford system | The synchronization idea from Ford (invisible conveyer line) Kanban as 'incomplete synchronization' | Productivity benchmarking with Ford Modified Taylorism | Adoption of Detroit-type automation where feasible U-shape layout as 'incomplete transfer machine' | Suggestion system from Ford Training within industry Statistical quality control | | |

Table 10.3 (continued)

| | Just-in-time | Multi tasking with product-focus layout | Jidoka and flexible equipment | Kaizen and TQC | Black box parts | Heavyweight product manager |
|---|---|---|---|---|---|---|
| Imperative of forced growth with resource shortage | | Limit of permanent work force after the 1950 strikes 'Forced' productivity increase in the 1960s | Shortage of investment fund: low cost automation had to be pursued | Shortage of supervisors replacing craftsmen-foremen = needs for TWI | High production growth and model proliferation created pressures for subassembly and design | |
| Imperative of forced flexibility with small and fragmented market | | | 'Forced' flexibility of equipment due to small volume | | Product proliferation of the 1960s created pressures for subcontracting out design jobs | Product proliferation with limited engineering resource created pressure for compact projects |
| Imperative of shortage of technology | Lack of computer production control technology in the 1950s and 1960s | | Lack of adaptive control automation: Jidoka needs human intervention | | Lack of electric parts technology at Toyota in 1949 (separation of Nippondenso) | |
| Ex post capability of the firm | | Flexible task assignment and flexible revision of work standards to better exploit opportunities of productivity increase | | Toyota maintained momentum for TQC by creating organizations for diffusing it to suppliers | Toyota institutionalized a version of black box parts system that could better exploit competitive advantages | Only Toyota adopted heavyweight product manager system from the aircraft industry as early as 1950s |

non-routine ways over time. Thus, I believe the evolutionary framework proposed in this chapter substantially adds to our understanding of why certain manufacturing practices have emerged at Toyota.

A company's decision-makers should certainly attempt to solve problems rationally, but they also should not assume rational plans always solve those problems. The actual process of system change is essentially emergent. And no matter how successful a company has been in the past, it needs to develop an organizational culture of 'preparedness': it must convert both the intended and unintended consequences of its actions, the lucky breaks and the well-laid plans, the temporary successes and failures, into long-term competitive advantage. This is the key ingredient of an effective evolutionary learning capability. After all, Fortune favours the prepared organizational mind.[5]

## NOTES

1.  Population ecology models may be applied more effectively in the case of the earlier phase of automobile industrial evolution, in which many births and deaths of individual automobile manufacturers were observed. See, for example, Abernathy (1978) and Carroll et al. (1996) for the case of the US auto industry.
2.  Note that I am using the term 'neo-Darwinism' broadly here as synonymous with the so-called Modern Synthesis, the prevalent theory in biological evolution that includes revised Darwinism and Mendelian genetics.
3.  Neoclassical decision theory further assumes that the economic actors are equally capable and face the identical environment.
4.  Similar concepts include static versus dynamic routines (Nelson and Winter, 1982), absorptive capacity (Cohen and Levinthal, 1990; 1994), as well as dynamic capability (Teece and Pisano, 1994). The current concept of evolutionary capability is different from these similar concepts in that the former emphasizes the non-routine and emergent nature of the process for creating routines.
5.  The original phrase was made famous statement by Louis Pasteur: 'Fortune favours the prepared mind.' The relevance of this phrase was suggested to me by David A. Hounshell (Carnegie Mellon University), as well as Cohen and Levinthal (1994).

## REFERENCES

Abernathy, W.J. (1978), *The Productivity Dilemma*, Baltimore, MD: Johns Hopkins University Press.

Barnett, W.P. and R.A. Burgelman (1996), 'Evolutionary perspectives on strategy', *Strategic Management Journal*, **17**, 5–19.

Burgelman, R.A. (1994), 'Fading memories: a process theory of strategic business exit in dynamic environments', *Administrative Science Quarterly*, **39**, 24–56.

Carroll, G.R., L.S. Bigelow, M.L. Seidel and L.B. Tsai (1996), 'The fates of de novo and de alio producers in the American automobile industry 1885–1981', *Strategic Management Journal*, **17**, 117–37.

Clark, K.B. and Fujimoto, T. (1991), *Product Development Performance*, Boston MA: Harvard Business School Press.

Cohen, W.M. and D.A. Levinthal (1990), 'Adaptive capacity: a new perspective on learning and innovation', *Administrative Science Quarterly*, **35**, 128–52.

Cohen, W.M. and D.A. Levinthal (1994), 'Fortune favors the prepared firm', *Management Science*, **40** (2), 227–51.

Fujimoto, T. (1995), 'A note on the origin of the "black box parts" practice in the Japanese motor vehicle industry', in H. Shiomi and K. Wada (eds), *Fordism Transformed*, Oxford: Oxford University Press.

Fujimoto, T. (1999) *The Evolution of a Manufacturing System at Toyota*, Oxford: Oxford University Press.

Hannan, M.T. and J. Freeman (1989), *Organizational Ecology*, Cambridge, MA: Harvard University Press.

Hounshell, D.A. (1984), *From the American System to Mass Production 1800–1932: The Development of Manufacturing Technology in the U.S.*, Baltimore, MD: Johns Hopkins University Press.

Levitt, B. and J.G. March (1988), 'Organizational Learning', Annual Review of Sociology, **14**, 319–40.

Mintzberg, H. and J.A. Waters (1985), 'Of strategies, deliberate and emergent', *Strategic Management Journal*, **6** (3), 257–72.

Nelson, R.R. and S.G. Winter (1982), *An Evolutionary Theory of Economic Change*, Cambridge, MA: Belknap Press.

Teece, D. and G. Pisano (1994), 'The dynamic capabilities of firms: an introduction', *Industrial and Corporate Change*, **3** (3), 537–56.

Womack, J., D.T. Jones and D. Roos (1990), *The Machine that Changed the World*, New York: Rawson Associates.

# Index